A Confetti of

PAPERS

Joseph L. (Jack) May

Acknowledgments

I am grateful to Harris Gilbert, Esq. (for Shamus history), to Dr. Robert D. Collins (for Old Oak history), to Kerry Griffee Lance (for proofreading), to Lynn Hewes May (for a lot of proofreading, and putting up with a lot), to Roxie Gibson for encouragement, to David Routon for drawing of J. May, to my brothers Robert Kinloch Massie and Walter Kimball Massie (for they were the Old Times) and to many writers, named and unnamed (for inspiration and a little plagiarism).

© 2008 by Joseph L. (Jack) May

All rights reserved. No part of this book may be reproduced or transmitted in any form or by any means, electronic or mechanical, including photocopying, recording, or by any information storage and retrieval system, without prior written permission of the Publisher, except where permitted by law.

Text and cover design by Armour&Armour
armour-armour.com

*To Dorothy Fishel, Natalie McCuaig,
Lynn Hewes, and Nancy Brown—
all endured the writing, and
still served up the meals*

Contents

Contents	7
Introduction	9
Ten Shamuses and Alfred Levine	15
Suicide: The Case of Meriwether Lewis	37
The Battles of Marathon	63
Two Connecticut-Bred Yale Men Who Volunteered to Spy During War Time and Became Heroes	81
a brief, sad, and lower case of e e cummings	107
May Hosiery Mills	127
The Score After Three Score	143
Solyman Brown	177
Draft Riots of the '60s: Tet and the Battle of Nashville	193
What a Berg!	211
Some Rothschilds	231
Marilyn Monroe	249
Karl Marx	271
The House of Hasmon	283
Angelo and Peter	297
The Battle of Nashville, 1864	315
Old Times Old Tales	335
Why Jacob May Was a Republican	351
Shamus Synopsis	365

The Old Oak Club, December 1903. Among the notables in this group are J.H. Kirkland, chancellor of Vanderbilt University; John Bell Keeble, lawyer; G.H. Baskette, editor; C.B. Wallace, head of Wallace Preparatory School; and James C. McReynolds, later a U.S. Supreme Court justice.

Introduction

NASHVILLE MAY BE unique in this respect: It seems to me that it has an unlikely number of men's intellectual societies of surprising longevity. The Old Oak Club was founded in 1888, and the Shamus Club was founded in 1927. There are other groups: Zodiac, Coffee House, Round Table, Old Goats, and The Gang of Six, to name those that quickly come to mind. Are there parallels in Jacksonville, or Louisville, or any-other-damn-ville? Somehow it does not seem likely.

Perhaps Nashville is special because it has been an energetic commercial town with a large and first-rate university. It must be rare that these two communities come together in such a happy town/gown interaction. This has been a good, even delightful, circumstance.

The papers herein, with the exception of one prepared for the Nashville Public Library on the May Hosiery Mills, were written for evening meetings of either the Old Oak Club or the Shamus Club. One might ask for the differences between these two clubs. There is very little. The Shamus Club is smaller, limited to twelve rather than the thirty in the Old Oak Club. The Shamus Club includes home hospitality meetings and certain one hundred percent circumcision.

The meetings take place around a meal, after which a paper by one of the members is read. The responsibility of a paper is taken seriously. It gives the member an opportunity

The Old Oak Club, 1988. Back row: Allen Patton, Hugh Graham, George Paine, Clay Bailey, Joe Thompson, Ward Dewitt, Bob Collins, Neil Bass, Bill Finch, Kent Syverud, Wendell Holiday, Charles Thorne, Bill Turner, Jim Sandlin, and Bob Brandt. Front row: Jack May, Walter Durham, Joe Wright, Erwin Hargrove, Bob McGaw, George Cate, Jack Allen, Jack Voegli, and Cliff Meador.

periodically to sit down and organize his thoughts on some topic of general interest. I was never really eager to write a paper, but, as with many of life's responsibilities, once it was done, I was glad to have had the opportunity.

The papers were written to be read aloud one time. They were never meant to be published and the writing critically perused. Some of the looseness of the paper could be corrected by ad lib during the reading. Any errors found herein (there are some) I feel surely must have been corrected orally at first reading.

As to the listeners: They were old men who had just finished a drink and a marvelous meal on a weeknight. Blessedly, some of their critical facilities were somewhat muted.

Also excuse the titles herein. It was a practice to make them somewhat cryptic to forestall front-running research or embarrassing pedantry by the questioners at the end of the paper. They were not above this sort of thing.

I hope that this volume will recall some of those rich evenings and preserve a few papers. Perhaps interest in them may be even preserved down the years of the future. I know of no more vivid picture of Nashville a little over a hundred years ago than Dan May's paper, "The Score after Four Score." In order to include a third generation, there is a paper by son Andy. It too is a fascinating history.

The papers are of a great variety. I would hope that the reader will pick among them, enjoy them, and if they're not of interest, move to the next paper with alacrity. I have lived my life in the abject fear of ever boring anyone. Please let this not be you. I have chosen for inclusion in this canon some of what I consider to be the better papers. There are others that I did not include that will have to go into the

The Shamus Club, December 19, 1990. Back row: A.T. Anderson, Robert Eisenstein, Dr. Fred Goldner, Rabbi Randy Falk, Dean Sam Richmond, Joe Kraft. Front row: Herb Shayne, Joseph May, Bernard Werthan Jr., Richard Eskind, Dr. Eric Chazen, Professor James Blumstein, and Harris Gilbert.

Introduction

Apocrypha. The last entry in this volume is a synopsis of some of those that are not included.

So here goes. Before shelving this book, I hope that you will find something herein to give you delight.

The Shamus Club, 1936. Back row: Charles Gilbert, Dan May, Julius Mark, Ernest Eskind, Herman Spitz, and Lawrence Goodman. Front row: Bernard Fensterwald, Herbert Kohn, Jacques Back, Alvin Kornman, and Alf Levine.

Dan loved people in general but was never reluctant to call attention to the faults of those around him. This sometimes hurt people's feelings, but generally they loved him for his insight and even for his bluntness. This Shamus paper is a tour de force looking at the small group as he recalls its members after some forty years of being in the club. It is only right that we enjoy the pleasure that Dan took in his friend Alf Levine. So let's enjoy.

Ten Shamuses and Alfred Levine

by Daniel May (1898–1982)

Read to the Shamus Club in June 1961

WHILE I STILL have some of my wits left, I thought it might be worthwhile to write something about the early days of the Shamus Club. Especially a paragraph or two should be given to each of the Founding Fathers and their contributions to this august group.

Some of the aforementioned contributions were negative. Some were like the fellow whose banal personality was

The Shamus Club, circa 1950: Bernard Fensterwald, unknown, Bernard Werthan, Alf Levine, Manuel Eskind, Charles Gilbert, Jacques Back, and Dr. Albert Weinstein.

so blah that when he entered the room you had the feeling that someone had just left. But since I am no longer running for public office—as a matter of fact I am not running at all but barely creeping—I will tell the tale of the early Shami (with one exception) as I remember portraying them with their moles as well as their dimples. Only one of the original twelve is still in the club, namely, our nonagenarian friend, Jacques Back. I will omit all reference to him, and I will leave his biography to some future historian.

The first meeting of the club was in April 1927; I became a member in June 1927 after the departure of one of the original twelve from the city. I married Dorothy Fishel in that same month and missed my first meeting as I was in California on my honeymoon. Of the twelve, four are still living; namely, Lawrence Goodman, Julius Mark, Herbert Kohn, and Jacques Back. Herb left Nashville, and his spot was filled by Judge Charles Gilbert. Herbert was the last of the amateurs in the Center business. Ever since his departure, we have had professionals, who, as a group, have not improved. They all are way out left, and all (with possibly one exception) would be marching side by side with the Chicago Seven in thinking, if not in fact. In other words, those who work in the centerfield really belong in left field. So when Herb left, your author and historian and self-appointed archivist of the club opposed any of Herb's successors as potential members of the club.

Herbert was brought to Nashville to take charge of the Y by Lee J. Loventhal, of blessed memory. He came from Louisville and was related to the Shapinsky family (all of whom have removed the Jewishness of their names by becoming Hapins, Sapensleys, and God knows what else).

Herb was different; he carried his Jewishness with dignity, but not with impudence. He was the youngest man in the original club—he was about twenty-seven, two years younger than Mark and I. He never quite forgave me for my first contact with him. He spelled his name K-O-H-N but pronounced it *Kahn*, as did his parents and his brothers. I walked in his office in the old YMHA at 712 Union Street and said very originally, "I'm glad to meet you, Mister Cohen." He replied, "I am glad to meet you too, but my name is Kahn, not Cohen." To which your irrepressible author replied, "If K-O-H-N is Kahn, then M-A-Y spells November." I never apologized but will one of these days.

Herb was a graduate of Ann Arbor. He always wrote interesting papers. Herb's papers were serious and thoughtful; he was a Democrat and a New Dealer (parenthetically he is now an extreme right-wing Stennis-type Democrat). He was not blessed or cursed, depending upon how you consider it, with original humor but really enjoyed it in others. He could laugh with you—God help those who can only laugh *at* you.

BERNARD FENSTERWALD WAS my best friend from my marriage to his death. He was a Phi Beta Kappa from Vanderbilt and one of the laziest men I ever knew. Part of his avoidance of work was possibly because his health was never too good—he was 4F in World War I because of hypertension and tachycardia. He claimed, facetiously, that he made Phi Beta without ever reading any fine print in any textbook. Stories about his avoidance of work are legion—two are worth retelling. He lived in the old Lindauer house on West End until his wife Blanche decided that she wanted a home on the corner of Leake and Belle Meade Boulevard. He reluctantly agreed. The first thing he did after moving was to change the lock on the front door so that it would be the same as that of his store, thereby avoiding the need to carry two keys. The other story refers to his habit of checking the extension on every invoice that Burk and Company received. He did it with a hand-driven Monroe calculator that had two handles, one to change the decimal and the other to revolve to get the product. Bernard was not stingy, actually one of the most liberal and charitable men I have ever known, but he refused to purchase a motor-driven Monroe. He was a reticent man (but more about that later), and for years he refused to tell me why, lazy as he was, he still would crank and rotate his old Monroe. Finally he told me. A motor-driven calculator, he said, would move too fast and might accelerate his whole tempo of living.

Bernard's closed-mouth laconic trait was most evident at Shamus Club meetings, where he would remain silent for long periods. I remember well one night when Alf Levine suddenly said, "I don't mind people who talk a little bit too much, but people who talk continually like Bernard Fensterwald get on my nerves." Poor B hadn't said anything for an hour, but he really laughed out loud then. Bernard loved good humor and fun—his papers were interesting but, as you might suspect, were short and to the point without any embellishments.

I am not taking these pioneers in any order, either by age, alphabet, or relative intelligence. Which brings me to Stanley Rich. Stanley was a dentist and a kindly man but still a Rich. The family was cursed with a strain of mental illness that expressed itself in depression and disorientation. The old gag goes that the only thing more stupid than a stupid doctor is a bright dentist, but this did not apply to Stanley. He was a kindly fellow, wrote dull papers, thought babies came from kisses, and was completely unworldly in every way. He was pleasant and agreeable, but he gradually developed mental disease—it crept on him so gradually that some of the club members did not notice the change. Finally he became so sick that he left the country and spent a year or so near London. He returned somewhat improved, but his appearance at Shamus meetings was painful to us all, although some of the group were not too kind.

ONE OF THE most famous of the Alf Levine stories, of which more later, involves Stanley Rich. Alf was completely irresponsible—his home, his appearance, his bank account, his everything was unique in the most pure use of that much-abused word. The club was to meet at Stanley's home one Thursday and Anna Rich, his wife, was a charming person, both in looks and conduct. Alf, in his usual careless manner, failed to show up after having confirmed the date with Mrs. Rich. She was so anxious to have a nice party, as she realized that possibly it would be the last one at her home because of Stanley's illness. Next day, I called Alf, told him of his gross rudeness in words of one syllable, and he was completely abashed and promised that he would send Mrs. Rich a dozen roses and a letter of apology. Knowing how Alf failed to keep his promises, made ever so sincerely, I asked him to mail me a copy of his letter. Next day, I received the letter, and the first two paragraphs were beautiful, as Alf had the gift of writing beautiful prose. Then I read the third. It read something like this: "I am deeply mortified at my failure to come. I realize that Stanley is losing his mind, which makes my bad manners all that much worse." Realizing how sensitive Anna Rich was, I reached for the phone and upbraided Alf for five minutes. He apologized, but insisted that it was the truth. Two days later, he had his stenographer call me to tell me that the third paragraph had been added only to my copy of the letter. Could anyone dislike Alf—even his creditors?

HERMAN SPITZ WAS an M.D. who, for one reason or another, specialized in doing laboratory work for other doctors. He was a doltish man, and his papers were uniformly dull and lengthy. His first paper for the club was on the life of Pasteur, and the paper was as long as Pasteur's life and as uninspiring as a *Banner* editorial. For years afterwards in the club the word "pasteurizing" was used not to describe a method of sterilizing milk but to describe a paper that was a soporific. Spitz was supposed to have heart disease, and one night at Charley Gilbert's he had an attack. Al Weinstein hustled him to the hospital after giving him a shot right in the living room, which I thought would become a dying room. His illness was diagnosed as heart disease, but a few months later Herman died, and it was discovered that he had a rare disease of the kidneys, which he had had from birth.

Herman did not have a pleasant life as his only daughter gave him very little pleasure, and his position in the profession was not the highest. He was put on probation by the local Academy of Medicine for prescribing a cancer drug that was totally worthless. I liked Herman—all of his faults were of the head and not of the heart, even his illness.

A Confetti of Papers

I KNEW DOCTOR Irving Simon but slightly. He was in the club only two months when he left Nashville to move to Pittsburgh. He was a doctor specializing in renal and allied diseases. I knew his mother better than I knew him. She was a mean and disagreeable person and had been a widow for years. Irving was a confirmed bachelor, but when he was about forty married Margarite Eskind, which marriage lasted but a few months. She still lives in her father's old home on Twenty-first Avenue surrounded by stores and filling stations. She was once a beautiful girl; she could now play the lead in *A House Is Not a Home* extemporaneously. I took his place in the club, and even my worst enemy would have to admit that I was an improvement, which would be the minimum in compliments. There was never a worse mismatch in local Jewry than Margarite and Irving. He was dour, humorless man; she was never serious; he was stingy, she adored jewelry. One could go on running the whole gamut of traits using the antonym in each particular.

For reasons that still escape me, we have always had a rabbi in the club. I might remark in passing that in these early days, we never had two at one time, which may give some credence to the phrase, the good old days. Seriously, there are a lot of unpleasant things one might say about the profession, but even the worst anti-Semite would have to admit that graduates of the Hebrew Union College are uniformly men of superior mentality, far superior to those turned out by any other denomination. And that was true of Julius Mark. Alf Levine always referred to him as Parson Mark; Julius, being very young in 1926, did not relish the appellation. Our bright young preacher had arrived in Nashville in September 1925, just three months before his twenty-eighth birthday. I was then and still am quite an admirer of Julius Mark. He was, like all his successors at Vine Street, a scholar, widely read and a good fellow. I doubt if he was ever a very devout man, and my friend Alfred Starr always thought he was an atheist at heart. Julius's papers were excellent except when he wrote on economics, for he was, like all his cohorts of the cloth, a socialist and believed that the Russian Revolution was a great advance in man's quest for a better life. He was one of the first men I knew who went to Russia after the Revolution. He went in the thirties, and he was not disillusioned by the trip. Not until Hitler's treaty with Stalin that made World War II a certainty did his love affair with communism cease. At about sixty, he finally was convinced (I believe) that socialism is nonproductive and always leads to a lower standard of living and loss of freedom. His moving to a right-wing synagogue did not convert him from socialism; Julius was always independent in his thinking and, while in Nashville, to his everlasting credit, he stood up to the richest men in his congregation whenever a question of conscience was involved. He was a good fellow, and his attendance at Shamus meetings was regular and pleasurable.

ERNEST ESKIND WAS a sport in the family. I am using "sport" in the biological meaning—a mutation. He was noisy, full of fun, and only slightly overweight. I was extremely fond of Ernest and always enjoyed his company. His early death just ten years after the formation of the club saddened me greatly. He was a Phi Beta Kappa and a practical one. It was he who was responsible for the naming of the club. At every meeting, after dinner, some thirty minutes would be devoted to "naming the club." Ernest's window-rattling laughter would dominate the scene, and we would go around the room asking each member to suggest a name. Because of our number, names like Zodiac and Dirty Dozen were suggested, and when a member passed without a suggestion, Ernest would blast forth with something like this: "You are such a big Shamus everywhere else, why can't you think of something now?" In Ernest's dictionary, "Shamus" and "Jewish male" were synonymous, and, finally, the name stuck without any formal approval. His papers were extremely good. He stuck to subjects he knew well and prepared his paper with care. He added much to the club, and his raucous laughter still rings in my ears.

THERE WERE TWO Goodmans in the club, not related by blood or any other way. Lawrence (who still lives on Woodmont) was a piano teacher. His wife too was a music teacher. She, along with the wives of the other Goodman and Alf Levine and Stanley Rich, were all non-Jews. The old gag about the couple who had one son, one daughter, and one musician could have had Lawrence in mind—not as to his sex, but rather to his complete unworldliness. Bernard Fensterwald was his self-appointed guardian for years, and Bernard never referred to him except as "The Nut." Examples of his eccentricities were many. I will recount only two. Prior to his marriage, he had given many concerts in which formal wear was required, but it was many years later before he discovered that a dress shirt could be laundered. He bought a new one for each concert! I will never forget the other incident. He was a totally impractical man, the very antithesis of a business man, yet he wrote a paper on the stock market at a Shamus meeting in 1928 and invested a large part, if not all, of his meager savings in some of the most overpriced issues before the 1929 debacle. He had another distinction, as he was the only man ever to resign from the Shamus Club. His wife Alberta, a very fine and brave lady, was a devout Roman Catholic. At one meeting Alvin Kornman, at the request of the paper assignment committee, reviewed a book that was very critical of the Church of Rome. In the discussion that followed, Lawrence became very indignant and claimed that the comments were personally directed at him and announced that he was resigning. This was in 1953, I believe, and I tried on three occasions to get him to forget his hurt, but he never returned. He was and still is "a nut," but there was nothing mean or small or ungentlemanly about Lawrence. The ordinary rules that apply to sock-sewers, lawyers, preachers, and others are not controlling for musicians and other artists. Alf always called Lawrence "the piano tuner," and his papers, except when he wrote about music, were sheer nonsense. He had the gift of perfect pitch and could name immediately any note one pressed on the piano on any of the keys, white or black. After a series of heart attacks, peptic ulcers, and a whole list of other physical, financial, and family problems, he still survives. He was gifted, he was humble in the good sense, and he enjoyed the low humor that Alf and others inflicted on the club, but he was and still is "a nut."

ROSWELL OR ROSSIE Goodman was an alcoholic. He was an attorney of sorts whose reputation for brilliance never became apparent to me. He had little humor, and alcohol wrecked whatever else he may have had. He was picked up by the police on more than one occasion, and his selection as a member of the club was a mystery to me. Alf chose him for no apparent reason. Alf would tell me how brilliant Rossie was, but I found no need to wear dark glasses in his presence. While a member of the club, he married a putative prostitute whose appearances at our annual ladies nights were an embarrassment. He quit coming to meetings and, before long, his obituary appeared in the paper.

ALVIN KORNMAN HAD a sharp and quiet sense of humor. He had all the brains of the family; he was not talkative but would often bring forth a remark that was to the point, and even Alf was bested often. His papers were not distinguished, yet were usually thoughtful and provocative. Financial troubles plagued him throughout the Depression years as he attempted to manufacture clothing here after the wholesale business disappeared. He was host at a Shamus Club meeting at his home about 1950. He told all the departing members good night and thereupon had a heart attack and died before midnight. Sam Riven reported him D.O.A.

JUST A LINE about some of the Shamus brothers who came later and who have gone. Sam Sandmel was the most versatile man ever to be in the club. He occupied the Hillel Chair at Vanderbilt until he was seduced away under false pretenses by Nelson Glueck of the Hebrew Union College. Sam is possibly the only past member of our club who will be remembered by scholars in the future. Sylvan Schwartzman too was a rabbi and one of my favorite people. A wonderful sense of humor was what attracted me, but somehow or other he never rose as high in his work as I thought he would. Sonny Kunian was a member for a short time until he moved to Atlanta—a good mind, but completely unorganized. He added but little that I remember.

I doubt if there was ever a more popular member than Charley Gilbert—a distinguished judge, a kindly man, and liked by all. And Bill Silverman, a bright rabbi, was absolutely devoid of humor, very intense but said to be a good teacher. Albert Weinstein, my good friend, who worked his way up from a stereotype yokel (whom I met at the Union Station) to possibly one of the five best physicians in the city before his early death, was a wonderful fellow.

THE ONE REMAINING individual was truly individual. Alfred Tennyson Levine, whose only brother was Wendell Holmes Levine, was *sui generis*. He, more than anyone else, was responsible for the formation of the club, and it was his humor and wit that kept the evenings stimulating. His papers were prosaic and rather dull; he was not a well-read man outside of the law, and even in that limited field, his knowledge was not extensive. But his jocularity served him as well in his law practice as it did in the Shamus Club.

His wit was spontaneous, never studied or contrived. Furthermore, his face was funny in itself; he was homely, a bit pop-eyed, and his expression added zest to his wit. Alf was short by present day standards—possibly five foot seven, rather dark, a poor athlete, uncoordinated, and rather clumsy.

I believe this is the place to list some of his stories and anecdotes for posterity. His father was a magistrate who was elected on a death ticket a half-dozen times. From the time

Jake Levine was sixty, Alf campaigned for him on a platform saying, "Poor Poppa is getting old, so let's keep him for one more term." He died in the high eighties, and he was still a squire even after the magistrate courts were abolished and their duties limited to service in the old Quarterly Court.

His mother was one of the "literary" people. Those who remember her tell me she was quite queer, as her selection of her son's name might indicate. When Jake came home after his first election to the high office of magistrate, his wife is reported to have asked him, "Now that you are a squire, what does that make me?" To which he replied, "The same damn fool you've always been."

Misdemeanors and civil cases involving less than five hundred dollars were tried before the magistrates. They would rent an empty storefront and call it a courtroom. Almost all of them were crooks, but Jake Levine was an exception, if any were. They were not paid salaries, but collected fees from the losing participant in a civil case and from the defendant in criminal causes. If a magistrate found an alleged culprit innocent, neither he nor the deputy sheriff nor the sheriff would receive a fee. The sheriff's income was dependent upon arresting the poor and having a Justice of the Peace find them guilty. Their title was abbreviated to J.P., which some said stood for "Judgment for the Plaintiff."

Jake Levine's usual opening remarks were to ask the defendant, "Guilty or not guilty? You had better say 'guilty'—if you weren't guilty you would not be here." On civil matters, the defendant had little chance, too.

Squire Jake had a small paperweight on his desk, a replica of the famous trio of monkeys who were free from evil. After hearing both defendant and plaintiff in a civil case, one young attorney asked to be allowed to speak for thirty minutes on his client's behalf. Squire Jake said that that was all right, but he was going out to get a haircut and when the young attorney had finished, he could find the court's judgment under the monkeys.

A Negro prostitute appeared in Jake's court once and wanted a man arrested for giving her gonorrhea. Jake said that he didn't believe that this was an indictable offense, then hesitated a moment and said, "We'll arrest him for arson; he set your place of business on fire."

I include these tales in this history because Alf blamed them on his father. Like all wits, I believe they were Alfred originals, and Alf relayed that they are better received if accredited to someone else. Alf said that on another occasion, a white girl wanted a criminal warrant against a young man whom she accused of raping her while she was asleep. Her story was that the culprit climbed into her bed while she was sleeping soundly. Squire Jake asked her how far he penetrated her before she awoke and she replied, "Eight or nine inches." The squire replied, "Young lady, don't go to sleep in this court—I don't believe there is anyone around here who could wake you up."

Other items of the Levine genre should be related for future generations. Some of my favorites are so ribald that they cannot be written even in this permissive age. And they would not be as funny if told by anyone other than Alfred.

Texaco many years ago was considering employing Ed Wynn on a radio program in the years before TV. He was in a Broadway show, and a Texaco advertising man was seen at the show in a chair in a box facing away from the stage. He wanted to see if Ed Wynn would be funny if you couldn't see his facial expressions. He was still funny, but not to the same degree. The same was true of Alf.

Alf did not have a good life. He married young—to a Catholic girl named Ida Beard from a Cajun family in New Orleans. She is still alive, as are Alf's son and daughter. Ida Levine was without doubt the worst housekeeper in the civilized world. She was personally dirty, her home was actually filthy, and animals, of which she was extremely fond, roamed around the house. Dogs, cats, monkeys, and parrots were everywhere, and at one Shamus Club dinner a cat (or was it a dog?) jumped on the table during dinner and walked slowly its whole length. Meals were at any hour (or totally omitted), and Shamus dinner started at any time from seven to ten-thirty. At one never-to-be-forgotten Shamus dinner, Alf's Negro "Butler" came to the living room door at nine p.m. and announced in solemn tones, "Gentlemen, dinner is not served."

A few of the unprintable stories were typed by me, not my typist. They could be printed today in the avant garde publications—are there any other kind?

I called Alf one day for an appointment on an important matter. "Sorry, Dan, I can't see you today, I have to (bleep) a friend." And he didn't see me, but I doubt greatly if that was the reason.

Alf told of a divorce case he handled where a rich Irish couple had employed Alf. It was a case full of rancor and hate, but still Irish. The husband shouted to his spouse, "When I married you, all you had was your ass and your Bible." To which she replied, "Yeah, and if you had given half as much attention to my Bible as you did to my ass, you'd be Pope by now."

And I would be derelict if I did not include some of the sobriquets that Alfred bestowed upon his brother Shamuses. He mooched liquor from Manuel Eskind for more than a decade, yet he always called Manuel "Tocus Face." And though I promised to exclude Jacques Back from these annals, Alf always said that Jacques—a much younger Jacques—looked like a constipated owl. I was always referred to as "the Sock Sewer" and Lawrence Goodman as "the Piano Tuner." Stanley Rich was called "Painless Stanley" after a quack local dentist who advertised as "Painless Winfrey." Alf always divided the club into the rich bastards and the poor gentlemen, he being the leader of that latter group. And he insisted that when he voted Albert and Bernard Werthan into the club he thought he was voting for Joe Werthan, with the hope of becoming attorney for that affluent corporation.

The original home, now The Regency condominium on Woodlawn, was rebuilt and enlarged by about fifty percent, and the family lived in the house while the work was going on amidst indescribable filth.

Alf was my attorney and did an excellent job. What he lacked in knowledge of the law, he more than made up by his wit, his many friends, and his remarkable perceptiveness. His mind was sharp and clear and organized. But his dress, his habits, and his finances were completely disorganized. Even in 1932, at the depth of the Great Depression, he had a large income from his practice—large for those dismal days. In spite of that, he was always in debt, was considered a bad risk by every retailer in Nashville, and was always in financial trouble, largely because of the extravagance of his wife, son, and daughter. On that grave March day in 1933, the bank holiday, I sat in his office. I was horribly gloomy. Alf's office was in the American Bank Building on Fourth and Union, and that bank had just taken over the defunct Fourth and First, which had been our largest bank. Every bank was closed, and the new President, Franklin Roosevelt, stated on radio that the government would guarantee the deposits of those banks solvent enough to open, but many would not. Rumors were floating around that the American was not to reopen, and I asked Alf what he thought. Without as much as a nod, he called to his secretary and told her to get Paul Davis, the bank's president, on the phone. The conversation was brief. Alf stated this "Paul, I hear a lot of disquieting rumors about your bank. Tell me if they are true because if they are, I'm going to move my overdraft to the Third." I was told later that Davis said that this conversation was the only bright spot in these troubled days.

On the occasion of his father's eightieth birthday, Alf gave a party. Jake made a speech as to how he had arrived in American from Hungary (I believe) without a cent, how he learned the cigar-making trade and worked alongside Samuel Gompers, the founder of the America trade union movement, and on and on. He ended up extolling what a great country America is—by the way, you wouldn't dare to say that today before a Jewish audience—and his final sentence was, "Here I was, a penniless immigrant and now a few short years after, I have a son who owes one hundred thousand dollars—God Bless America!" And it was true.

The Shamus Club in its early days was strictly dry. Ernest Eskind insisted that no liquor be served to break the rule. Alf was the first one to break the rule. Alf always had to be different—his only drink was gin and Coca-Cola.

Gradually one by one started serving highballs, but I believe Ernest never did.

Most of Alf's pranks were of the visual type. His favorite target was poor Herman Spitz. I will never forget poor Spitz's disgust when Alf showed him how to "turn an orange into a peach." Alf always spoke before he thought. Alf was always toastmaster at every ladies night, and Sylvan Schwartzman only last week reminded me of the famous one at the Werthan farm just after his resignation from the Vine Street pulpit. Alf put the orange inside a big napkin, stretched the napkin from the bottom of his unzipped fly and said to poor Herman, "Isn't that a peach?"

Alf's ready and insane responses brought him much trouble. He was the attorney for a half-dozen trade groups like the Oil Men Association and the Tennessee Hotel Association, but he lost most of them either because of some silly insult or some sloppy law work. He was one of the founders of the old University Club that succeeded the very select Hermitage Club on Sixth Avenue just south of the Hermitage Hotel. The club went broke because Alf told them that they did not have to pay federal excise tax, and he was wrong. He walked into my home one night at dinner time and asked if he could eat with us. It seems that when he arrived home, Ida introduced him to a lady whom he had never seen before by the name of Weakley. Alf replied, "Glad to meet you, Mrs. Weakley. How's your monthly?" And then he turned on his heels and came to my house for dinner.

Alf considered himself a master chef and belonged to a club of amateur cooks who met to prepare dishes and drink whiskey. He claimed to have been the only person to whom Nashville's famous restaurateur, Faucon, had entrusted the secret of his salad dressing. Alf would prepare it himself just prior to every Shamus dinner, and there were among us some unkindly souls who insisted that the large wooden bowl into which Alf dived with both hands had not been cleaned since the last Shamus dinner, thereby imparting a delicate flavor unobtainable by any other mixer. Clean or dirty, it was excellent.

Alf *was* the Shamus Club. With him the period before dinner, during the dinner, and the pleasant interval before the paper, became alive. He was a clown in the best sense of the word—a funny man like Red Skelton, whose humor had no cosmic importance, was rarely dependent upon contrived situations, and was completely devoid of rancor or guile. For example, in the twenties and early thirties of this century, the Ku Klux Klan was rampant in the Midwest and South. It was anti-Jew, anti-Catholic, and extremely anti-Negro. While others were trembling either from fear or anger or both, Alf's summary was simple, "The Ku Klux Klan loves me—I was born a Jew, married a Catholic, and look like a nigger."

The *Banner* one day had a streamer headline on the front page: "HITLER SAYS JEWS IN WORLD-WIDE CONSPIRACY." Alf's response was to call Rabbi Mark at once. "Look here, Parson, just because I married a Catholic, that's no damn reason not to let me in on this conspiracy."

Alf died rather young of cancer. His doctor was never paid, and he never even saw the inside of a hospital. His record of poor pay plus his wife's devotion to all forms of superstition doomed him. I visited him regularly, and I can still recall my last visit. He was sitting on the porch of his home, horribly filthy (both as to his person and his environment).

His funeral was on a cold winter day, with a chilling rain and the thermometer just above freezing. Alf always insisted that he was a Jew, but his family had a Catholic priest bury him, who apologized to the audience for the type of service. It was brief and implied that Alfred was doomed to eternal torment because of his refusal to accept his wife's religion. If he was correct, I will wager that Hell is a happier place for Alf's being there.

The Old Oak Club, 1914

Wherein there are long quotes to profile and adumbrate, an impertinent suggestion is made, whilst our theme is suicide.

Suicide: The Case of Meriwether Lewis

Read to the Old Oak Club April 27, 1972

SO FAR AS I can discern, Meriwether Lewis spent only one day of his life in Middle Tennessee. That day was in early October when the natural beauty of our beloved region was at its fullest and the bounties of nature at their most ripe. Unflatteringly, he ended the day by shooting himself in the chest and head.

At the time of this enormous act, Lewis was America's greatest hero. I believe that we have had none since to match him. One might argue for a Charles Lindbergh, an Admiral Byrd, John Glenn, or Buzz Aldrin, *et al.*, but in terms of resolution, physical privation, political high place, personal discipline, group leadership, and national consequence, none of these great men rise more than shoulder high when measured against Meriwether Lewis. And so, if my prejudice is right, a mighty hero's suicide in the midst of our soft and golden hills is worth our evening's reflection and contemplation. For as I read this paper I know that here is a tale, that if I were wise and able enough to tell with knowledge and depth enough, it could release a human significance far beyond history's footnote. I regret most that no hoary metaphysician, no psychiatrist, no criminal investigator, no poet, nor even novelists have addressed themselves to this bit of history. The material available is either from journalists of an oriental hue, or from historians who, faced with perishing, reluctantly and desperately published. Predictably, their works are factual skeletons having neither bowels nor soul.

Our general topic will be suicide. Rare is the man amongst us who has not known of, and been surprised by, a suicide of someone close, someone tied to us in an emotional way. It is usually only in retrospect that there is predictability.

But in retrospect there is often a powerful logic. Had we but a warning, had we but an opportunity to break the ineluctable chain of circumstance with a word of love, reason, or wisdom, couldn't we have changed the bleak course of events leading to the final irreversible action? What were the right words for Meriwether Lewis, and who was there to say them?

MERIWETHER LEWIS WAS born in Albemarle County, August 18, 1774. The families of both his parents, William Lewis and Lucy Meriwether, were established among the Piedmont elite. Their peers were no less than the Randolphs, the Jeffersons, and the Monroes of the Charlottesville

Suicide: The Case of Meriwether Lewis

community. The family home, Locust Hill, was proximate enough to Monticello that Jefferson devised a heliograph to summon his young friend when he wished his company. Meriwether's father William was a patriot. He served with distinction and without pay in the Continental Army. Traveling in mid-November of 1779, he forded a swollen stream; then, proceeding drenched and fatigued, he contracted pneumonia and died within forty-eight hours of the drenching. Meriwether was five years old. He had an older sister, a younger brother, and a mother who was a widow at twenty-seven. Lucy Lewis was also quite a woman and wise. Within six months of her husband's sudden death, she married John Marks and shortly after the Revolution moved the family to Georgia.

Young Lewis remained in Georgia with his stepfather until he felt himself to be an adult. He was then fourteen, and he returned to Albemarle County where he claimed and managed his father's land by right of primogeniture. He did have the aid of his uncle until the age of eighteen.

His formal education was meager. He had a number of tutors, at least one of whom was disagreeable to the point of sadism. He seems to have learned only grammar, and his creative spelling of the King's English was so rich and free that it may be best explained in the revolutionary spirit of the age. A classmate, Peachy Gilmer, gives us this perceptive portrait of Lewis as a boy:

> *He was always remarkable for perseverance, which in the early period of his life seemed nothing more than obstinacy in pursuing the trifles that employ that age; of a martial temper and great steadiness of purpose, self-possession and undaunted courage. His person was stiff and without grace; bow-legged, awkward, formal, and almost without flexibility. It bore to my vision a very strong resemblance to Bonaparte.*

But if his book learning was short, his training in the out of doors left little to be desired. By the time he was eight he liked to hunt, alone except for his dog, and by night. There is a story of his Georgia days that once, when the Cherokees were on the warpath, he was with a body of settlers hiding in the woods. One of the men stupidly kindled a fire, giving away their location to the Indians. A shot was heard; the men panicked. Here and there they ran, grabbing up rifles while silhouetted by the cook fire. Only young Meriwether had the presence of mind to dash a bucket of water on the fire to prevent his elders from becoming sitting-duck targets for the hostiles.

Ten years after this amazing episode, this active, action-oriented lad opted to farm rather than continue his formal education at William and Mary. And as gentleman farming became the excuse to avoid the tedium of education, two years later, at the age of twenty, the alternative of the military became the excuse to avoid the tedium of plantation life. In answer to President Washington's call, he was one of the first to enlist in the Virginia Militia and take out after the disenchanted Pennsylvania farmers in the Whiskey Rebellion of 1794. Lewis loved his first taste of soldiering. He wrote his mother, "We have mountains of beef and oceans of whiskey, and I feel myself able to share it with the heartiest fellows in camp." When he became eligible for discharge, he re-upped. Again writing to Mother Lucy, he apologized for his quixotic rambling and concluded, "I am quite delighted with a soldier's life." For the next seven years he served with distinction and gradually rising responsibility. One rough spot involved being court-martialed and acquitted on a charge of drunkenness. Most of his duties took him into "the frontiers." He sharpened his woodsman technique. He assiduously applied himself to Indian tongues and ways, and he learned the discipline of command, which would in time elevate him to the heights of greatness. Then at the age of twenty-eight, the fates interceded. There are few army captains so fortunate to have a neighbor elected President of the United States. And fewer still for whom such familiarity breeds esteem with the result that shortly after his election, Thomas Jefferson, then President, requested Lewis's commanding general to release him to become his private secretary.

For two years, Lewis served as aide-de-camp, legman, and confidant to the President. He was fully privy to affairs of state and other affairs of some delicacy. His evenings were spent in long conversation with the best of the nation. His days were often spent in the downstairs, map-filled study with the President where the seminal dream of western adventure coalesced.

By January of 1803, Jefferson had sufficiently nurtured the dream to request an appropriation from Congress. The message to Congress was secret, and Jefferson's real intent was further concealed. Ostensibly, the President wished to search out new Indian land for purchase and to find posts for trade. Only incidentally did Jefferson mention that the Pacific might be reached by a "single portage." Thus the third President started the final chapter of a story commenced by Christopher Columbus over three hundred years before. That is, exploration westward to find a route to the Orient. Two years later on the Pacific shore at the mouth of the Columbia River, appropriately named for the first of the Western explorers, did the last of this list know for certain that there was no Northwest Passage, no easy route to Cathay. Jefferson's hope of short passage was in fact a two-hundred-mile stretch across the mighty, rocky, rugged cord of mountains that stretched virtually from the Arctic to the Antarctic. The mighty Amazon, like the mighty Missouri, would yield no passage. Although it took three hundred years for Lewis to end the dream of Columbus, it was only one hundred years after Lewis that a twentieth-century Eastern establishment Harvard man created an alternative to the lost dream. Teddy Roosevelt just blasted a hole in the Isthmus of Panama. Columbus to Lewis to Roosevelt.

Later in 1802, Congress approved the western expedition of Meriwether Lewis and financed it to the extent of two thousand dollars. The sum bears mentioning because its meagerness fixes the remoteness of the era. It was at a time when Lewis could complete his unfinished education in all of the world's sciences in one place and in only a few months. He went to Philadelphia to the American Philosophical Society, a body founded by Benjamin Franklin sixty years before. He studied mathematics, navigation, cartography, medicine, meteorology, surveying, the natural sciences, and even some interestingly advanced anthropology. A checklist of information on the Indians, requested by the Society, was to complete a survey of Indian attitudes on sex, suicide, murder, food preservation, disposal of the dead, medicine, and the "affinity between their ceremonies and those of the Jews."

By the time Lewis was ready to embark on his journey, he was well prepared. He was well versed and keenly honed in the ways of the wilderness, the ways of men, and now in the ways of the institute. He went west well prepared for the unusual trials of nature and self. But he returned ill prepared for the usual trials of pettiness and tedium that were to be his portion.

SO WEST HE went. The story of the Lewis and Clark Expedition is well known to every schoolboy. The trip took three summers and two winters. It overcame the unpredictability and rigors of myriad different Indians, geographies, climates, animals, mountains, insects, and subordinates. Over fifty people were attached to the trip at various times. There was but one casualty; Sergeant Floyd died of a ruptured appendix. But had he been in Philadelphia in the care of the nation's finest physicians, he could not have been saved in 1805. Although thousands of Indians of varying degrees of hostility were encountered, only two of these were shot, and that was in the act of stealing all of the expedition's horses. The entire cost of the adventure, including salaries and logistics for fifty men, over a period of two and one-half years, was under forty thousand dollars.

No less remarkable than the expedition and its survival were the journals kept by Lewis and the others as each day passed. The diary is valuable not only for its clarity of observation and the encyclopedic inclusion of detail but more so for our purpose in that it provides for us an excellent insight into the character of the author. It is really our only firsthand means of exploring the parameters of Meriwether Lewis's personality. I include here some random entries for this purpose. Listen carefully to these bits of diary. How could this man so bent on the safety and survival of his men and of himself, and so successfully involved in the totality of life, be dead by his own hand (as surely he was) less than five years after the writing?

The journal entry of August 19, 1805, is a good example of Lewis's journalistic anthropology as he observed both his own men and the Indians.

> *The Shoshonees may be estimated at about one hundred warriors, and about three times that number of women and children. They have more children among them than I expected to have seen among a people who procure subsistence with such difficulty. There are but few very old persons, nor did they appear to treat those with much tenderness or respect. The man is the sole proprietor of his wives and daughters, and can barter or dispose of*

either as he thinks proper, a plurality of wives is common among them, but these are not generally sisters as with the Minnitares & Mandans but are purchased of different fathers. The father frequently disposed of his infant daughters in marriage to men who are grown or to men who have sons for whom they think proper to provide wives, the compensation given in such cases usually consists of horses or mules which the father receives at the time of contract and converts to his own use. The girl remains with her parents until she is conceived to have obtained the age of puberty, which with them is considered to be about the age of thirteen or fourteen years. The female at this age is surrendered to her sovereign lord and husband agreeably to contract—and with her is frequently restored by the father his daughter; but this is discretionary with the father. Sah-car-qar-we-ah had been thus disposed of before she was taken by the Minnitares, or had arrived to the years of puberty, the husband was yet living with this band, he claimed her as his wife but said that as she had had a child by another man, who was Charbono, that he did not want her.

They seldom correct their children particularly the boys who soon become masters of their own acts, they give as a reason that it cows and breaks the spirit of the boy to whip him, and that he never recovers his independence of mind after he is grown. They treat their women but with little respect, and compel them to perform every species of drudgery. They collect the wild fruits and roots, attend to the horses or assist in that duty, cook, dress the skins and make all their apparel, collect wood and make their fires, arrange and form their lodges, and when they travel pack the horses and take charge of all the baggage; in short the man does little else except attend his horses, hunt and fish, the man considers himself degraded if he is compelled to walk any distance and if he is so unfortunately poor as only to possess two horses he rides the best himself and leaves the woman, or women if he has more than one, to transport their baggage and children on the other, and to walk if the horse is unable to carry the additional weight of their persons, the chastity of their women is not held in high estimation, and the husband will for a trifle barter the companion of his bed for a night or longer if he conceives the reward adequate though they are not so importunate that we should caress their women as the Sioux's were, and some of their women appear to be held more sacred than in any nation we have seen. I have requested the men to give them no cause of jealousy by having connection with their women without their knowledge, which with them, strange as it may seem, is considered as disgraceful to the husband as clandestine connections of a similar kind are among civilized nations, to prevent this mutual exchange of good offices altogether I know it impossible to effect, particularly on the part of our young men whom some months abstinance have made very polite to those tawney damsels, no evil has yet resulted and I hope will not from these connections.

The expedition, as the moon trips one hundred sixty years later, were military in organization. Lewis was the leader. It was to him that the men looked for example, discipline, morale, and survival. This journal entry of June 7, 1805, illustrates his cool and his capacities as chief. For the record, the military equality of William Clark was a fiction. The fiction was invented by Lewis and maintained with the complicity of Jefferson. Lewis was the leader in seniority, rank, and fact, but he chose that his men and history should be told otherwise.

> *It continued to rain almost without intermission last night and as I expected we had a most disagreeable and restless night. Our camp possessing no allurements, we left our watery beds at an early hour and continued our rout down the river. It still continues to rain the wind hard from N.E. and cold. The ground remarkably slippery, in so much that we were unable to walk on the sides of the bluffs where we had passed as we ascended the river, not with standing the rain that has now fallen the earth of these bluffs is not wet to a greater depth than two inches; in its present state it is precisely like walking over frozen ground which is thawed to small depth and slips equally as bad, this clay not only appears to require more water to saturate it appears on the other hand to yield its moisture with equal difficulty.*
>
> *In passing along the face of one of these bluffs today I slipped as a narrow pass of about thirty yards in length and but for a quick and fortunate recovery by means of my espoontoon I should precipitated into the river down a craggy precipice of about ninety feet. I had scarcely reached a place on which I could stand with tolerable safety even with the assistance of my espoontoon before I heard a voice behind me cry out oh god Capt. what shall I do on turning about I found it was Windsor who had slipped and fallen about the center of this narrow*

pass and was lying prostrate on his belly, with his right hand arm and leg over the precipice while he was holding on with the left arm and foot as well as he could which appeared to be with much difficulty. I discovered his danger and the trepidation which he was in gave me still further concern for I expected every instant to see him lose his strength and slip off although much alarmed at his situation I disguised my feelings and spoke very calmly to him and assured him that he was in no kind of danger, to take the knife out of his belt behind him with his right hand and dig a hold with it in the face of the bank to receive his right foot which he did and then raised himself to his knees; I then directed him to take off his mockersons and to come forward on his hands and knees holding the knife in one hand and the gun in the other this he happily effected by my orders and waded the river at the foot of the bluff where the water was breast deep.

It was useless we knew to attempt the plain on this part of the river in consequence of the numerous steep ravines which intersected and which were quite as bad as the river bluffs, we therefore continued our rout down the river sometimes in the mud and water of the bottom lands, at other in the river at our breasts and when the water became so deep that we could not wade we cut foot steps in the face of the steep bluffs with our knives and proceeded. We continued our disagreeable march through the rain mud and water until late in the evening having traveled only about eighteen miles and encamped in an old Indian stick lodge which afforded us a dry and comfortable shelter. During the day we had killed six deer some of them in very good order although none of them had yet entirely discarded their winter coats. We had reserved and brought with us a good supply of the best pieces; we roasted and ate a hearty supper of our venison not having tasted a morsel before during the day; I now laid myself down on some willow boughs to a comfortable nights rest, and felt indeed as if I was fully repaid for the toil and pain of the day, so much will a good shelter, a dry bed, and comfortable supper revive the spirits of the wearied, wet and hungry traveler.

In dealing with the Indians, Lewis was ever flexible. He was pragmatic and intuitive to the point of perfection. He would appeal in turn to the Indians' curiosity by gifts of trinkets and by the display of a black human (the slave York). He would appeal to their pride with generous donations of peace medals from Jefferson, the Great White Father. He would in turn appeal to their fears with gratuitous displays of riflery. And should the occasion demand, he could appeal to their souls with a diplomatic, Old Testament stem-winder, of which an example follows. This peroration closed a speech to the Otos August 3, 1804:

Children, do these things which your Great Father advises and be happy. Avoid the councils of bad birds, turn on your heels from them as you would from the precipice of a high rock, whose summit reached the clouds and whose base was washed by the gulf of human woes, lest by one false step you should bring upon your nation the displeasure of your Great Father, the Great Chief of the Seventeen Great Nations of America, who would consume you as the fire consumes the grass of the plains. The

> *mouths of all the rivers through which the traders bring goods to you are in his possession and if you displease him, he could, at pleasure, shut them up and prevent his traders from coming among you and this would, of course, bring all the calamities of want upon you. But it is not the wish of your Great Father to injure you; on the contrary, he is now pursuing the measures best calculated to insure your happiness.*

At another time, August 1805, to other Indians, the Shoshones, the situation required that he sleep beside the chief rather than lecture him. He recorded his thoughts thus:

> *My mind was in reality quite as gloomy all this evening as the most affrighted Indian but I affected cheerfulness to keep the Indians so who were about me. We finally laid down and the chief placed himself by the side of my musquetoe bier. I slept but little as might be well expected, my mind dwelling on the state of the expedition which I have ever held in equal estimation with my own existence, and the fait of which appeared at this moment to depend in a great measure upon the caprice of a few savages who are ever as fickle as the wind. I had mentioned to the chief several times that we had with us a woman of his nation who had been taken prisoner by the Minnetares, and that by means of her I hoped to explain myself more fully than I could do signs. Some of the party had also told the Indians that we had a man with us who was black and has short curling hair, this had excited their curiosity very much, and they seemed quite as anxious to see this monster as they were the merchandize which we had to barter for their horses.*

Suicide: The Case of Meriwether Lewis

The same man could wax meticulously descriptive, as he told posterity of the minute characteristics of the Mountain Hemlock on Wednesday, February 5, 1806.

Fir No. 2 is next in dignity in point of size. It is much the most common species, it may be said to constitute at least one half of the timber in this neighborhood. It appears to be of the spruce kind, it raised to the height of 160 to 180 feet very commonly and is from 4 to 6 feet in diameter, very straight round and regularly tapering, the bark is thin of a dark color, and much divided with small longitudinal interstices; that of the boughs and young trees of the white pine of our country. The wood is white throughout and rather soft but very tough, and difficult to rive. The trunk of this tree is a simple branching diffused stem and not proliferous as the pines and firs usually are but like most other trees it puts forth buds from the sides of the small boughs as well as their extremities. The stem usually terminates in a very slender pointed top like the cedar. The leaves are petiolate, the footstalk small short and oppressed; acerose rather more than half a line in width and very unequal in length, the greatest length being little more than half an inch, while others intermixed on every part of the bough are not more than a 1/4 in length. Flat with a small longitudinal channel is the upper disk which is of a deep green and glossy, while the under disk is of a whitish green only; two ranked, obtusely pointed, soft and flexible. This tree affords but little rosin, the cone is remarkably small not larger than the end of a man's thumb soft, flexible and of an ovate form, produced at the ends of the small twigs.

A Confetti of Papers

The last of these random quotes from this man of many parts is his reflection upon his thirty-second birthday. These are not the words of Emerson in Boston, nor those of Saint Francis in his cave, but those of a man a year and a half beyond Saint Louis in unexplored land about to ascend the cruel Bitterroot Mountains where survival itself was scarcely assured. Listen:

> *This day I completed my thirty first year, and conceived that I had in all human probability now existed about half the period which I am to remain in this sublunary world. I reflected that I had as yet done but little, very little, indeed, to further the happiness of the human race or to advance the information of the succeeding generation. I viewed with regret the many hours I have spent in indolence, and now sorely feel the want of the information which those hours would have given me had they been judiciously expended, but since they are past and cannot be recalled, I dash from me the gloomy thought, and resolved in future, to redouble my exertions and at least endeavor to promote those two primary of talents which nature and fortune have bestowed on me; or in future, to live for mankind, as I have here to fore lived for myself.*

So with these fragments the sensitivity, intelligence, and variety of the man are proclaimed. And so the Corps of Discovery got to the Pacific, and so the Corps of Discovery returned. It was a fearful trip. The American people realized it, and we had a towering hero. Lewis was lionized by the President and by Eastern society. While Lewis lectured and rewrote his notes, Clark concerned himself with Cupid and quickly married. In this regard, Lewis was less direct and puzzlingly unsuccessful. His affairs with the lasses each time progressed from hope to infatuation and thence to disillusion and withdrawal. In the fall of 1807 he wrote his half-brother:

> *My little affair with Miss A-n R has had neither beginning nor end on her part; pr. contra, on my own it has had both. The fact is that, on enquiry, I found that she was previously engaged and, therefore, dismissed every idea of prosecuting my pretensions in that quarter and am now a perfect widower with respect to love. Thus, floating on the surface of occasion, I feel all that restlessness, that inquietude, that certain indescribably something common to old bachelors, which I cannot avoid thinking, my dear fellow, proceeds from that void in our hearts which might, or ought, to be better filled. Whence it comes, I know not, but certain it is that I never felt less like a hero than at the present moment. What may be my next adventure, God knows, but on this I am determined, to get a wife.*

So in love, determined he was, but successful he was not, and early in 1808, he arrived back in St. Louis as His Excellency the Governor of Louisiana. He was alone, without a wife, and now without Clark or even friends.

THE ST. LOUIS experience could only be described as sordid. The issues and personalities were petty and the outcome tragic. Those qualities of character that were appropriate to a military leader failed among the ward-heeler types of the territorial capital. Above all he was bored. He quarreled bitterly with his second in command, Frederick Bates. The selfish and the greedy were ascending. If politics were sour, the state of his private finances was yet more sour. He had no competence. In his attempt to obtain a fortune through land speculation, he lost all of his capital and had to pledge his income for years to come. Things were so bad that he was regularly humiliated by having to borrow trivial sums of a few dollars for doctor fees, medicines, and even a gambling debt. The final straw came when the Washington bureaucracy contested a draft of several thousand dollars sent in the administration of the territory. Upon arrival of this news he determined to salvage his honor by a direct appeal to Washington in person. Having so determined, he sold all his property to the payments of his debts, delegated his administrative responsibilities, and left St. Louis by boat, bound for Washington via New Orleans, on September 4, 1809. Five weeks later, he ended his life.

Nothing is known of the boat that carried Lewis down the Mississippi. He did have with him his servant, Pernier, and sixteen notebooks containing the as-yet-unpublished journal of the expedition.

One week out of St. Louis, at a brief stop in New Madrid, he executed a will, apparently his first and only, leaving all to his mother after payment of his debts. Four days later, September 11, the boat reached Memphis (then Fort Pickering) and Lewis left the boat. He was too ill to continue and would wait at the fort until he was stronger. At that time, he decided not to continue via New Orleans by boat, but rather to proceed via Nashville by foot. The two reasons for this, he wrote lucidly to President Madison, were fear of the British in New Orleans confiscating his original papers,

Suicide: The Case of Meriwether Lewis

and also a fear of the late summer heat in his weakened condition. He was indeed very ill. He was physically weak and mentally disoriented. But if he was ill, what illness did he have? The historians are poor diagnosticians. Variously, they suspect malaria, alcoholism, hypochondria, opium addiction, depression, fevers. At any rate, for the first six days in Memphis, the fort commander reported Lewis in a state of mental derangement. He watched him carefully as the crew of the riverboat had reported that he made two attempts to kill himself on the trip. By September 29, all symptoms of mental aberration had disappeared. He left Memphis that day with James Neely, an Indian agent, who was fortuitously going his way. They were accompanied by a number of Chickasaws, and each man had a servant.

The little caravan moved due eastward from Memphis through the swamps and canebrakes along the Tennessee-Mississippi border until they reached the Tennessee River.

Here they rested for two days, as Lewis appeared deranged at times. Resuming their journey they reached the Natchez Trace and camped the night of October 9. During the night, two of the horses strayed. Neely stayed behind to round them up, and the Governor and the two servants proceeded on, promising to wait for Neely at the first house inhabited by a white man.

The events of the last twelve hours of Meriwether Lewis's life have been reported by dozens of reporters and historians. None I have read has done better than the biographer, Richard Dillon, and I quote:

> *Near Little Swan Creek in the bosky hill county of south central Tennessee, Lewis turned his horse off the*

shallow swale of the Natchez Trace where it skirted a hacked-out clearing in the oaks. From this new meadow rose a haze of chimney smoke, mingling with the soft light on sunset. As he left the canopy of oaks and maples, Lewis saw a pair of rude log cabins, at right angles joined by a 12- or 15-foot dogtrot or breezeway. He greeted the lone woman who stood awaiting him and learned that this was Grinder's Stand, seventy-two miles from Nashville and on the very border of Indian Territory. Lewis dismounted, took off the loose robe, or duster, striped blue and white like mattress ticking, which he wore, and looked over the establishment. The cabins were rude, indeed, and the only other signs of civilization were a barn and stable and the stumps of cut trees in the clearing. But it would do.

The woman identified herself as Mrs. Robert Grinder and explained that her husband was away, helping with the harvest at their Duck River Farm some 20 miles distant. Lewis inquired if he might have lodging. Mrs. Grinder assented of course, but asked, "Do you come alone?" No, the Governor told her, his servants would be along shortly. After taking his saddle into the cabin which the woman indicated would be his, the Virginian asked Mrs. Grinder for a glass of whiskey. But when she brought it, he drank very little. Shortly, the servants rode up and Lewis asked one of them about powder for his Pistols, saying that he was sure he had some handy in a canister. The servant's reply was indistinct but Lewis, instead of seeing to the priming of his arms, began to pace back and forth before the rude oak door of his cabin, obviously upset, talking to himself. At times, he would walk up almost to his startled hostess, then wheel on his heel and stride away, wrapped in thought and anger as he rehearsed his upcoming confrontation with Secretary of War Eustis.

When Mrs. Grinder announced that supper was ready, the Governor sat down at the table but did not lose his agitation. After eating only a few bites, he started up, his face flushed with a fit of anger, muttering something to himself as he considered anew the injustice of his treatment by Washington. Finally, he lit his pipe and drew a chair close to the door, remarking, "Madam, this is a very pleasant evening." He smoked for a time, then got up and resumed his impatient pacing, traversing the yard this time. Regaining his composure once more, he took his seat, filled his pipe and lit it. Blowing clouds of smoke and staring toward the west, he observed, "What a sweet evening this is."

In the meantime, Mrs. Grinder was preparing a bed for her guest in the cabin. However, the Governor stopped her, explaining that he preferred to sleep on the puncheon floor. He sent one of the servants for his bearskins and buffalo robe, which were spread on the floor. Since it was now dark, Mrs. Grinder took her leave of the gentlemen in order to make her own bed down in the hayloft, 200 yards away. But Mrs. Grinder did not sleep. According to her later testimony, the frenetic and puzzling pacing of her visitor so unnerved her that she lay awake for a long time, during which time she could plainly hear Lewis talking aloud, "like a lawyer," as he walked back and forth in the adjoining cabin.

Suddenly the woman was brought fully awake by the loud report of a firearm nearby. It was followed by a thud *in Lewis's cabin, like the sound of a heavy object hitting the floor. Then she heard the words, 'Oh Lord' followed by the explosion of another shot. A few minutes later she heard her guest at the kitchen door crying out pitifully, "Oh madam give me some water, and heal my wounds."*

It must have been 3 A.M. when the woman peered through the chinks between the logs of the kitchen wall. She saw Governor Lewis staggering backward in the dark, to fall against a stump left by Grinder between the kitchen and the sleeping cabin. Then he crawled on hands and knees a short distance to a tree and with its support, pulled himself painfully up into a sitting position. After resting thus for a moment, he lurched and shuffled his way through the shadows and back into the cabin. But he was soon at her door again, scratching feebly at it, not speaking now. She next heard him scraping in the bucket with the gourd as the gunshot wounds made his body beg for water. But there was not even to be the solace of water for Lewis. The bucket was empty.

Mrs. Grinder, as she later told her story, was terrified. In any case, she did nothing for the dying man who scratched at her bolted door, begging help. At daybreak, hours later, she sent two of her children to the barn to arouse the servants who had apparently heard nothing.

Pernia and the Negro came up to find Lewis lying on the bed, which he had spurned the night before. He was wounded in the head and side by pistol balls (and perhaps cut with a knife or razor; the accounts differ), was in great pain and fitfully conscious. According to one of the several versions which Mrs. Grinder gave interrogators,

Suicide: The Case of Meriwether Lewis

Lewis uncovered his side to show then the dreadful wound where a bullet had entered. In addition, a pistol ball had torn off a portion of his forehead, not causing much blood but exposing part of the brain. Lewis, according to Mrs. Grinder, begged them to take his rifle—presumably because he had emptied his pistols into his own body—and blow out his brains. If they would do this for him, he said, he would give them all the money he had in the trunk. According to the strangely timid frontiers woman, the Governor, who had been unable to kill himself with two heavy-caliber pistols, begged Pernia not to be afraid of him assuring the Creole that he would not hurt him.

Meriwether Lewis's last words on earth came as the rising sun tinged the treetops to the east with light. They were, "I am no coward, but I am so strong. It is so hard to die."

THE POST-MORTEM REPORTING of the hero's death are interesting chapters in themselves.

We, who are so close in time to the Warren Commission and Police Chief Garrison, are aware of the pitfalls of reporting a public tragedy. The firsthand report came from Mrs. Grinder, by Neely, to ex-President Jefferson. There was no doubt by these three that suicide was the cause of death. Jefferson wrote that Lewis "had from early youth suffered from hypochondriac affections . . . inherited from his father" and while serving as his personal secretary, had been subject to "sensible depressions of the mind." Thus, Jefferson concludes, when after his monumental journey he returned to sedentary occupations did his mental disorder return and eventually "did the deed which plunged friends into afflictions and deprived the country of one of her most valued citizens." So general was the presumption of suicide that no official inquiry of any kind was made.

Two serious attempts were made privately to reconstruct the incident. These were eighty-two years apart, one in 1811 and one in 1893. Both, coincidentally, by distinguished ornithologists. The first, Alexander Wilson, corroborates that of Neely as he debriefed, at length, Mrs. Grinder on the particulars of the melancholy events. The second, Elliot Coues, gave national dissemination to a *Nashville American* newspaper interview with an elderly woman who, forty years earlier, knew a girl who had been employed at Grinder's Stand that night. Her story was that Robert Grinder had murdered Lewis with a motive of robbery. With the money thus obtained, he bought land on the Duck River near the present town of Centerville. Ultimately, the N.C. and St. L. Railroad terminated a spur line of this allegedly ill-gotten property. From this sod in our own day sprang Minnie Pearl, the philosopher of Grinder's Switch.

Once the Sunday supplements opened the door of the murder theory at the turn of the century, the vulgar populace and the sentimental historians found it irresistible. Bill Alderson will find for you in the State Library no less than fifteen newspaper articles from 1891 to 1904 supporting the murder hypothesis. This mostly proves that journalists know what builds circulation. In the structured society of 1900, who wants a complex and messy hero? Horatio Alger and Frank Merriwell don't shoot themselves when the going gets tough. But the legend of murder is a powerful one, and its mythology filters into high places. The current *Encyclopedia Britannica* and the *Dictionary of American Biography* both conclude that it was a felony murder for reason of gain. But we Old Oaks know better.

MERIWETHER LEWIS WAS raised by a strong mother. He lost his father at age five. He fled his foster father at fourteen. He never married. His attempts at courtship were embarrassing and ineffectual. His sixteen-year relationship with William Clark was an obvious source of great satisfaction to him. This relationship ended abruptly when Clark married immediately on his return from Clatsop. Without wallowing in the pleasures of historical Freudianism, it is possible, I submit, that the broken shaft monument erected by the State of Tennessee at his death site in 1845 might connote more than a shortened life.

And if there is an emotional aridity in the Freudian landscape, bleaker still, it is that determinist Marxist scene. Lewis's economic realities were depressing. Debts, no income, no fortune, and no prospects. The banality of financial arithmetic ensnares the exalted as certainly as the profligate. Who is immune to its dismal truth?

So a simple progression of circumstances led to a corner without perspective. A situation that to the outsider, be he friend or academic, seems trivial in the totality of a life and its accomplishments must continually seem immense and encompassing from the inside. Or maybe the explanation is more in the momentary than in the cumulative. The action must take place at an instant of time and here, as so often it is, in the late night. Perhaps just the late night itself is explanation enough. There are few suicides after breakfast.

But and yet if a man is to die by his own hand, who is to second guess? Is there any other court where the facts are so totally known? Here, within one skull, is the accuser and defendant, the prosecutor and defense attorney, the judge, the jury, and governor with the pardon standing beside the executioner. Who, outside that bone, can interpose a knowledgeable judgment. Who is so callow as to even say "Why?" or "He shouldn't have done it." The one who did it knew the whole and incommunicable truth. He knew, and he did it. But the victim, our hero or our friend, is then mute. Really all is moot.

Did you ever do it again?
"He who does not climb Mount Fuji is a fool. He who climbs it twice is twice a fool."—Japanese proverb

The Battles of Marathon

*Read to the Shamus Club June 21, 1979,
and to the Old Oak Club February 28, 1980*

NEBUCHADNEZZAR IS A good place to start. You recall, Nebuchadnezzar was the King of Babylon (Shadrach, Meshach and Abednego). About 590 B.C. Nebuchadnezzar subjugated all the world worth subjugating. This included the Jews. He destroyed their Temple, led their leadership off into exile in Babylon and, except for Jeremiah and a few miserable remnants who escaped to Egypt, destroyed the Kingdom of Judah. But it was not just the cream of the Jewish people who were brought to Babylon; it was the cream of the known world. This was the largest and most powerful kingdom since legendary times. Nevertheless, Nebuchadnezzar was only a man, and in 561 he died. As often happens in the wake of the great, there were weak successors. For about a decade, four of these kings of Babylon struggled to maintain the far-flung kingdom.

It was around 550 B.C. that out of the northern mountains of Medea there rose a military and organizational genius known as Cyrus. Along with almost all of the known world, Cyrus eventually subjugated Babylon. This was one of the great watersheds of history. It marked the first victory of vigorous northern Aryans over the Semitic people of the desert. Cyrus was not only a great military leader, but he apparently was an emotional genius as well. He restored the Jewish people to their estate, and he organized trade and tax patterns that allowed for autonomy, and that made Persia the ruling power of the world from India in the east through Egypt in the west.

After the death of Cyrus the Mede and his son, Cambyses, who died mysteriously in Egypt, there arose to seize the reins of power a distant relative, Darius the First, a third giant in a century of giants. Persia still controlled almost the entire world, including the Aegean Coast of Turkey. Darius did not, however, control Greece. In fact, it is not at all certain that he had even heard of it. However, in time, squabbling among the Ionian coastal provinces brought the attention of Darius to the western world and Greece. It was thus in 490 B.C. that Darius with a navy and a mighty military expedition force mounted the entire power of his world against the little Greek state. He brought his cavalry by ship with ten thousand troops to the plains of Marathon, some twenty miles east of Athens. Herodotus gives a stirring and mystical description of this battle. There is no doubt that the Persians felt they could win easily. They were flush and confident with their victory over Eritrea. They had a wide flat plain for their army to maneuver in, and they had the advantage of intelligence, with the Greek traitor Hippias directing their invading army. At the same time, the Athenian troops were commanded by an unusual military table of organization. There were ten generals, and each of the ten rotated by days in command of the troops. This was a most unusual and unwieldy situation for running a war. It did become apparent, though, to all of the Athenian leadership that they must have help. With this in mind, they dispatched a professional long-distance runner, Pheidippides, to run about one hundred forty miles to the city-state of Sparta to get reinforcements against the eastern hordes.

According to Herodotus, Pheidippides along the way ascended a mountain and there met the god Pan, who called him by name. The god Pan asked the runner why the Athenians had been neglectful of him when he had been so friendly to them in the past. In appreciation for this most unusual appearance of the god, the Athenians after their victory built a special shrine to Pan under the mountain. After the brief interlude with the god, Pheidippides arrived in Sparta and asked for their help. He implored them not to stand by while the most ancient city of Greece was to be crushed by a foreign invader, as even now the Greek cities east of the Aegean had been enslaved. The Spartans were moved by the entreaties of Pheidippides. However, it was the ninth day of the month and, according to tradition, they could not leave for a military expedition until the moon was full. While they waited for the full moon, the treacherous Hippias guided the Persians on at Marathon.

Hippias himself the night before the battle dreamed that he was sleeping with his mother. He interpreted this dream to mean that he would return to Athens and recover his power and die peacefully at home in old age. This was only his first interpretation. On the following day when he was acting as a guide with the invaders, he became seized by a violent fit of sneezing and coughing. As he was an older man, most of his teeth were loose. One of his teeth fell out upon the ground; he searched and searched in efforts to find it, but it was nowhere to be seen. He then turned to his companions with a deep sign and said, "This land is not ours, we shall never conquer it, and the only part I have ever had in it, my tooth now possesses." The dream was then clear to him.

Although the Spartans did not come, about a thousand crucial men from the city of Plataea did come and joined with the Athenian troops. Herodotus makes much of the Plataeans as the faithful friends in contrast with the Spartans, who proved to be dilatory in their friendship.

The divided Athenian command could have been fatal had not the general of the War Archon, Miltiades, implored the other nine generals to effect a uniformed front. Through compromise, they agreed upon a battle plan and, under Miltiades, a decision was made to attack without waiting for the full moon and the Spartans.

For those interested in military history the battle has great significance. The Athenian infantry felt they could not face the Persian cavalry on the plain, so they narrowed the distance between the enemy by felling trees at night and moving them as obstacles to the plain. The Persians decided to remain on the defensive, expecting the impecunious Greeks to attack and thinking they could then outflank them with their cavalry.

Shortly before dawn, Athenian intelligence reported that the cavalry was away. Where they were is not quite clear, but perhaps they sought fertile grounds for feed and water elsewhere. On hearing this, Miltiades saw his chance. He thinned his forces at the center and strengthened the wings of his infantry line and then charged from the weak center across the plain and struck the Persian infantry with strong momentum. Although they were outnumbered considerably, the Greek infantry had longer spears and swords and heavy bronze protective armor. The Persians wore tunic, turban, and trousers and carried only wicker shields. As the Greek center was their weakest point, they had to depend on running for their momentum. The Greek wings were their strength, and they defeated their opponents. While they were doing this, the Persian counter-attack drove the Greek center backward. But the Greek wings wheeled in and outflanked and defeated the Persians.

The spot is marked to this day by a high mound covered with the ashes of the Greek dead. The Persians fled in disorder and, as the Greeks pursued with vigor, the Persian fleet came ashore Dunkirk-like to rescue their fugitives. The Persian fleet then sailed for Athens. The Athenian army marched rapidly home and arrived in time to prevent any landing at the city itself. The Persians departed beaten. According to Herodotus the Persians lost six thousand four hundred men compared to only one hundred ninety-two of the Athenians.

The battle is of enormous historical importance because it meant the preservation of the West, a Europe free and clear of the Eastern domination. The sequel to the battle comes ten years later, when the largest army ever assembled (the largest ever, that is, until the twentieth century), some 2,500,000 men returned in 480 to try again to conquer the Greeks, this time under the generalship of Darius Xerxes.

He too was to be defeated in a long series of battles recorded by Herodotus at Salamis, Artemisium, Thermopylae, and the rest. After the eventual withdrawal of Persian army there begins classic Western history. The Greek Golden Age ensued. About a hundred years later, under Alexander, the Greeks themselves turned the process about and conquered all of the eastern world.

One can only wonder at the tiny city of Athens and its victory. It is even remarkable from our perspective. History is replete with examples of small nations defeating great armies. The Finns stopped the Russians, the Vietnamese stopped the Americans, and the Maccabees stopped the Greeks, to name a few instances. I have pondered this somewhat. I think the best explanation is by the modern biologist/anthropologist Robert Ardrey. He points out the essential territoriality of the animal species. Whether it is the robin singing in the spring to let all others know his territory or the lion protecting his ground on the African veldt, there is something basic in all animal species with regard to land and territoriality. A people protecting their own land have their effectiveness multiplied by some factor. There is a parallel negative effect upon an invading army, which must bring far greater force to bear than the small defender. The power of man on his own land is enormously magnified. It is a lesson of history that seems to be continually repeated for lack of understanding.

One popular footnote to the battle of Marathon is the Pheidippides myth delineated by Plutarch, a Roman writing some five hundred years after the event itself. He tells the well-known story of the runner Pheidippides who, after the victory at Marathon, ran some twenty miles back to Athens, announced, "We are victorious," and dropped dead. This is undoubtedly fancy. Pheidippides would have had no trouble running this distance. He had, after all, run all the way to Sparta before the battle and had returned the following day, stopping along the way to talk to the gods. Since there are no contemporaneous reports of this event taking place, we must label it myth. If indeed he was a finely trained runner, sudden death is most unlikely, as we shall see.

I HAVE NEVER been much of an athlete. I was a fair high school tennis player and basketball player, but nothing really special. I am very proud that I hold one Nashville Interscholastic League record that I doubt will ever be equaled. In the school year 1946–1947, I scored exactly one point in NIL football and one point in NIL basketball. This one extra point and one foul shot for an entire year's production must surely stand the test of time. My career was continually plagued by a bad right knee. George Carpenter operated and removed the medial meniscus, the semilunar cartilage, when I was a high school junior. The operation was not successful, and the following year, my senior year when I set these unforgettable records, he operated again. My freshman year at college, I went out for the freshman basketball team. I was the last man cut, the thirteenth man on a twelve-man squad. Needing some exercise, I started jogging laps in the gym. It has become a lifelong habit. I have run distances along the dikes dividing rice paddies in Korea, the length of the Boardwalk in Atlantic City, the circumference of Hyde Park in London, along lonely beaches, and at the foot of the Tetons. I don't travel without my running shoes. It is a convenient way to exercise. It is inexpensive and portable. One doesn't need to find a friend of comparable ability with whom to play. One never has to agonize over why he lost or why his stroke is out of groove. It can be done in any weather, at any time of the year, at any time of night or day, at almost any place on earth. It takes a minimum amount of time, and it does not generate stories with which to bore one's friends concerning the perfect overhead smash or the exquisite bunker shot. While it is not without its drawbacks, such as dogs, vehicular traffic, and the disdain of one's neighbors, it can be accomplished with little investment of time or money.

As I approached running in my middle years, I was intellectually fortified to do so by two cardiologists. Doctor George Sheehan and Doctor Kenneth Cooper have both been extensively published and widely read. As much as anyone else, Doctor Cooper's books on aerobics are responsible for the enormous increase in jogging, which is to be seen everywhere around us. Largely the result of Doctor Cooper's efforts, there are ten million regular joggers in America today. His books have been translated into most of the major languages, and in some places where there in no direct translation for "aerobics," it is known as Cooper's. Doctor Cooper's point with aerobics was that regular rhythmic and extended physical exercise has a positive effect on the cardio-pulmonary functions. Doctor Cooper has published charts whereby an individual can earn points from extended exercise. He set a minimum of good cardiovascular help at thirty points a week. This could be earned by walking, cycling, jogging, swimming, or other similar repetitive-type physical activity. The commitment need not be great. Ten brisk walks of twenty-two minutes each is enough to earn the thirty points. Personally, the point system gave some structure to exercise, and for the past ten years, I have been earning my thirty points per week. Doctor Cooper came to his conclusions on aerobic exercise by working with fitness programs in the Air Force. He had an enormous amount of statistical information published in his books. He is a great advocate of the stress test for heart-sufficiency diagnosis. He also has a self-test of a mile-and-a-half run. For a man of sixty to have a good rating, he should be able to go a mile and a half in 16½ minutes. With proper conditioning, this not too tough. Since I was converted by Doctor Cooper, I surely would like to proselytize further among the uninitiated.

Doctor George Sheehan, on the other hand, was an athlete and runner before being a doctor. His plea for running is based on far broader basis than just the health of one's heart, blood vessels, and lungs. His books are of superb reading. He quotes liberally from Ortega, Santayana, and the like. He too agrees that running is the best exercise. He cites the ease of doing it. It is the physiologically perfect exercise. Running uses the large thigh and leg muscles in rhythmic fashion at a controlled rate. Beyond that, it also has good results for other body areas, including the mind. It reduces the weight. It lowers the blood pressure, it decreases cholesterol and triglycerides and, perhaps most importantly, it helps with psychological stability. Whereas golf is a tension-building activity, running is a tension-releasing activity. After a little training, take long jogs. There is very little exercise as tough as jogging a half-hour or as pleasant as jogging for a hour. There is oxygen, which has a palpable psychological effect. Running will not only make you well; it will make you happy.

Beyond these two writers, there is an enormous literature on jogging and running. Much of it is claptrap, but all of it I find interesting. There are those who would tell you that it can peel away the layers of civilization and return one to the jungle for the primal human instinct of running across the African savannahs—primal because running separated us from the arboreal apes. I find quite the opposite to be true. It is the daily activities at the hosiery mill that are closer to the jungle, and the running that is closer to the sublime.

Having jogged for so many years and seeing around me a national fad develop late in the day of my long history, I decided that the time had come to do something wherein the accomplishment could be measured. I made up my mind to run a marathon.

THE MODERN MARATHON was first staged in the revival of the Olympic games in Athens in 1896. Although the distance of the modern marathon has now been standardized at 26 miles, 385 yards, the first six races were at varying distances. It was in the 1924 marathon in London that the race extended to its present distance, because the British Olympic Committee wanted to start the race at the royal residence at Windsor Castle and finish in front of the Royal Box in London. Thus the British peerage made again its authority felt in the modern world. Today marathons are common. There are over three hundred of them that are American Athletic Union-authorized and run in this country every year, including the famous Boston Marathon on the 19th of April, Patriot's Day, commemorating Paul Revere's ride. People of all ages run marathons. Records show a five-year-old boy and a hundred-year-old man. Records are kept for each age and for both sexes. The best modern time for the twenty-six miles is about two hours and nine minutes.

The current world champion is an American, Bill Rogers. His marathons are the equivalent to running four-minute, fifty-five-second miles, twenty-six of them back to back. Over one hundred marathoners ran the Boston last year under two hours and twenty minutes. You can't even qualify this year unless you run it under two hours and fifty minutes. This is almost like sprinting the entire distance. The speed at which these runners move is impressive if you try to keep up with one for even one hundred yards. Rogers's record is the equivalent of forty-six eighteen-second hundred-yard dashes. The figures are no less impressive when you see the numbers of people doing it.

I worked my training into my after-work routine and regular long Sunday runs through the beautiful courses over the hills in Percy Warner Park. I would leave my car at Sam Fleming's wall and lope to the park, then around the 11.2-mile course and back, in about two hours. That is one-half a marathon, and the rest of Sunday was still before me. My race was sponsored by the Marathon Oil Company. It is known on the racing circuit as the Marathon-Marathon. It takes place at Terre Haute, Indiana. Terre Haute is a nondescript, homely little town on the Illinois border of Indiana. As far as I know it has no distinction other than being the place where Indiana State University is located. Indiana State is similarly undistinguished, other than having been NCAA runner-ups in basketball last spring with their great shooting forward, Larry Bird. The town is situated on U.S. 41. Enormous trailer trucks go up and down the main street so that it is noisy all day long and all though sleepless night of marathon eve. The name itself, Terre Haute, is somewhat ominous as hills are a distinct problem for the distance runner. Nevertheless, I have never seen a hill in Indiana and assume that the name is simply something given by a imaginative early French trapper.

THE DATE WAS June 2, A.D. 1979. The time the race was to begin was 7:00 A.M. Dawn came early. By race time the sun was high above the flat eastern horizon. By 6:15 hundreds of cars had arrived at the Indiana fairgrounds. The starting line was on an auto racing drag strip. There is a rural raunchiness about all fairgrounds that is intense enough during the fair itself to survive through the rest of the year. There was no place to sit, and the some thirteen hundred entrants shifted around nervously with their families or friends. A hedgerow separated the edge of the fairgrounds from the neighboring residential area. In the hours before a race all marathoners heavily ingest fluids. It was behind this hedgerow, in view of the hopefully sleeping residents, that most of the thirteen hundred entrants relieved their bladders. The six portable toilets provided were hopelessly inadequate. The marathoners further relieved their nervousness by going through various stretching rituals and by trading light trade talk with the other entrants. In the heavy early morning light, the scene was colorful. No two people had the same type running gear. There were participants of every age and each sex. I saw a girl of about seven and a man obviously in his late sixties. The only common denominator is that there were no fat people. Most were extremely thin, and the faces generally portrayed an intense, nervous intelligence. I saw one man who looked like a pirate with a shaved head, anchor tattoo, and a solitary earring in his right ear.

The weather was not good. There were no clouds in

the sky and, in spite of this, there was some ground fog. The morning temperature was about sixty degrees, and it was humid. The forecast the night before had been given as sixty degrees at starting time rising to seventy-five at noon. The humidity was also predicted. The great enemy of the long-distance runner is heat. The depletion of fluids through strenuous exercise is of course aggravated. The one great health danger is the exhaustion of body fluids. The likelihood of heat exhaustion is multiplied by each ten degrees of temperature. Temperatures in the forties and fifties are considered ideal. Temperatures of eighty degrees are quite dangerous. Further, the cloudless sky also bespoke the problems of sunstroke through long exposure, adding to the problem of heat exhaustion. I was glad I had a hat.

In a moment of reflection, I realize I was seized with an acute case of cold feet. After all, I am past fifty now, well into middle age, with substantial business and family responsibilities. And there is the shadow of anonymous death—in Terre Haute!—in short pants, without dignity. "An advanced case of adult infantilism," I could hear my father saying. Nevertheless, there is the honor of my group, and I have come this far and trained this long, and there is the starting gun, and here we go. The surging mass of thirteen hundred runners waddled forward at a duck's gait. After twenty seconds, I had reached the starting line. The mass of participants was at this stage one animal, a mighty millipede. One body and twenty-six hundred legs. The worm began to elongate, but even a mile down the road it was still one body. By the time, I reached the mark at one mile, the column had spread out perhaps a thousand yards.

The demeanor of the mass was grim. There were

obviously not many friends or acquaintances among the mass. Most had come from far away as I had, and all were strangers one to another. Nevertheless, as in many times of stress, a dark humor was to be heard. An older gentleman passed me and said, "Just my luck, a cloudless day and my wife forgot to pay my insurance premium." Ha. Ha. The two-mile mark came so quickly that I couldn't believe it. I was high as a kite. The adrenaline was flowing, and so was I. I wasn't even breathing hard, let alone noticing any personal discomfort. I had plotted my time for each mile along the course. I hoped to finish the first six miles in nine-minute intervals, the middle twelve miles in ten-minute intervals, and the last six in eleven-minute intervals. This pace would bring me in at four hours and a half. Hardly Olympic quality but enough to be certified for my maiden effort—the outside requirement is five hours. The race is officially over at that point, and the course is cleared. My task for the day was to finish the race under five hours, hopefully under 4½ and, on the other hand, not to perish while so doing. The morning was young and time would tell. At 2½ miles came the first aid station. Along the route children swarmed with cups of Gatorade or water and with sponges heavily soaked with ice-cold water. We had been admonished to drink heavily and often.

I did this. But I did not know how delicious the feel could be of cold water sponged over the body, its purpose to externally control body heat. The faster runners took advantage of these aid stations without even breaking stride. Drinking at full running speed is a learned skill. For me, it was enough to walk and to experience the meaning of refreshment. At a little over four miles, I voided behind

The Battles of Marathon

I ran the marathon in a T-shirt with the Shamus Club on the front and the Old Oak Club on the back.

a tree. The human body produces a urine at a constant rate. For marathoners of both sexes and all ages, it is a contest in which modesty loses to necessity. I am told that the helicopter doing news footage of the start of the New York Marathon on Staten Island over the Verrazano Bridge had to destroy the newsreel tapes because all they had was thirteen thousand participants peeing off the bridge. I had been on the course for one hour at mile seven and was nicely ahead of my schedule. I still felt fresh and was even beginning to enjoy the race with the help of the blessed aid stations each 2½ miles. At mile nine, the leader of the race on this out-and-back course passed me heading for home. I have never seen anybody running so fast nor with such an expression of zombie-like intensity. At least at this point in the morning, I was having more fun than he was. At about twelve miles, I became conscious that the mile markers were getting farther apart. Where is that halfway sign?

Eventually it came. Thirteen miles in under two hours. This meant I had three hours to do on the way back what I had done coming out in two. A piece of cake. I figured if I could just make it to mile fifteen, the rest would be my regular Sunday morning, 11.2-mile course through Percy Warner Park. I had done that often enough to know I could do it for a certainty. But the sun was getting hot, and there was no mistake about it: I was not running as fast as I had been. There were a few hills, and I decided to walk wherever I could find some shade. At mile eighteen, I had walked for ten minutes. At mile twenty, the time was exactly three hours and twenty minutes, right on my schedule. At this point, I knew that I could get back even if I had to crawl the last hour and forty minutes. I also experienced what is known to the marathoners as "the wall."

This is the time when the body has used up its sugar, glycogen, and is now having to burn body fats. My legs were fine, my breathing was fine, but I simply had no energy left. It was if I had weights on my feet. Other than the fatigue, I was still totally rational and still able to joke with those who were dragging along with me.

At this time, I decided that I would walk for five minutes and then jog for five minutes over the last six miles. The race was getting to be two hours past the time the winners had finished. The roadblocks that kept out the heavy traffic had been lifted. The few straggling runners were competing for road space with tractor-trailers. The rural Indiana countryside was now changed to grim manufacturing businesses, and the day was still hot and sunny. Eventually and surely, I arrive at the Banks of the Wabash festival-grounds. I checked the twenty-six-mile marker and only had 385 yards left. Here I noticed a historical marker to Paul Dresser, the brother of Theodore Dreiser. It was Paul who wrote the haunting turn-of-the-century song, *On the Banks of the Wabash*. Armed with this piece of information, wondering about why the brothers spelled their names differently, I headed for the barn. The last 385 yards were not a distance of exhaustion but one of exhilaration. I suddenly felt fresh and glided with what grace I could muster to the finish line to the deafening applause of the only two interested spectators, Natalie and Maria May. I was handed a marked tongue depressor as I crossed the finish line and found that I had finished 835th, my time 4 hours, 44 minutes. I made it, and I knew that my group would be proud.

Some four hundred people did not make it at all, and Natalie told me that the ambulances and rescue squads got increasingly busy during the later morning hours as the

heat took its toll of the runners and her anxiety mounted. My goals were accomplished. I didn't die. I did finish. There were ten "runners" behind me. My time was not double the time of the winner by about eight seconds. All in all it was okay. I will continue to jog. Marathoning, well, that was a bit quixotic. I won't be doing many more of those. But unlike Pheidippides, I didn't die. It didn't kill me, but it did kill an evening.

This was written soon after Jack Downey's release on my best information and beliefs. There are a few inaccuracies; i.e., Jack's books came from his mother and from the prison library. Jack has never written anything about his twenty-one years, and many of the details remain hazy. Whether this is from effacing modesty or from innate greatness, I don't know. So we remain in our own confinement as to our curiosity. Was he tortured? Was there shame? Was there despair? How much hope? Had I written this now, thirty-five years later, there would not be much more amplification. And, as W.S. Gilbert suggested, I have added merely corroborative detail to give artistic verisimilitude to an otherwise bald and unconvincing narrative.

Two Connecticut-Bred Yale Men Who Volunteered to Spy During War Time and Became Heroes

Read to the Old Oak Club February 26, 1976

IT OCCURRED TO me while writing the petit memoir that a little history lesson might be helpful and in the

Bicentennial year downright obligatory. In any case, my own story has at least for me a pleasing circularity and, as a ring is more impressive when borne upon a cushion, so might my little story be shown off best nestled upon the soft cushion of history.

On September 21, 1776, Nathan Hale was captured by British soldiers. He survived only fifteen hours after capture. It was not a pleasant fifteen hours. His captors were both savage and unkind. The generally compassionate British soldier in this regard acted in a manner uncharacteristic and unworthy. But this is the historical expectation of the spy. Nathan Hale during the night watch of his death requested a clergyman, and this was denied. He requested a Bible for a few moments of devotion, and this was denied. He was not allowed a letter to a friend or parent. Alone on Manhattan Island without acquaintance or companion, without an amiable word from an arrogant enemy, he was hanged by dawn's light. Only his famous statement of patriotism was to survive him. "I regret," he said, "that I have but one life to give for my country."

Nathan Hale's career as a spy lasted only seven days. One week before he was captured, he had been a young captain attached to the Continental Army under General George Washington. On September 14, he was stationed in that part of Manhattan known today as Harlem, then Harlem Heights. The Continental Army had just retreated from Long Island and had left the British in full possession of its entirety. Washington did not know the British intentions. It was natural that he should be anxious, lacking information as to which way they would continue their operations, if indeed they would continue them at all. He simply did not know whether to defend the city of New York or to make strategic retreat to a more defensible area. He wrote "as everything, in a manner, depends on obtaining intelligence of the enemy's motions, I do urgently entreat General Clinton to exert himself to accomplish this desirable end. Leave no stone unturned nor do not stick at any expense to bring it to pass. I was never more uneasy than on the account for my want for knowledge on this score."

Washington was in vital need of having answered such questions as: Will the British directly attack the island of Manhattan? Will they land on Manhattan? At what point? Will they drive across the island from the East River or from the Hudson River? Will they arrive at Turtle Bay or Bloomingdale? Do they intend to slip behind the four thousand troops I have left there?

The answers to these questions could not come about by divination. Somebody had to go out and find out firsthand. The search was undertaken for someone both competent and willing to undertake such a perilous mission. A young officer did appear, pale from recent sickness, and said, "I will take it." It was the voice of Nathan Hale. He told his friends that he felt that he owed this to his country in that so far while he had been in the army he had done little to help in any way. He certainly told them he had no expectation of promotion or reward. He simply wished to be useful.

He had been in the army nearly one year. During that time, he had done very little except exist. It would seem that the need to alleviate boredom is one of the motivating factors leading men of imagination to undertake difficult or dangerous missions. As we will see later in our story yet to unfold, a parallel takes place in a more recent war.

A Confetti of Papers

He left with the above questions and instructions in his mind and walked through Westchester to lower Connecticut and, near the town of Norwalk, took a small boat. He crossed Long Island Sound by night and landed in Huntington, Long Island. He stepped ashore at daylight. One can only wonder about his anxieties. He had chosen the cover of being a schoolmaster. Indeed, he had been one in the brief time between his graduation from Yale and his enlistment in the Continental Army. As he walked ashore not knowing where he was, he came upon a farmhouse and ventured to ask the whereabouts of work. He was told that there may be some as the British troops were eager for labor. He walked westward from Huntington to Oyster Bay. There he did find that there was an opportunity to help in loading carts for various British logistics as they moved westward toward Manhattan. Along the way, as he worked the wagon trains, he inquired as to how many troops were in each place and if more were expected, how long would they remain, and where did they expect to be going. He continued to work his way westward on the island and ultimately crossed into Manhattan to help with the unloading. When he arrived near the Battery, he found that the British already had crossed the river in large numbers and were fortifying sections of the lower city. He mingled among them and elicited enough information to make him feel that his mission was complete. Then on the fateful morning, just six months less than two hundred years ago, he started to make his way northward to find his commanding officer and friendly troops.

Apparently coincidentally, a mammoth fire broke out in lower Manhattan on this same morning. How Hale spent his day or if he used the confusion of the conflagration to hide his northward trip, we do not know. I imagine him under huge pall of smoke, making his way to the Harlem River. The British from Long Island sent boats to inspect the fire. One of these patrols came near Manhattan in the vicinity of what is now Ward's Island in the East River. A Captain Quarme decided to set ashore in a small patrol boat. Through the smoke Nathan Hale saw the small craft and unfortunately did not see the larger one from whence it came. He broke the basic rule of a spy; that is, never to act in a manner inconsistent with one's cover. In his anxiety, and his apparent wishful belief that the small patrol was actually his own troops, he exposed himself and was captured. As recounted, he lived only fifteen hours longer.

There was no published account of the above tale until twenty-three years after the event. It was some thirty years after that before any circulation was given to the story of Nathan Hale. Much of what is said above has been taken from letters, and no solid history or historian was contemporary to give much flesh beyond what I have related. We do know that he was an honest and upright preacher's son who had attended Yale and was much loved by his classmates. That he chose to be a spy during the Revolution was not in itself unique. There were many others. The fact is that it is simply impossible successfully to wage war or even diplomacy without accurate knowledge of the enemy. And as to the men and women who enter careers in this hazardous work, they seem to have common denominator of mostly admirable traits. A Revolutionary War historian summed up the spies of that war as follows:

Men or women who enter upon such a career must

possess strength of character and be bestowed with all qualifications of both good soldier and a commanding officer besides. A soldier must possess bravery and courage, but a spy must not only be brave and courageous but also must have what is called nerve, poise, self-possession, absolute control of facial expressions, fearlessness, tact, and discretion unequal. For his is the most hazardous of all undertakings. Discovery means death, the penalty afflicted alike by all nations.

And with these heavy words, we conclude our debt to the Bicentennial. The curtain can now be lowered to denote a passage of time. We skip ahead in our story, one hundred seventy-eight Yale graduating classes. It is now 1951.

———o———

JAPAN WAS TO that generation, what Paris had been for the generation that preceded mine. At the time of the Korean War, it was a foreign place but at once both familiar and exotic. That was a time and that was a place that combine the excitements of war overlaid upon a foreign geography both ancient and rich. To experience these circumstances at a time of life when new-found maturity and incipient adulthood make all experience more intense and heightened, more delicious and more painful, is to have something that those who entered graduate schools or the family foundries will forever be denied. So it was that Jack Downey, Jim Lilley, and I found ourselves in Japan. Our story begins on a particular weekend in the fall of 1952. We had made a date to leave our various posts in suburban Tokyo for a weekend in that great and second-most cosmopolitan of all cities to be together in youthful release. In Tokyo, it was fun in a very special sense. In coming into the twentieth century, Japan aped the United States as we imitated Europe two centuries before. Street lights and traffic signs were entirely familiar. Kids on vacant lots played baseball. Dozens of words were derived from everyday American English. At the same time, the Japanese copies of Chinese characters and the oriental appearance of the people continually reminded one that he was in a foreign place. Nothing so symbolized this dichotomy to me as seeing massive steam shovels driven by obviously competent, ordinary blue-collar types who always had flower arrangements in their cab. We were in a tougher and a gentler place.

Against this backdrop, Jim, Jack, and I embarked on what was to be, both in anticipation and the remembrance, a very pleasant weekend. We planned to go to see sumo wrestling. Both Lilley and Downey had been superior college athletes. Both were big, bright, and attractive. Both were superior by any standards. Their fellowship was of the best, and our spirits were high as we went to the Sumo Arena.

Grant me a digression on sumo. It is a sport most similar

A folding nickel

to wrestling. Two gigantic men face each other in a circle some ten yards in diameter. The object is for either man to push the other out of the circle or to cause any portion of his body, other than the bottom of his feet, to touch the mat. If he does so, he is the winner. This is a sport that requires no stamina, only an extreme burst of momentum and energy, released quickly. This burst, combined with a sense of balance and a knowledge of the martial arts, enables the better athlete to win or lose almost immediately. Wrestlers are men of huge weight, some over three hundred fifty pounds. They smack together in the middle of the ring and, within a few seconds, the bout is over one way or another. The only American sport that has a similarity is the line play of a football team. As a human endeavor in terms of subtlety and

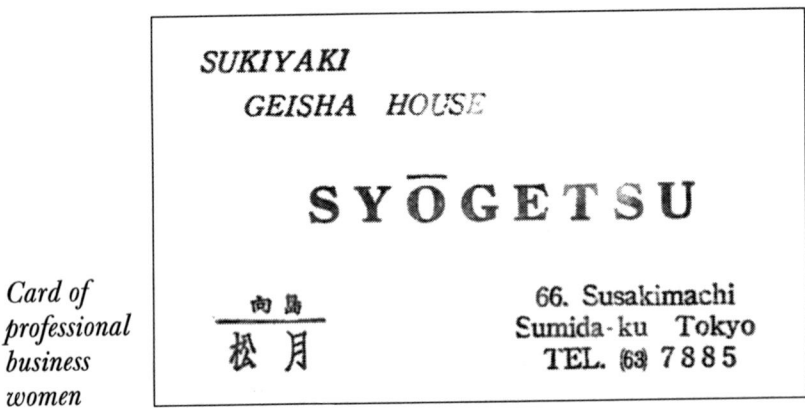

Card of professional business women

endurance, it quite contrasts with the practice of espionage. So we sat the afternoon out, watched with interest, ate our sashimi, and looked forward to the evening to follow.

After piling out of the crowded arena, we hailed a taxi in the fall twilight and sped away to the delights of the famous Yoshiwara section of Tokyo. We had a evening of entertainment in a modified geisha house. After a delicately sufficient dinner, the early evening was passed in childlike games of fun. Then the later evening was spent in more honest activity. Japan is the only place in the world where a trip to a whorehouse could be called a spiritually uplifting experience. Sunday morning then came bright and beautiful with no sense of degradation but instead only a sense of proportion and rightness that goes with so much that is Japan. We spent a quiet Sunday in Tokyo, eventually walking around the University, kicking at leaves as we had done in the four falls in New Haven. Late that afternoon in Tokyo station, we departed for our respective billets, and the weekend was completed. I was to spend other happy weekends with Jim Lilley. But the next week, Jack Downey disappeared, and I was not to see him again for twenty-two years.

A LITTLE BACKGROUND might be helpful. The three of us, Lilley, Downey, and I, had volunteered prior to graduation senior year at Yale for service in the CIA. I am not sure what motivated my friends, but for me it was a rational act of patriotism. I can remember discussing into the night with my own roommate that I had learned nothing in college that so rang of the truth as the American experiment as expressed in the sentiments of the Founding Fathers. I had found nothing so antithetical to this as the Communist Movement, particularly the Asian version with its gloomy debasement of the human panache. Besides that, I was sick as the devil with the academic routine, and what the hell. A number of our other classmates so volunteered, and with them I had gone to Washington. I was eager. I did not wait for commencement. They could mail me my diploma. There was a war on!

A Confetti of Papers

The elementary training was four intensive months. The areas covered were diverse. They included bureaucratic administration on the one hand to the running of espionage nets on the other. Some were trained in executive-type action such as sabotage and psychological warfare. This executive-type activity was not so practical as it had been in World War II. The main difference was that this was Asia. Whereas the OSS could drop men to the France resistance, it was almost impossible to lose a six-foot blond in Central China. The bravest among us obviously could not be used in these capacities, and motivated indigenous personnel had to be employed.

It was to one of these parachute-type organizations that Jack Downey had been assigned. His primary function was to train agents for dropping behind the lines to get military, political, and economic intelligence and to exfiltrate them at some time after the parachute drop. These agents could come out either by working their way to the coast to be picked up by small boats or through the technique of an air snatch pick-up. This involved sending over a propeller-driven aircraft with a harness from a goalpost-looking device and literally picking the man off the ground into the airplane. Whether through boredom (remember Nathan Hale) or through devotion to a particular agent who was going to infiltrate or for whatever reason, Jack Downey decided to make an overflight north of the Yalu River. Over Chinese territory the plane came in low at the landing site. The trap, however, had been set. The Chinese had found out about the mission. A plane flying low and under a hundred miles per hour is an easy target, and it was shot down. The C-47 crashed on a barren Manchurian hilltop.

Two Connecticut-Bred Yale Men Who Volunteered to Spy

The scene as Jack later described it could only be called comic as is so often the case with terror recalled. Man was not designed and can't be trained for moments of confusion and fear. As the plane crashed, everyone was strapped into their bucket seats, and miraculously no one was killed. There was a sound of machine gun fire, the cracking of branches, the scream of steel as it ripped apart, the shouts of high-pitched Chinese, and small-arms fire. In the midst of all this, Jack started running as hard as he could. It was some seconds later he discovered that he was still in the place where he had been sitting and had neglected to undo his seat strap. He was quickly taken into custody and immediately put in jail, where he was to spend the next twenty-one years in isolation. For those of us on the outside, there was total silence for two years and an assumption that he had been killed. With a deep and a heavy heart, we all wrote letters to his mother.

Our bereavement was authentic. I wonder if there is any truer sense of mortality than that which comes with the loss of that first close contemporary.

Jack was a New Englander. He was born and grew up in New Britain, Connecticut. His mother was a schoolteacher; his father, I believe, died when he was young. The family was of modest means. Although Jack did have a famous uncle, the Irish tenor Morton Downey, he had to have financial aid to get through Yale. He worked hard in various menial positions that were provided by the school to the scholarship student. His academic achievement was high, as was his esteem among his classmates. He believed that sacrifice leads to accomplishment. He once expressed to me bewilderment in that he played his best football game for Herman Hickman after having been out for his first and only time ever before a Saturday game to drink beer with his friend. I remember him as an undergraduate with a good sense of humor and a sense of proportion both about himself and Yale that was rare among his classmates.

During the year following the shooting down of the airplane Jack was placed in a Northern Chinese prison and was interrogated intensively. One can assume that some torture was involved. It was not uncommon in this period simply to chain someone to a bed and leave him there. Usually after two days or two weeks he was willing to say whatever was known. It is the practice among intelligence services to no longer attempt to have their agents maintain secrets by silence. What thumbscrews could not drag forth from a man Sodium Pentothal now accomplishes. As a defense against this type of interrogation, most intelligence services just tell people what they "need to know." The "need to know" system implies that once an operative is compromised he is expected to tell all that he knows, but through his limited knowledge, all he knows is compartmentalized only to his immediate area of activity. Much of the rest of the organization's activities are thereby protected. Jack did in fact tell all he knew. He has since told me that he described me so well to the Chinese Communists that they knew every necktie I owned. He was so voluminous in his disclosures that the Chinese at one point assumed that he was manufacturing the whole thing as no one could remember that much detail.

After this period of long debriefing on our intelligence practices, the trial was held for those men who were captured. Jack assumed that the Chinese had all they wanted and would, after a token sentence, release him. Jack was either more naive than Nathan or the times appeared less dangerous to the revolution. He remembered standing in front of the judge thinking, *Well, here goes three years of my life.* At this point, the judge started passing sentence on the Chinese who were captured on the airplane and, as he came down the line of people in the dock, the judge sentenced by saying death, death, death, death, and at this point, he reached Downey and said life imprisonment. Jack remembers only a feeling of exquisite relief. The fact of life seems sweet after the prospect of death, which was given to the unfortunate Chinese. Those others captured, the lesser officer and pilots, were given sentences in the five- to twenty-year range. There is no time off for good behavior or anything else under the Chinese system.

Jack was taken off to a prison in Peking and there set about spending his life in a foreign jail. It was effectively a solitary confinement. He did not see any of the others captured with him or any other Americans. The exception to this was his two hours out of doors each day on the exercise ground. He was neither allowed contact with the Chinese jailer, nor was he ever allowed to speak anything except English. The study of the Chinese language was denied to him.

IN THE HOPELESSNESS of this situation, Jack did survive, and survived fairly well. His first technique for this survival was to make a daily routine to which he adhered exactly. He arose in the morning, did sitting-up exercises, cleaned out his cell, went to a propaganda session given by the Chinese, set aside time for running during the exercise period, and spent the rest of the day in reading and at other chores that he devised for himself. He did not deviate from his daily structure. He survived twenty years of solitary confinement and made it seem possible. His mother sent him paperback books, many of which he received. His survival strategy became one of running and of reading. He would run two hours on the playing ground to maintain a good physical condition, and the rest of the day would be spent in reading and reflection.

The reading consisted of the *belles-lettres* as well as lesser modern works at least up until the 1930s in America. He read and he read. He read *War and Peace* seven times, every third year while he was in prison. He read the great books so often that the structure of the author's concept would be revealed and the fabric of the books would fall apart. I asked Jack what author held up best. He said without hesitation, Scott Fitzgerald. He could not get enough of *The Great Gatsby* and would reread it constantly, always finding something new in its pages. Another surprising choice of his was an American book called *Drums Along the Mohawk*. I bought it when Jack told me of its excellence but was unable to force my way through this adventure story of the American Revolution.

He got no news of the outside world, but he was aware that the war was going on in Vietnam. The propaganda that he listened to was extremely heavy-handed and, even through years and years of captivity, it made little impression upon him. (How about that, Patty Hearst?) Jack said that under torture they can make you say anything but make you believe nothing. If the Chinese knew techniques for brainwashing, they certainly were not successful in this instance. The shape of the world was so distorted from the Chinese point of view that he really never had any concept of the geopolitics of that long period from 1952 to 1973. Once a month he got a mail package from his mother, which could only contain magazines of sports or college interest. They sometimes included the Yale alumni magazine. He was allowed to write one letter a month. The magazines and the letters were through the courtesy of the Red Cross. His letters were written on a piece of stationery that measured one inch high and one and one-half inches long. He wrote microscopically on both sides, and he would send his mother messages always of good humor. His knowledge of great events came often from inferences. In one Yale alumni magazine he saw that you could send off for a stamp showing a first-day cover of man's landing on the moon.

His treatment varied over the years, often as reflection of internal stresses and external concerns of the Chinese. During the episode of the Red Guards his food was far worse than in periods of relatively good times.

In 1958, Jack felt that he could have been released if John Foster Dulles had simply taken one opportunity to admit that he had been in the CIA. He felt his release could have been obtained quickly. As it was, he had to wait until Henry Kissinger's visit to China in 1971. The Chinese asked only the admission of his participation in Central Intelligence Agency activities. Ultimately Nixon did this in a news conference, and Jack was released in 1973 at Hong Kong.

My own assumption had been that the Chinese were simply using him as a trading pawn and that he would be released either for some captured Chinese agent whom they wanted returned or some military advantage such as the return of Quemoy and Matsu. It turns out such was not the case. I expect his release was due to vast global political movements and to antipathy toward the Soviet Union, which meant a need for bridging the gap with the U.S. Jack was the most-ready token with which to express these needs. I am told that Kissinger said that Nixon would not make the trip unless the release of this man was obtained. So in spring of 1973 out came Jack.

He was unchanged to the casual eye. His health was good, his weight was the same as it had been when he went in and, except for a dental problem or two, he was as fit as any forty-two-year-old could expect to be. He was flown to Hartford and met at the plane by a number of dignitaries. Among those meeting him was my old roommate and Jack's closest friend, Bob Longman. Downey's first remark to him on stepping off the plane was hardly profound. "Has anybody seen *Deep Throat?*" said Jack.

After Jack's short convalescence and debriefing by various officials, it was time to have a party. Bob Longman on Long Island arranged it, and Nat and I drove up to New York to spend a happy evening of reunion. A number of Jack's football and wrestling contemporaries were there. In a word, he was fine. He was jocular and happy. I had enough hours with him to know that he was and remained a whole person. One remarkable fact about him was that he was rich. There are two ways to get rich: one is to make a lot of money and the other is not to spend any. Jack took the latter route. He had hardly been in a position to spend any money, and his pay simply piled up in his account at J.P. Morgan during the twenty-one years of his absence.

His brother had become a financial manager and evidently managed his funds well. We were making about seven

Jack Downey, Jack May, and Jim Lilley at Langley Headquarters, June 25, 1998. (Photo by George Tenet)

thousand dollars a year at the time of his capture, and I guess this must have risen over the period to almost a quarter-million dollars.

The day I saw him, he had just gotten his prisoner's pay from the government. Evidently, the U.S. Government pays two dollars a day additionally to anyone who is prisoner of war. Jack was so considered. He therefore had something over eleven thousand dollars' worth of these two dollars. He also had massive amounts of accumulated vacation. I think this amounted to something over four years, which he could take at full pay and spend in any manner he liked. When I saw him he was toying with the idea of teaching in his old prep school or perhaps going back to graduate school. He in fact chose the latter. He is now at his third year at Harvard Law School, and doing very well. He married last year. The girl is a microbiologist on the Yale faculty. She is a Chinese-American, and I'll let the Freudians among you ponder that one.

I asked him the usual questions. He said the next person who comes up to him and says, "Well, Rip Van Winkle, what do you see that is different?" he is going to have to give him a bust in the nose. But he did admit to only two things that were different. One was the speed of the automobiles on the Interstate highways. He just simply couldn't get use to going to seventy-five miles an hour. The second thing that he was unable to adjust to was the electronic music that had become standard of a new generation. For a person who had always been a jazz buff, it was hard even to conceive of rock as music. Although he did not say so in so many words, he felt some results of the sexual revolution. He was something of a celebrity, and his opportunities with girls were expanded far beyond what he could remember from generations before. He had many proposals of marriage, including at least four from ex-nuns who thought he sounded like a good prospect. He was also trying to get his fill of ice cream. The craving for familiar food denied takes longer to sate than other desires where catching up is quicker.

When I saw him, it was two months after his return. He was spending his days identically as he had spent them in jail. He would run in the morning and read in the afternoon, often driving from New Britain to New Haven to use the Yale Library. But his regime was identical.

He listened with interest to the progress that his old classmates had made. He said that he envied none of it except their families. His younger sister had been married and had children. They were the happiest things he had found. As far as the classmates' careers, he found little to interest him in any of it. Hard to believe anything made much difference, he said to me. "You know it is going to be awfully hard for me to believe any of it is important enough to make me really care."

So I left Jack and left Natalie with her mother and started to drive on home. First night, I stopped in Washington to visit with friend Jim Lilley, whom you remember from the early paragraphs of this long tale. Jim's wife Sally cooked a marvelous dinner and we reminisced about old times. I told them much of what I have told you tonight. Jim had remained with the CIA. He worked hard, studied long, and had become one of the most successful rising young career men in the organization. He told me that instead of going into Eastern Europe his assignment had just been changed. He had spent the weekend before at San Clemente in an intensive briefing session with Henry Kissinger. Jim was to leave the following week to go to Peking. He was in fact, to open China for the CIA. I said, "Even after I have told you that every detail of your existence is in dossiers in Peking, do you still intend to go?" Jim laughed. He said. "Well, sure. They know who I am and what my connections are. This has all been cleared well in advance with Chou En-lai." The fact was that Chou knew that Jim Lilley was one of the most knowledgeable Chinese experts in America and wanted him in the Embassy. The fact that he was Central Intelligence at this level did not faze the Chinese in the slightest. The only thing that Jim felt concerned about was keeping the above confidential, not so much as to protect him, but to protect the Chinese hosts from being embarrassed by a CIA man coming to light in a high place. Had not Jim's presence since been revealed by that great slime columnist, Jack Anderson, I would not be telling you tonight.

A Confetti of Papers

AND SO MY little story comes to an end for the three of us who spent a weekend in revelry in 1952 in Tokyo. One had spent twenty-one years in solitary in Peking and had come out only to find another going right back into Peking. I hope that you find this symmetry interesting and its circularity, in some mystic way, profound. I am an admirer of both Jim Lilley and Jack Downey. They are both made of stern stuff. Rare.

Before closing maybe I should cover just a few more points beyond the story just completed. First I would like to thank the Old Oakers for the indulgence of a personal remembrance. Listening to a story of one's past is always for the listener like having to watch a good friend's trip slides. No matter how good the friend or how good the slides, there is always the hope that the bulbs will burn out. I am almost through.

You might wonder after my obvious admiration for these men and for our cause why I left the intelligence business after only four years. I like to remember that decision as one of principle. First of all, I did not want to spend my life making war, cold or hot. Secondly, I detested the bureaucracy. Those organizations that are not subject to the discipline of the marketplace are always political, often in the worse sense. Since there is no objective way to evaluate individual performance, life becomes one of convincing the echelon above of the worth and merit of the individuals and projects of the echelon below. It is not how good you are, for indeed there is really no way to measure that—it is how good your superiors think you are. It is this impossibility of performance evaluation that make so fundamental the manure, both chicken and bull, that is commonly associated with bureaucratic structure. Never had I known as many able men assembled in one place and never had I known so many motivated men put together in one organization. At the same time, never did I see so much waste of talent as within the bureaucracy, and the profligacy with money was incredible. If this is true for the CIA's dedicated, even inspired, workers, what must it be at the Bureau of Mines? The typical CIA professional was brilliant, scholarly, and serious. Were you to ask me who among our Old Oak group was most stereotypical of my colleagues in CIA, I would unhesitatingly rejoin, "Surely Harry Ransom," and from the Shamus Club, "Sam Richmond." Instead of the attention and energy of these men being focused on the external tasks, all heads are turned backwards as if swept along by the paper blizzard of reports, always self-serving, blowing toward the Great Wastebasket on the Potomac.

So I did at least two things in my life on principle. I joined the CIA, and I got out of it and went to making socks. The scope of manufacturing socks is exceedingly narrow as compared to the world-view problems of Central Intelligence Agency. But nevertheless, the frustrations are much less. Decisions are possible, and the result is a humble but useful product. A sock functions well and sells at a low price. At the end of the year one can look at some numbers and see how well you did it. For those of you outside of the marketplace, you can never be this sure.

Of course, your reader this evening has strong feelings about the essential need for intelligence, the need for a strong and alert America, and our need to have a place in Asia. But all of these things are beyond the scope of this evening's personal presentation. Events in Southeast Asia and the recent disclosures concerning the CIA are hardly surprising to me;

however, the absence of surprise in no way diminishes my sense of loss at the conquest of a nation, any nation, and my sense of anxiety grows over America's even greater need for intelligence in the world where evil seems ascendent as it has at no time since the 1930s.

The CIA, or at least its predecessor, was conceived in the shock and surprise of Pearl Harbor. There will be no redemption from another such surprise. My prayer is that the nation will survive. But to do so the government must be organized in its intelligence services more to overlook and discourage the James McCords, Gordon Liddys, and Howard Hunts, and more to find and encourage the Jack Downeys, Jim Lilleys, and the Nathan Hales. Can it do so? I don't know.

I'll work on it for my Tricentennial paper.

Epilogue (2004)

As a postscript, here is an update on CIA, Lilley, Downey, and me.

The CIA remains a government agency. We did have another shock and surprise. The 9/11 attack killed twice as many people as we lost at Pearl Harbor. Thank God that there may be a redemption from this surprise. But maybe not the third time. Whatever else bureaucracies are, they are not nimble. I have no contacts left in Washington. Whatever feelings I have are just adumbrations from the shadows. My guess is that the CIA was filled with Soviet experts, Russian-language speakers, and Kremlinologists at the time the Wall fell in 1989. Government bureaucracies are inert. After the first World Trade Center bombing in 1994 it was clear to the dullest eye that we needed Arabists and needed them fast. However, what in the world do you do with all of these employees who were fighting the Cold War and will be undigested until their retirement? The CIA had neither the energy, money, nor will to turn on the necessary dime.

Jim Lilley went on to a distinguished career in diplomacy. He was the United States Ambassador to Beijing at the time of the Tiananmen Square riot and atrocities. He is *the* American expert on China. He makes continual appearances on the networks and cable news channels when a China issue comes up. This great man is currently finishing his memoirs, to be published later this year.

Jack Downey was, incredibly, refused admission to Yale Law School. He did, however, go to Harvard Law

This advertisement for James Lilley's superb book China Hands *includes a picture of Jack May and Lilley in Japan, here enlarged.*

School and did very well against his classmates a generation younger. He attempted to run for the United States Senate. The liberal governor of Connecticut, Ella Grasso, had taken him under wing. In this quest, he failed. He returned to New Haven. He lives on St. Ronan Street, across from my cousins, the Osterweises, in a big, comfortable house. He became a judge and he has worked for years with inner-city youths as a juvenile court justice. He was honored last year by the New Haven Bar when they named the new courthouse in his honor.

Yale, however, continues to ignore this hero and refuses to honor him for fear that the nut-left faculty will attack the school or anyone who honors America. "For God, for Country and for Yale" has gone away. It is now for political correctness to the exclusion of all else.

Some of us have written letters to get Yale to give Jack an honorary degree. But it ain't gonna happen.

Finally, Jack May. Jack has managed to go on to his thirtieth year in Shamus.

Two Connecticut-Bred Yale Men Who Volunteered to Spy

GEORGE BUSH

March 7, 2003

Dear Jack,

I appreciated your letter of February 26 "seconding the motion" for a letter of endorsement on behalf of Jack Downey. Jim Lilley wrote me about this a couple of weeks ago and I immediately fired off a letter to Yale.

I have great respect for Jack Downey, and I hope he gets this well deserved recognition.

Thanks for checking in.

All the best,

G Bush

Mr. Joseph L. May
Attorney at Law
Post Office Box 190628
Nashville, TN 37219-0628

P. O. BOX 79798 · HOUSTON, TEXAS 77279-9798
PHONE (713) 686-1188 · FAX (713) 683-0801

Some of us have been trying to get Downey an honorary Yale degree. It ain't gonna happen.
— J. M.

With debt to Richard S. Kennedy's *Dreams in the Mirror*, a jazz life is superficially examined with some poetic residue provided. College roommate in 1950, John Rawlings wrote and produced a musical of "IXI." It was performed once and was the best theater I have ever seen.

a brief, sad, and lower case of e e cummings

Read to the Old Oak Club November 23, 1983

A SKETCH WILL follow outlining an interesting life. Particular emphasis will be upon some high adventures during World War I and low adventures during three marriages. The life of e e cummings, though of interest, is a life somehow cramped, stunted, and crabbed. Perhaps therefore this evening (as with his life itself) can be redeemed in its tangible residue: the poems, the poems themselves. I will read a few of these at end of this paper. A few that have given me pleasure through the years. Maybe in indulging me the fun of reading these poems, you too will take some pleasure. In the late 1900s, the material and the sensual have too quickly filled the poetry void as poetry left our lives. It is a circumstance for regret.

edward estlin cummings (1894–1962) was a certifiable giant of twentieth-century letters. As an innovator he stands alongside T.S. Eliot, Ezra Pound, and James Joyce. He, in his own way, revolutionized modern literary expression. Beyond his assured status as a poet, he was a man of various and developed parts. He was a Cubist painter, a pianist, and a brilliant conversationalist. He was a romantic, if irrational, curmudgeon. He started his life as an idealistic intellectual, but as that life wore on and as his health grew frailer and his experience deeper, he became more and more embittered.

He hated much of that which he saw around him, and he saw quite a bit. These hates were universal, contradictory, and consuming.

By the end of his life a list of those things that he did not like was long and various. He did not like Communists, socialists, or fascists. He did not like conservatives or Democrats. He did derive pleasure from a few things, but the pleasure that he did find in friends, in nature, and in his family was random and occasional.

He professed to love only that which was innocent and not foolish, that which was childlike, not childish. Most of his adult life was spent in Greenwich Village. But the bleakness of the city and the crassness of its people always grated. In some ways those most successful of all New Yorkers, the Jews, particularly riled his sensibilities. Of course, true to fact and to cliché, his best friends were indeed Jews.

a brief, sad, and lower case of e e cummings

Some anti-Semitism:

a kike is the most dangerous
machine as yet invented
by even yankee ingenu
ity (out of a jew a few
dead dollars and some twisted laws)
it comes both prigged and canted

Personally, he was a man of enormous erudition and could be charming to boot. His good friend John Dos Passos described him as the most entertaining man he had ever met. In his younger days he could be a dreadful show-off. Social occasions called for a performance. He loved to entertain with his brilliant and mordant wit. He played the piano like fireworks and talked the same way. Archibald MacLeish describes a visit to cummings in 1924 when he put on a virtuoso performance. He talked for eight solid hours. He continued—always entertaining, never boring. His head was a storehouse of memorized verses. He quoted Sappho in Greek, Laforgue in French, Horace in Latin, and Lowell and Longfellow in English. He could weave the various poets and languages together with a spontaneity of wit that could be at once beautiful and funny. The consummate punster, he could blend scraps from ancient and foreign languages punctuated with common and slang phrases. He was a painter as well as a poet. This fact may account for his acute sensitivity to nature. He lived in a period when artistic experimentation was in full flower. The influx of new ideas came in waves from Europe. Cubism, Fauvism, and the full spectrum of

Abstract Impressionism can be traced over to the intellectual exercise of his poetry in a rather straight-line relationship.

In personality he was, even to his close friends, modest and retiring. Once outside that circle he was almost pathologically protectively wrapped within himself. Another figure of the era, Charlie Chaplin's tramp, is a close analog.

But if it is true that he loved art and love and innocence, by the end of his life he hated almost all else. He was a common grouch, a tireless grumbler. He somehow blamed the Korean War on Franklin and Eleanor Roosevelt. When Kennedy invited him to the White House, he scornfully turned it down. He who for years had heaped scorn on American values was totally of America. Like his hometown of Boston, he was as good at building tradition as at tearing it down. Acerbic and mordant to the core, his apple had enough cinnamon for traditional apple pie.

Some anti-FDR. Shrapnel gets through where philosophy doesn't:

plato told

him:he couldn't
believe it(jesus

told him;he
wouldn't believe
it)lao

tsze
certainly told
him,and general
(yes

a brief, sad, and lower case of e e cummings

mam)
sherman;
and even
(believe it
or

not)you
told him:i told
him;we told him
(he didn't believe it,no

sir)it took
a nipponized bit of
the old sixth

avenue
el;in the top of his head:to tell

him

---

cummings was born in 1894 in Boston. His father was a Unitarian minister. Boston was the Unitarian town of Emerson and Lowell. Edward Cummings the father was the minister at the church of the Harvard establishment. A puritan Brahmin. His house was learned and pious. The home environment was as rich and solid as the Harvard Cambridge atmosphere that surrounded it. Young cummings attended the finest schools, Cambridge Latin and ultimately Harvard itself. He did not make Phi Beta Kappa as had his father and uncle. But he did graduate *magna cum laude* in English with emphasis in Greek and Classics. His AB degree came in 1915, and he stayed another year to get his master's in English in 1916. He might have continued in academics, but there was a war on.

As did many classmates (Dos Passos among them), he volunteered for the Red Cross Norton-Harjes Ambulance Corps. Support for the war was strong at Harvard. President Lowell urged participation. The ambulance service provided the vehicle for many. This interest, even eagerness, is in marked contrast with my own experience at Harvard fifty-two springs later.

As well as I can judge, the students of 1916 were also pacifistic in nature. If this were true, the ambulance corps' being non-combatant answered that objection. This service had other advantages. The drivers were classified as officers without the burden and responsibility of command.

Although there was little danger, the prestige of the drivers was high. It was easy. There was no training if you could drive. And the enlistment was short, just six months. Above all it involved sharing in the great experience of their time. To be there and to be there with little regimentation probably explains the Harvard volunteers.

On the boat trip over, cummings met Slater Brown, a recent graduate of Columbia. The two found that they had much in common and became fast friends. They were both twenty-two years old. On the train trip across France to Paris the two became separated from their group when the rest got off at the wrong station. Brown and cummings reported separately from the balance of the contingent and were told to come back when the rest arrived. In the ensuing snafu their records were lost. It took six weeks to find them, and in the meantime the two youths had a Paris holiday. As with so many of this generation they had a romance with this city. They enjoyed all of its delights, aesthetic ambience, culinary expansion, and sexual initiation.

a brief, sad, and lower case of e e cummings

Some porn:

> she being Brand
>
> -new;and you
> know consequently a
> little stiff i was
> careful of her and(having
>
> thoroughly oiled the universal
> joint tested my gas felt of
> her radiator made sure her springs were O.
>
> K.)i went right to it flooded-the-carburetor cranked her
>
> up,slipped the
> clutch(and then somehow got into reverse she
> kicked what
> the hell)next
> minute i was back in neutral tried and
>
> again slo-wly;bare,ly nudg.   ing(my
>
> lev-er Right-
> oh and her gears being in
> A 1 shape passed
> from low through
> second-in-to-high like
> greased lightning just as we turned the corner of Divinity
>
> avenue i touched the accelerator and give
>
> her the juice,good
>   it
>
> was the first ride and believe i we was
> happy to see how nice she acted right up to

the last minute coming back down by the Public
Gardens i slammed on
the

internalexpanding
&
externalcontracting
brakes Bothatonce and

brought allofher tremB
-ling
to a:dead.

stand-
;Still)

When at last they did report to their unit, they were unprepared for the squalor of the backwash of warfare. The days were filled with boring make-work among insensitive mates. The two Ivy Leaguers held themselves aloof. Apart from their equals, they scoffed at the system. It is another repetition of the conflict of the intellectual with the military. After World War II Herman Wouk laid it out fictionally in the conflict between Queeg and the college officers in his underrated novel, *The Caine Mutiny.*

Of course they got in trouble. The case against them was documented by the censors. Brown wrote home of poor French morale and made sport of the French leaders. With this evidence both men were arrested and interrogated. When asked if they hated the Germans, they did not respond. That was enough for the authorities, and off to prison they went. A minimum security facility, but surely a prison. This concentration camp was several hours by train west of Paris at La Ferté Mac. The other inmates were petty criminals and assorted misfits, both male and female, who were caught one way or another as Kafkaesque flotsam of war. cummings kept copious notes while confined and three years later published *The Enormous Room.* The book is still in print in Modern Library.

Aphoristic truth:

*a politician is an arse upon
which everyone has sat except a man*

In the fall of 1917, both of the inmates were released. This was accomplished after no little string-pulling at levels as high as the U.S. cabinet. Both were immediately sent home. Typically, while the American boys were going "Over There," cummings was headed over here. He landed in New York and spent the winter of 1917–1918 enjoying the intellectual and ethnic pleasures of the city. One particular favorite for intense delight was the Yiddish theater. But with the war still raging, these pursuits did not last. He was drafted in the spring of 1918 and was sent to Fort Devon, Massachusetts. At this stage of maturity he was able to handle the army life well enough, but he deeply detested it. In his correspondence he waxed bitter about the stultifying bureaucracy, the coarseness, and the boredom. Finally, this pacifist's life as a warrior ended with the armistice.

THEN IN NOVEMBER 1918 cummings headed for New York and fifteen years of romantic adventure and professional frustration. He, in those fifteen years, accomplished ten books and three wives.

The first of his wives was Elaine Elliot Orr Thayer. The girl and the romance itself are a perfect evocation of the era: the American 1920s, subset Greenwich Village bohemia. Elaine was the orphaned daughter of a rich man. At an early age she was sent to boarding school, first to Westover and then finished at Miss Bennett's. She was a beauty, graceful and demure. She was perfect in coiffure and in dress. A pre-war appearance (see Charles Dana Gibson) with a post-war flapper attitude (see John Held Jr.).

Her story is a full one and might best be followed diagrammatically. In this period, she (A) marries (B) but lives off and on with (C) with B's acquiescence. A gets pregnant by C and has the baby. After the baby A divorces B and marries C. On the honeymoon with C she falls in love with (D), whom she marries later the same year after divorcing C.

The cast of this drama are first Schofield Thayer (B), an intellectual entrepreneur. He started a little magazine, *Dial*, in Chicago. He and Elaine married in 1916. cummings (C) met the couple before their wedding and before he left Harvard. He was smitten with the bride but wrote a long wedding poem idolizing both of the partners. When he returned from France he again took up with the couple. With the husband traveling, Elaine got pregnant and had Nancy, cummings's only child, in 1920. The young poet, in the face of this, expatriated. He spent two and a half years in Europe writing. Upon his return he married Elaine in 1924. While on the boat for a European wedding trip she met a rich intellectual banker from London named McDermott (D). She fell in love and in months left cummings. cummings did, however, adopt his daughter, and she took his name. The legal struggle to accomplish this took years and much emotional capital.

Five years pass until his second marriage. In this interim, the shy Puritan managed to cut a swath in the circle where New York society and literati intersect. During this period cummings had his innings with Emily Vanderbilt. This was at the time she was divorcing William H. Vanderbilt (ours?). Soon after she was linked with Scott Fitzgerald and Thomas Wolfe *seriatim*. Then in 1925, cummings met Anne Barton. She, aged twenty-six, was the daughter of a policeman and wife of Ralph Barton, a man about town and illustrator of Anita Loos's *Gentleman Prefer Blondes*, who had himself just taken off with an actress.

Morrie Werner, cummings's longtime companion, introduced him to Anne at the end of a difficult five-year period. The acrimonious legal battle with his first wife over his rights with regard to his daughter Nancy continued to drag on. Anne's child Diana served as a surrogate during the course of the romance. The three spent summers together at Silver Lake near Chocorua, New Hampshire, where the elder Cummings had kept a summer home.

Anne was herself a genuine flapper. She was a heavy smoker, witty, vivacious, and mischievous. They finally married in 1929. Once more on a European honeymoon cummings encounters McDermott in a chance meeting, this time with Elaine, stolen on a previous wedding trip. They all go to dinner. After all, this was the late twenties, and we are civilized.

In 1931 cummings went to Russia alone. He left Anne behind and pregnant. She in loneliness or bitterness aborted the child. The next year found cummings back from Russia.

A Confetti of Papers

His bride, once dazzling, had become a harpy. Her tongue, while still entertaining, had turned vicious. She had become sexually restless and was drinking heavily. His flapper bride transformed into bitch wife. The whole mess resolved suddenly when Anne ran away, got a Mexican divorce, and married a doctor.

Meanwhile, cummings's Russian experience resulted in a book, *EIMI*. He detested the Communist state. In contrast to many intellectuals and academics of the era between the wars, cummings was too clear-eyed and honest to see the Soviet monolith as anything other than the stultifying anti-human institution that it always was and still is.

Super love sonnet:

> *if i have made, my lady, intricate*
> *imperfect various things chiefly which wrong*
> *your eyes(frailer than most deep dreams are frail)*
> *songs less firm than your body's whitest song*
> *upon my mind—if i have failed to snare*
> *the glance too shy—if through my singing slips*
> *the very skillful strangeness of your smile*
> *the keen primeval silence of your hair*
>
> *—let the world say "his most wise music stole*
> *nothing from death"—*
>   *you only will create*
> *(who are so perfectly alive) my shame:*
> *lady through whose profound and fragile lips*
> *the sweet small clumsy feet of April came*
>
> *into the ragged meadow of my soul.*

---

cummings's third wife was Marion Morehouse. She was a Midwesterner, twelve years younger than he. He met her in 1932 backstage when she was playing in the Ziegfeld Follies. She was the toast of Broadway and, like his other women, a great beauty. They stayed together until his death in 1962. Although there was no record of a marriage, they always referred to each other as husband and wife, and the marriage was real enough for thirty-five years. Marion was, each in its time, his mistress, his companion, and his nurse. It was a celebrated love and a true marriage.

Throughout cummings's life, through the ups and downs just described, he struggled as a poet. He was always poor. His annual income was sometimes as little as three thousand dollars, even in the late forties and fifties. Toward his later years he did a little university lecturing at Harvard and poetry reading at the New York YMHA. His books never sold well, and the lack of money plagued him continually. Poverty can be embittering and made doubly so by ill health. He was never strong. He suffered from leg and back pains for the last thirty years of his life. He insisted on living in Greenwich Village, which enhanced his misery. Fortunately, each summer he took his leisure in New Hampshire. His love of the natural and the removal from the city renewed him year after year.

cummings died in 1962, and America lost a major poet. He had burst upon the scene in the 1920s with his unique visual and typographical style. He had some imitators, but his place in American letters is assured. He was a hard-working craftsman. Writing poetry was really all he ever did. He worked at his craft every day and remained sparkling and witty until the end. Yet at the end he was still racked by isolation, bad humor, and alienation. So miserable was his spirit that it makes the origin of his genius the more puzzling. From this meanness sprang the love of love, the love of nature, and the love to create, to delight, and to entertain. More generally, four themes seem to braid through his life and art. First, primitiveness and simplicity, shown by his focus upon ordinary people, nature, and the "little man." Second, creativity and uniqueness. He was and is an innovator and pattern breaker. Third, recognition of reality and experience. He got his hands into war, sex, travel, scholarship, city life, and flowers up to the elbows without gloves. And fourth and last, independence and freedom; he despised authority, U.S., Russian, public, or private in whatever form he perceived it. But most of all he gave some joy, at least to me.

A comment on racist, xenophobic brutishness, but funny:

> *ygUDuh*
>   *ydoan*
>   *yunnuhstan*
>   *ydoan o*
>   *yunnuhstan dem*
>   *yguduh ged*
>   *yunnuhstan dem doidee*
>   *yguduh ged riduh*
>   *ydoan o nudh*
> *LISN bud LISN*
>   *dem*
>   *gud*
>   *am*
>   *lidl yelluh bas*
>   *tuds weer goin*
> *duhSIVILEYEzum*

a brief, sad, and lower case of e e cummings

Two early poems with spring themes, childlike with innocent joy. In the first, note the words positioned like locomotive smoke. In the second, the balloonman represents the strangeness of the adult world amid the other wonders of spring:

---

the
   sky
      was
can dy lu
minous
    edible
spry
   pinks shy
lemons
greens   coo   l   choc
olate
s.

  un   der,
 a lo
co
mo
  tive   s pout
       ing
          vi
         o
        lets

---

in Just-
spring   when the world is mud-
luscious the little
lame balloonman

whistles   far   and wee

*and eddieandbill come
running from marbles and
piracies and it's
spring*

when the world is puddle-wonderful

*the queer
old balloonman whistles
far   and   wee
and bettyandisbel come dancing*

from hop-scotch and jump-rope and

*it's
spring
and
    the*

*   goat-footetd*

*balloonMan   whistles
far
and
wee*

Take this, Louis Untermeyer:

*mr u will not be missed
who as an anthologist
sold the many on the few
not excluding mr u*

a brief, sad, and lower case of e e cummings

Here clearly the typography is the message, a grasshopper out of the corner of the eye.

---

                              r-p-o-p-h-e-s-s-a-g-r
               who
a)s w(e loo)k
upnowgath
        PPEGORHRASS
                       eringint(o-
aThe):l
    eA
       !p:
S   a
           (r
rIvIng   -gRrEaPsPhOs)
                            to
rea(be)rran(com)gi(e)ngly
,grasshopper;

Cleanth Brooks uses this to explain mood and character.

Buffalo Bill's
defunct
    who used to
    ride a watersmooth-silver
                    stallion
and break onetwothreefourfive pigeonsjustlikethat
                                 Jesus

he was a handsome man
                      and what i want to know is
how do you like your blueeyed boy
Mister Death

> A rollicking delight attacking religion, politics, and business. Are they all the same?

it was a goodly co
which paid to make man free
(for man is enslaved by a dread dizziz
and the sooner it's over the sooner to biz
don't ask me what it's pliz)

then up rose bishop budge from kew
a anglican was who
(with a rag and a bone and a hank of hair)'d
he picked up a thousand pounds or two
and he smote the monster merde

then up rose pride and up rose pelf
and ghibelline and guelph
and ladios and laddios
(on radios and raddios)
did save man from himself

ye duskiest despot's goldenest gal
did wring that dragon's tail
(for men must loaf and women must lay)
and she gave him a desdemonial
that took his breath away

all history oped her teeming womb
said demon for to doom
yea(fresh complexions being oke
with him)one william shakespeare broke
the silence of the tomb

then up rose mr lipshits pres
(who always nothing says)
and he kisséd the general menedjerr
and they smokéd a robert burns cigerr
to the god of things like they err

a brief, sad, and lower case of e e cummings

Sweet and lovely. Hypocrisy on the home front:

my sweet old etcetera
aunt lucy during the recent

war could and what
is more did tell you just
what everybody was fighting

for,
my sister
isabel created hundreds
(and
hundreds)of socks not to
mention shirts fleaproof earwarmers

etcetera wristers etcetera, my
mother hoped that

i would die etcetera
bravely of course my father used
to become hoarse talking about how it was
a privilege and if only he
could meanwhile my

self etcetera lay quietly
in the deep mud et

cetera
(dreaming,
et
   cetera, of
Your smile
eyes knees and of your Etcetera)

Last poem. No better epitaph–gravest one gravestone:

one

t
hi
s

snowflake

(a
  li
    ght
       in
g)

is upon a gra

v
es
t

one

This was written and read when requested by Mary Glenn Hearne of the Nashville Room of the Public Library at Green Hills on May 13, 1973, and was published in *Some Paragraphs from the Nashville Story* in 1974.

May Hosiery Mills

Jack May

THE MAY HOSIERY Mills was founded in 1896, seventy-seven years ago in Nashville. The story of its founding starts many years before in a small European village. The tale is an oft-paralleled story of the coming of age in America. It is the tale of an immigrant leaving limited opportunity for the vast possibilities of a new world. Here, in the blessings of freedom, liberty, space, tolerance, and opportunity, any man, perhaps for the first time ever, could realize his potential. Time and time again, immigrants came to avail themselves of these blessings.

Jacob May was born in the town of Höchst, Odenwald, Hesse-Darnstadt, Germany, on May 8, 1861. He was one of twelve children born to Loeserman May and Malcha Neu.

All twelve of these children survived and grew to adulthood. Six of them, Jacob being the first, immigrated to the United States. The others remained in Europe, and some ended their lives as elderly people in the massacres of Hitler in the late 1930s. Two were gassed.

Jacob May spent his boyhood in Germany. By the time he reached the age of eighteen, he had completed his high school education, which was somewhat unusual for the time. It required a twelve-mile trip to the nearest institution of education. He, in spite of his education and extremely flat feet, was to be drafted into the Army to do both menial and degrading work. Apparently for this reason, he decided to leave restrictive Europe for the openness of America. He came in 1879 at the age of eighteen years. The trip was on a steamship, with sails added for speed. The entire voyage was spent in a filthy hole and lasted several weeks. When he arrived in New York City, Jacob May had seven dollars in his pocket. A minimum of five dollars was required for admission to Castle Garden at the Battery in New York. Consider the plight of a man without a knowledge of the language, without friends, and with only two dollars, embarking on life thousands of miles across the ocean from his home. It is certainly not a unique story, but one that deserves the reconsideration of each American generation.

After a brief stay in New York City, where a relative had a business, he moved to a town in New Hampshire, where another relative named Mayer had a retail store. From the savings of his brief New York days, he bought a horse and wagon and peddled around the New England farm counties. Typically, many German Jews got their start in the United States by peddling. Jacob May, however, was always proud that he never had to carry a pack on his back and that he had saved enough to buy a horse and wagon. He often recalled the hardships of riding in the New England midwinter of sub-zero temperatures, but remembered that only on one occasion did he have to sleep in a barn.

He married Rebecca Weingarten in 1890, lived in Farmington, New Hampshire, and eventually opened a store with Mayer in Laconia, which was and remains a hosiery town to this day. The mills were powered by the streams flowing out of Lake Winnipesaukee. In order to buy wares for his peddling wagon, it was necessary for him to make train trips to Boston. There he would buy from the Yankee wholesalers. Somehow, he conceived a clever idea. He convinced the hosiery mill manufacturers in Laconia to let him have samples. He sold the hosiery to the same Boston merchants from whom he bought supplies, thereby cutting down his travel cost and making profitable use of his trip both ways. He became more and more interested in the hosiery business and one day he saw an advertisement in a Boston newspaper advising that the State of Tennessee was taking bids for convict labor. With the help of a well-to-do New Yorker, Leo Kaufman, he placed a bid for fifty men at approximately fifty cents per day. Amazingly, the bid was accepted, and in 1896 Jacob May, his wife Rebecca, their sons Mortimer and Abraham, and three or four French-Canadian fixers (men skilled in the repair of knitting machines) moved to Nashville and started the Rock City Hosiery Mills inside the walls of the Tennessee State Penitentiary.

Jacob May moved his wife and two sons, Mortimer and Abraham, to a small cottage at 113 Belmont Avenue (now Sixteenth Avenue North). The site of the family home is now a parking lot. It was chosen by Mister May because of its proximity to the penitentiary, which was located on Church Street in an irregular piece of property bordered by McMillan Street on the west and Cedar (now Charlotte) on the north. At the turn of the century, the penitentiary was moved to the present West Nashville location. Then, in order to get to the penitentiary, Jacob May had to take a horse car down Broad Street to the Union Depot and then take a train to far West Nashville each morning.

There he was shaved at a barber shop where each customer had soap and a mug with the owner's name emblazoned on it in fancy gold leaf. The factory was located in the northeast corner of the prison yard in a three-story building. Two years after their arrival in Nashville, on Christmas Day, 1898, a third son, Daniel, was born. One of the original employees of the firm was the office manager, a young man named Morris Werthan. His family, of course, has gone on to prosper and to become an important factor in the industry and public life of Nashville. Another of the original employees was a man by the name of Napoleon Poiré, one of the fixers who had traveled to Nashville with Jacob May. His descendants remain to this day in Nashville. Napoleon married a local girl by the name of Balch. Soon after he changed his name to Perry and left the Catholic Church for a Southern Protestant denomination. This family, some seventy-seven years later, still has a number of its offspring at the May Hosiery Mills. Napoleon's wife was a widow with one son named Lewis. Together they subsequently had three sons, Napoleon Jr., J.D., and a posthumous child, Finley, who was the namesake of the Mills' bookkeeper and office manager of many years, Mr. I.C. Finley. The older Napoleon was a fine-looking man, a wonderful foreman, and a skilled knitter. His eldest son, Napoleon Jr., was brought into the mill as an infant and referred to as "Baby." He is employed to this day by May Hosiery Mills and is in charge of all maintenance in a 250,000-square-foot plant on Chestnut Street. He is still called "Baby" by all.

The mill always has manufactured socks, as distinguished from ladies sheer stockings, a close first cousin in the hosiery industry. The hosiery industry itself is ancient. Socks were found in the tomb of Pharaoh some two thousand years B.C. Hosiery is made by process of knitting, which is an art almost as ancient as weaving. The fact that the sock is knit, rather than woven, means it fits more comfortably close to the skin under the shoe. At the same time, being a comfortable item of under-apparel, it also has been subject through the years to vicissitudes of styling. The first sock made by May Hosiery Mills was style 228. This was a three-pound-per-dozen, one-by-one, ribbed stocking made on the 160-needle ribber, which was then transferred to a footing machine. The toe of the sock was closed on a looper. The loopers were not equipped with trimmers, and the socks had to be ravelled by young convicts.

The original capitalization of the factory was fifteen thousand dollars, of which Jacob May put in about sixty percent, the partner Leo Kaufman the other forty percent. Jacob and Leo never hit it off. Kaufman had been wealthy and was used to taking long vacations, while Jacob toiled long hours without vacations, working with the unskilled labor and forced to deal with the corrupt or corruptible politicians who ran the penitentiary.

Although the company lost money in the first year, it

A Confetti of Papers

In 1907 Jacob May (third row center) returned to visit his family in Germany some twenty-eight years after he left the village of Höchst. Also pictured are his father Loeserman May (second row center) and his sons Mortimer (front row center) and Dan May (front row right). One of the twin girls (third row right) is the grandmother of Lanie Preis Doochin Cook and Linda Preis Zeitlin of Nashville.

did not lose again thereafter. About 1901 Jacob May and Leo Kaufman had a falling out that was somewhat bitter. Kaufman was then bought out and he departed, and Jacob May became the sole owner. During the first six years of this century the mill became quite profitable, and in the days before the income tax Jacob May became what could then be called a rich man. Thus it was that in 1907, Jacob May, with his wife and children, some twenty-eight years after he left the village of Höchst, returned home to Germany triumphant. He was a man of wealth, full of enthusiasm and admiration for the great land of opportunity and liberty that lay across the ocean. One can imagine the pride and triumph of that journey in 1907. The dream was realized. Jacob May could account that he was well-off. He owned a mare, a buggy, and a telephone. Although he had no central heating in his home on Laurel Street east of Sixteenth, he did have Wellsbach burners for gas lighting and a servant who was paid about four dollars per week. He could tell them how he commuted to the penitentiary on the Belmont streetcar, which passed his home, for five cents, although it did involve transferring at Eighth (then Spruce) and Church Street and then taking the West Nashville Line all the way to the penitentiary. Maybe not idyllic in 1973 terms, but miraculous in terms of medieval Höchst.

On the tragic side, the middle May son, Abe, died twenty-four hours after the onset of meningitis. Rebecca never recovered from the sudden loss of her middle son. Also in 1907, the second renewable contract ran out, and the new contract with the State of Tennessee was lost in 1908. The loss of the contract and the loss of the son prompted Jacob to move his family away from Nashville to New York, where his wife had been born, on June 26, 1863. New York was no paradise, but Nashville was rampant in early years with typhoid, malaria, diphtheria, pellagra, and a host of other diseases now, happily, forgotten. However, before the journey to New York could be made, tragedy again struck. Mrs. May developed cancer, postponed surgery, and finally was operated on June 1910 at McGannon Infirmary at Eighth and Union. The family left Nashville in August and settled in New York in an apartment at 550 West 157th on the corner of Broadway. Mrs. May died on December 27, 1911.

Following the loss of the prison contract, Jacob May made a business arrangement with two friends, Julius Martin and Sol M. Gordon, to go into the hosiery business independently of the State. The two partners had recently lost a retail business but had managed to salvage some twenty thousand dollars between them. To this Jacob May added his machinery of similar value, and thirty shares each of common stock were issued. Jacob May received an additional ten shares of preferred, convertible into common at any time. The business was opened at a location on Brown Street at the present South Nashville location of the mill. Jacob May, after his wife's death, contributed to the management of the business from New York the best that he could from that distance.

The hosiery manufacturing during the second decade of this century continued to be heavyweight, long-length, ribbed socks for boys and girls. These were all made from natural fibers, usually one hundred percent cotton or part wool. The mill's chief supplier of cotton yarn was the Berryton Mills of Berryton, Georgia. The yarn was sold to the mills by Len Fite, of Nashville, who was the commission agent for the Berryton Mill. Socks were dyed in one color only, and that was black. This was made by the use of sulphur dyes using a hazardous process. The dye, being highly toxic, had to be done in a separate building.

The socks were sold by one of the principals of the business—either Jacob May, Saul Gordon, or Julius Martin. Customers were the great jobbing houses of the Midwest. Among these were Ely Walker and Rice-Stix of St. Louis, Marshall Field's and Carson Pirie Scott of Chicago, and William R. Moore of Memphis. Also important customers were a number of Nashville wholesale concerns largely centered around the public square. Among these were Neely-Harwell, J.S. Reeves, Harris-Davis, Eskind and Greenspan, W.S. Riddle, and Herman Bros., Lindauer. In 1910, the first variety chain store came into being in Memphis; this was S.H. Kress, which opened its #2 store in Nashville. F.W. Woolworth started shortly thereafter, and this was to be the beginning of the chain retailing revolution in the country and the start of the slow demise of the wholesaler and jobber.

DURING WORLD WAR I the mill began to prosper. The profits were large as there was no price control, and scarcities abounded. With the labor shortages of the war years the mill had to innovate. Julius Martin invented a quick method of transferring. The leg was jabbed on the footer in place of the skilled hand transferring. This trebled production. He also developed a line of part-wool socks, which he introduced, made of a twisted yarn with one end of cotton and one end of wool. At this time silk hosiery was fashionable. Coincidentally during the war years the Powder Plant developed in Old Hickory. This subsequently became Dupont and a center for rayon yarns. Rayon replaced silk in much hosiery. The use of pre-dyed yarns made patterns possible through reverse plaiting, a process of changing the front and back yarns while knitting the sock. In time, the mill expanded by purchasing Nashville Hosiery Mill, which was operating in the 1700 block of Charlotte (then Cedar). Another mill was started in 1918 in Lawrenceburg, Tennessee. This increased production of greige hosiery and fed the Nashville finishing mill until its close in 1930. Dan May also entered the business about this time, and has been active from the early 1920s to the present day. Dan's brother

Mortimer, the brilliant eldest son, was active in various administrative capacities in this period.

The twenties were a boom time for much of America, but there was little growth at the May Hosiery Mills. Jacob May, as well as Gordon and Martin, were past their prime, and the business was floundering. It was represented by the H.D. Thomas Sales Commission Agency, but sales did not meet anticipation.

It was at this time Mortimer and Dan May took control and in 1928 hired F.J. Olewine from their ex-agents, H.D. Thomas, and moved him to a New York office on the third floor of a building at 366 Broadway. All commissioned salesmen were fired, and the year 1929 was one of growth and profit. It was with the starting of the New York office that Montgomery Ward and Company became the number-one customer of the mill and has remained so until this day.

With the thirties came depression and hard times for the hosiery industry as well as most of American business. In spite, or because of, this a number of technological changes were made in the product. Rubber yarn was invented, and W.D. Davis of Fort Payne, Alabama, invented a process by which it could be inlaid in the top of men's socks. The days of the man's garter were soon gone. The mill developed other customers during the thirties, including the Boy Scouts of America, for which we have manufactured hosiery ever since. The mill became one of the first licensees of Walt Disney and put Donald Duck and Mickey Mouse on the cuffs of children's anklets. With innovative marketing and frugal manufacturing under superintendent O.A. Moers, the mill somehow survived those dark years of the Depression. Boys at that time were wearing knickers and with knickers wore long socks that were reverse-plaited. I think old hosiery mill people still hope for the return of male knickers. Most of the hosiery sold for ten cents a pair. The profit margin on them was minimum or non-existent. In spite of this, the mill hired two fine industrial engineers. One was Kurt Salmon who, after marrying one of the girls out of the office, went on to found the largest textile consulting firm in the world. The other man was Shepard Schwartz, who innovated in all areas of manufacturing. Upon Dan May's retirement in 1963 he became President. Interestingly enough, our looping room was air-conditioned in the middle thirties by the York Company. I know of no earlier industrial use of air-conditioning. Air-conditioning aided productivity in the long hot summer in the South and, perhaps more than anything else, should get credit for the boom development of our region.

The decade of the 1930s ended, but the Depression did not. Gathering storm clouds of war in Europe were real enough, but until the United States' entry into the war in 1942, the industry of the country, and certainly the hosiery business as a whole, suffered in the Great Depression. The war brought not only economic improvement, but also technological and social change. The nylon stocking revolutionized the ladies hosiery business. Men were wearing patterned argyles, and girls were wearing bobby socks. May Hosiery Mills used all of its available yarn to manufacture for the armed services. Also, the mill, under Shep Schwartz and Baby Perry, developed a machine shop capacity to manufacture hardware for the war. May Hosiery Mills was a prime contractor on mortar fuses. At its peak, the mill employed some twelve hundred persons at our South Nashville location.

With the end of the war, the May Hosiery Mills adapted to the great variety of new styles and made these from the new fibers now available. By this time it was the oldest, and perhaps the largest, sock mill in the South, where eighty percent of the industry had by this time moved. May Hosiery Mills had been the first, but by 1950, North Carolina was covered by hosiery manufacturing facilities. May's major customers at the time were the great chains: Woolworth, Kress, Spiegel, Butler Bros., and of course Montgomery Ward and the Boy Scouts. Regional and local sales had somewhat diminished but were carried out by the local office under Felix Dodd.

THE 1950S BROUGHT expansion into the branded hosiery field. The Vaughan Knitting Mills of Pottstown, Pennsylvania, was purchased. With this company came the acquisition of the name Nuweave and a line of branded socks that was sold to independent retailers across the country. Through the fifties and sixties the mill was making approximately one million socks per week (forty thousand dozen pair). This included a variety of infants, girls, boys, mens, and womens socks. The operation had grown enormously complex, and a vast variety of knitting machines had become available. In the dye house, colors had become complex, and a knowledge of chemistry was necessary to become a dyer. The fibers used were all of the polyesters, polypropylenes, and acrylics that were then on the market. A Swiss invented a stretch yarn that made one-size hosiery possible and also made the product almost impossible to wear out. The darning egg, which had aided mending many a sock for generations, became an obsolete artifact. One of the new products invented by May Hosiery Mills was a seamless, shoe-top-length foot sock without a heavy elastic band at the top, which was marketed under the name of Sonliner and received national recognition. Along with the Vaughan Mills came a marvelous hosiery style, 3715. This all-cotton, transferred-top crew sock was selected without solicitation by NASA to be worn by the astronauts on all their flights, including the trips to the moon. All astronauts in the Apollo program wore this sock. This gives May Hosiery Mills a monopoly on hosiery worn on the moon.

By the end of the 1950s, sales offices were under the direction of I.R. Ryerson. By now, the Girl Scouts of USA were depending upon us for their socks, as was Sears, Roebuck. With the decade of the sixties came further innovations. Socks were developed that went all the way to the waist and were joined together to make tights. This was a very practical and warm garment for little children. It had its counterpart in the ladies industry with the development of pantyhose. The styling combination of the miniskirt and panty stocking led to a number of profitable years of ladies hosiery business. By the time of the late sixties some fundamental styling changes had come into effect. Women for the first time in perhaps a thousand years stopped wearing skirts, and, for the first time in probably as long a period, boys, particularly college students, stopped wearing socks. In spite of these appalling developments in the hosiery market, innovation has continued. The sock that stopped at the waist continued now to the shoulder and became the bodysuit. The first garment of this type was worked out at May Hosiery Mills. Today, the body stocking has lost its legs and become the body shirt. This outer garment is still knit and is as comfortable and form-fitting as a sock. Today, the body shirt has become a main product of the May Hosiery Mills.

In the middle 1960s a merger was worked out with the Wayne Knitting Mills of Humboldt, Tennessee. The May stockholders took large portions of stock in this company and merged the business into Wayne. Wayne Knitting Mills is an eighty-year-old company founded in Fort Wayne, Indiana, in 1891. Wayne has been listed on the New York Stock Exchange since the middle 1930s and has not missed a dividend since. Wayne enjoys a fine reputation in the trade for its Belle Sharmeer ladies nylons. Subsequent to this move a number of other mergers have taken place. The Athens Hosiery Mills of Athens, Tennessee, was acquired by May Hosiery Mills and is now run as a parallel manufacturing operation. In 1968 the Wayne Knitting Mills acquired the H.W. Gossard Company of Chicago, a ladies intimate apparel manufacturer, and the corporation changed its name to Wayne-Gossard Corporation. All divisions of the company, which now include Heritage Sportswear in Marion, South Carolina, are involved with knitting garments both in hosiery, women's apparel, and outerwear, and each division is dedicated to the highest quality in each of the product lines that are now manufactured and marketed.

IN DRAWING THIS history to a close I feel remiss in not mentioning the employees. Many more people have worked at May Hosiery Mills than were in the entire population of Nashville when the mill began. The success of this mill is as much due to the loyalty and diligence of the Nashville working men and women as to any other one factor. While working at the mill, people married, had children, and some died. The reality of these thousands of lives is far more meaningful than the addresses and dates in this outline.

One also wishes there were time to preserve the myriad anecdotes that make the folklore of any institution. This paper will have to close without telling about the time Frank Austin stole the boiler, or about the time Ben and Baby had to eat catfish at knifepoint, or about the time Billy Martin put a live terrapin on Mister Finley's desk to replace his tortoise-shell paperweight. No mention will be made of the maintenance man who said, "The Mays don't pay enough to live on and if it weren't for the cheap lunches and the [girls] I sure would leave." Or Joe Muller who, complaining about an incompetent apprentice, immortally proclaimed, "I taught him all I know, and he still don't know nothing."

So, if we have been unable to give an institution human substance, let us just close with a few more facts.

May 1973 finds the May Hosiery Mills still vital and expanding. The two locations in Nashville and Athens occupy over three hundred thousand square feet of manufacturing floor space, employ about one thousand Tennesseans, and ship about forty thousand dozen pair of socks and body wear each week.

This seventy-seven-year history bridges a period of almost apocalyptic change. Looking back and then looking forward, it will be a brave man who will predict with any confidence where the future will lead. The vagaries of fashion, the impact of technology, the overtaxing of our planet's resources, both raw and human, and the nearness of new markets and new competition will surely perplex the thoughtful predictor. But through all of this, I expect this company to continue on its stable course. We have had only two sales managers in fifty years and only three chief executives in over three-fourths of a century. This stability has left a real heritage of adaptability and hard work that should carry us through.

If by some miracle I could come back when a like period of history had passed, the first thing I would want to see in the year 2050 would be the hosiery. What will men and women be wearing beneath their shoes and next to their feet and legs? We can't be sure, but whatever it is I have confidence that it will in some part be supplied by the May Hosiery Mills of Nashville, Tennessee.

Epilogue

The May Hosiery Mills did not last until 2050, but only to 1983. It was sold to Renfro Hosiery Mills of Mount Airy, North Carolina. Within ten years, the parent company, Signal Apparel of Chattanooga, and the largest customer, Montgomery Ward, went out of business. All three were no more as of the early 1990s.

It is now 2008, one hundred ten years since Dan was born in Nashville. That same length of time before his birth would put you within twenty years of Donelson and the ladies arriving here for the first time. I wonder if Robertson and Donelson would find the Nashville of Dan's youth as remote as Dan in his youth would find the Nashville of today. This is a good memoir of time long past. Dan uses the vehicle of the occupations of the members of the Shamus Club to remember those times.

The Score After Three Score

by Daniel May (1898–1982)

*Read to the Shamus Club in June 1961;
Walter Knestrick read a modified version
to the Roundtable in March 2008*

WHEN JUST TWO weeks ago, our fellow Shamus, the adipose dispenser of ethyl alcohol, in his usual dilatory and delaying manner, managed to unload his Shamus Club paper on your humble servant, I realized quickly that

The Shamus Club, 1956. Back row: Robert Teitlebaum, Sonny Kunian, Rabbi Bill Silverman, Albert Werthan, Dr. Albert Weinstein, Lou Silberman, Bernard Werthan, and David Steine. Front row: Judge Charles Gilbert, Rabbi Julius Mark, Jacques Back, Dan May, and Manuel Eskind.

time would not permit a review of a book or even a careful study of any subject.

I am now in my seventh decade on this sphere. The thought struck me that while my cerebral arteries are still functioning with some degree of normality, it would not be out of place to take a backward look at Nashville. As only two of my auditors were living in Nashville at the turn of the century and during the first decade of the twentieth, I thought that an analysis of the progress or retrogression of this area might be of interest. Rushed as I am, I hope Charley and Manuel will not find too many errors; if I have erred, I apologize to Charley—Manuel is getting off lightly as it is, and I don't want any adverse criticism from him.

My idea was to present a paper describing the society in which I grew up. When I sat down to write this paper, a gulf opened up before me that was so great that I was terrified. Surely to do this paper accurately would take months and months of research; but on the other hand, possibly general impressions have some value—so here we go.

Knowing my propensity for argument, you may rest assured that this will not be all history, but much will be conclusion. I have entitled this paper "The Score After Three Score." Not to keep you in suspense; I will let you in on the score. The game isn't over, but here in the middle of the lucky seventh, virtue is triumphing but the forces of evil always have another turn at bat.

I must briefly give a bit of family history. My father was born on May 8, 1861, just a hundred years ago last month, in a small village, Höchst, in Hesse, near the city of Darmstadt. This town is located in a country that looks like Middle Tennessee, with low, rolling hills known as the Odenwald.

The May family has lived in this town in the same house as far back as 1780, according to the records in the town hall. The family name was spelled M-A-I and, under the rule of primogeniture, the eldest son always inherited the house. Apparently the family had always eked out a meager living by cultivating a small "farm"—I have placed the word "farm" in quotes advisedly because it was merely an acre or so of ground that was truck-farmed to an inch of its borders. The family spending money came from trading in cattle, one of the few occupations in which German Jews could participate. The occupation was known by a combination of a Hebrew and a German word: *Bahameshaendler.* My father was one of twelve children, and the orthodoxy of the family can be easily verified when one considers the names of the six boys. They were Abraham, Isaac, Jacob, Moses . . . at which point I presume they ran out of Biblical names and named the last two Herman and Henry. My paternal grandfather, Loeserman May, was a rugged individual who lived to eighty-five. He had twelve children in the nineteenth century, and not one of the twelve died either in infancy or childhood. As a matter of fact, all twelve were alive at the time of his death. My paternal grandmother naturally did not live long after having twelve children. She was dead before I was born. She was a German whose name was Martha Neu, and she lived in a small village, Messel. She died of what apparently was tuberculosis shortly after her twelfth baby was born.

To complete the picture, I must devote a paragraph to my mother's family.

She was born in New York City on June 26, 1863, one of ten children, several of whom died in infancy as was routine at that time. Her name was Rebecca Weingarten.

Her father and mother both had been born in Germany. My maternal grandfather was a rarity among the German Jews who landed in America during that period, as he was an artisan and worked in shipbuilding on the Lower East Side of New York. He had the distinction of being one of the employees who built the Union battleship *Monitor*. The *Monitor* was the ironclad that engaged in the first naval battle between two such ships, the other being the ship of the Confederacy, *Merrimac*, in 1862. It was described at that time as a cheesebox on a raft. The family lived in the slums on the Lower East Side and managed to preserve appearances only by making each child go to work as young as possible. My mother told me how she started working in a sewing machine factory at 16, I believe, although my mind is hazy as to the exact ages.

My father Jacob, like so many German Jews, left Germany because of conscription. He managed to finish high school or, as it was called in Germany, gymnasium. Here we must ponder at the privation the family went through to send even two of the sons to gymnasium. The school was located some twenty miles from their town in Mittelstadt, and the boys had to go by train both ways. He was rejected by the Army because of a skeletal defect as he had fallen arches but later he was recalled for a second examination. The Jews were always relegated to the menial jobs in the Army, and none ever were officers. At this point, before the second physical, he left Germany and, like millions of other Americans, arrived at New York with a few dollars in his pocket and unlimited hope. He had a kinsman who had preceded him, a cousin by the name of Mayer. This is the history of almost all the immigrants who landed in New York—they immediately sought out some friend or relative who had preceded them and, from this point, started on their own. The cousin, Mayer, was living in New Hampshire and had developed a business by going through the countryside with a horse and wagon and peddling merchandise. Both Mayer and my father were proud of the fact that they had started, not as peddlers with a pack on their back, but even then had a degree of status for, from the very start, they had always used a horse and wagon.

My father would make frequent trips to Boston and New York to buy merchandise, where he met my mother and was married in the latter city. The young couple moved to Laconia, New Hampshire, and lived happily under very rugged New England conditions. Two sons were born there, Mortimer and Abraham, in 1892 and 1895.

Laconia was a large textile town with at least three hosiery mills. Incidentally, the largest manufacturer of knitting machinery is still located in Laconia. My father, on his trips to New York and Boston, discovered that traveling was very expensive, even in those days, and somehow or other he convinced the president of Samuel Tilton Company to allow him to take some hosiery samples on these trips in an endeavor to sell to some of the people from whom he was buying his supplies.

One day he noticed an advertisement in a Boston newspaper that the State of Tennessee was taking bids on convict labor in Nashville in 1896. He dug up another *landsmann* and together raised some twelve thousand dollars, put in a bid, and was the successful bidder. He came to Nashville and started the hosiery mills behind the old walls of the penitentiary, which was then located on the irregular plot at about

Fourteenth and Church. To be close to his work, he rented a house at 113 Sixteenth Avenue North (then called Belmont Avenue) at which point the third and last son was born on Christmas Day, 1898. This plant, the Rock City Hosiery Mills, was the first hosiery mill in either Tennessee or the Carolinas. Now in 1961, almost the entire industry is located in these states.

MY REARING WAS most atypical and violated everything recommended by Doctor Spock. When my brother Abraham died, my parents gave up housekeeping and moved to a downtown hotel, where I lived from 1905 to 1910, and it is these years that I will discuss particularly in this paper.

The Tulane Hotel, which was situated at the corner of Eighth and Church until it was razed about two years ago, was typical of Southern hotels. There were only three hotels in Nashville. The best one was the Duncan, located on the southwest corner of College and Cedar streets—now known as Fourth and Charlotte. Presently, it is occupied by the Negro YMCA but then it was our most plush hotel. The Duncan catered only to transient guests while the Tulane had both transient and semi-permanent guests. The third hotel was the Maxwell House, which was a third-class hotel, even during the first decade of the century. I shall not describe the Maxwell House as its interior and decor has been so eloquently delineated in O. Henry's best story, "A Municipal Report." If you have never read this story, you should, as its description of Nashville and its atmosphere is well-nigh perfect. At this time, Tennessee's governors did not reside in a state-owned "mansion" but all lived at the Tulane as well as most of the state legislators and many of the judges of the State Supreme Court.

My hobby as a boy was politics, and I attended the state legislature with my brother Mortimer almost daily for many sessions. I can still remember the first four names of the Senate Roll Call of the year when the Prohibition Act was passed, some time about 1908, as I attended almost every session. The roll call started Askew, Banks, Baskerville, Cummings. I remember that Mr. Cummings was from Chattanooga and an arch opponent of Prohibition; the leader of the drys had the inappropriate name of O.K. Holliday. Mortimer was opposed to the prohibition law and was very unhappy when it was finally passed. The governor, Ham Patterson, vetoed it but under Tennessee law, a majority can pass a bill over the governor's veto, and this was done immediately. I knew many of the governors, and my favorite hobby even at the age of ten was to sit around listening to political arguments in the lobby of the Tulane. Governor Frazier, Governor Cox, Governor McMillin, and Governor Patterson all apparently did not object to a boy listening in on their conversations. (I believe Governor Patterson was the first governor to live in the "mansion," which was located on the east side of Seventh Avenue between Union and Charlotte, where the War Memorial Building now stands.) Joe Byrne, who was later to become Speaker of the House in Washington, also lived at the hotel when first he became a Congressman. He was a more reticent man. He was successful in ousting from Congress the most pompous politician Davidson County has ever produced, John Wesley Gaines, about whom a most clever poem was written. Gaines was the Claghorn type of politician with a big black hat and a Prince Albert coat and a loud voice that was a political necessity before sound amplification was invented. The anonymous author of the poem has remained anonymous to this day. Only this month I discovered it again in Fadiman's *The American Treasury,* and it goes like this:

John Wesley Gaines,
John Wesley Gaines,
Thou monumental mass of brains.
Come in, John Wesley
For it rains.

Very fortunately Sulphur Dell was close by the State Capitol, and I would slip out of the Senate Chamber sometimes with a pair of field glasses to watch the early ball games in April. There were several special sessions of the legislature on Prohibition, and the ball park in those days had home plate in the opposite corner so that one could see the whole infield from the rear porch of the Capitol. My interest in baseball and politics has never diminished.

I THOUGHT POSSIBLY one way I could describe Nashville would be to approach it from an occupational viewpoint of each of the members of this Shamus Club. I will use this device to give you an idea of the society under which we survived during the period prior to World War I.

But, first, I must tell you something of the geography. The streets were named, not numbered, but the City Council finally put in a numbering system over the objection of the traditionalists. The avenues starting at the river were Wharf,

Market, Cherry, College, Summer, High, Vine, Spruce, and McLemore. This area was the limit of my wanderings as a boy except to go to football games on old Dudley Field at Twenty-first and West End. The visiting football teams stayed at the Tulane, and I would walk to Dudley Field and back to see the games. I also would go with my father on Saturdays to the penitentiary (which after about 1901 was at its present location) on the West Nashville streetcar and, with the exceptions of my trips to Vanderbilt and to the pen, the rest of my life lay between Wharf and McLemore. I attended the first school building ever built in Nashville, Hume School, which was located on Eighth Avenue near Broadway with Fogg High School immediately in front of it. Walking down Church Street, one would see in those days an entirely different vista. Hardly a single store remains that was in business in 1910. There may be some who have the same trade name, but there are no individuals left of the direct family. Zibart Brothers is the only exception I can think of. It was located then on the corner of Seventh and Church where Tinsley's is presently. Castner's was built about 1907, and Capitol Boulevard was not in existence. Deaderick Street came to an end at Fifth Avenue, and the fire headquarters faced directly down Deaderick at its termination.

The whole downtown area has changed. Office buildings on Church Street never thought of using the ground floor for anything except entrances, other than the corner store. The Jackson Building at Fifth and Church housed both my dentist and physician, Doctors Rich and Bromberg. The firm of Joe Frank & Company occupied the corner for years. Ernest Frank was the young man of the firm and, although he was younger in 1910, he was no prettier. The

Hitchcock Building also used the corner for a store, Decker's, which was the place to take your date around 1915. You drove up in your car on Sixth Avenue and received curb service. Skalowaki's was the soda fountain par excellence, first located on the west side of Fifth Avenue and then enlarged in real Hollywood style on Church Street next to McKendree Church. The soda fountain declined with the consciousness of weight by females, with the slim figure replacing the Rabelaisian type. There is much to be said for both.

I PROMISED EARLY in this paper to approach the analysis of the score by occupations represented in this group. First the liquor business. The open saloon was in its heyday in my youth, ranging from the worst type of joints to a palatial bar called Luigart's located where the Paramount Theatre is presently. The liquor trade then and now resisted any regulation irrespective of its wildness or stringency, and although there were laws limiting the hour of sale on weekdays, regulating the sale to minors, and requiring that they be closed on Sunday, all were violated to some extent then as they are now.

One method of dispensing whiskey has disappeared completely and that was the old barrel house. I still distinctly remember one of these elegant places on Church Street where the Telephone building now stands between Second and Third. It was owned by the mother of the uncle [by marriage] of the girl who was to become my wife, and it was a very lucrative business. Whiskey was sold from barrels at so much a shot. There were no bottles in the store and, although I am far from an expert on the subject, I understand that the potency of the product varied from the very worst to the very bad. Doors were removed in the summer, and I remember very distinctly the day in 1910 when Prohibition was to become effective at midnight. I stood across the street and it was a sight that I have never forgotten. Customers were three deep at the bar and the whiskey odor reached across the street. These barrel houses were numerous and especially vile in the Negro neighborhood on Fourth Avenue from Broadway south about three blocks, then known as Black Bottom. Two of the most famous joints in this area were run by individuals whose descendants, both collateral and direct, are still in our midst. I refrain from describing them or calling them by name, but these resorts were of the Barbary Coast variety, and their heirs are putting on airs. It's a great country.

Public drunkenness was more common, although I doubt if there was as much whiskey drunk per capita then as now. There was no automobile for a man to climb into when he was drunk and he had to wend his way home on foot. Parenthetically, I notice that New York now requires post mortems on all people killed in automobile accidents, and the report showed that of those people killed in automobile accidents after dark thus far this year in New York City, seventy-four percent had more than the alcoholic blood content that is considered the incompetent level.

Fifty years ago the inebriated gentry had to hoof it on foot, and I watched dozens go down Spruce Street from the side door of the Tulane bar. One thing for certain, the consumption of whiskey by women was small compared with present day. Women were never permitted in a bar, but eating places like Luigart's would serve drinks to women. The New Year's Eve party at Luigart's was always good for the female gossip department for at least two to three weeks each year. My good Aunt Nancy (my mother's sister) who was a fine person, but who loved what would now be called café society, was always the target of much criticism. My mother did not disapprove, but my father was very critical, not because of the morality but because of the waste of money. She never failed to attend Luigart's parties.

There were no first-class restaurants in town other than Luigart's and Faucon's. The latter, which was located on the south side of Union between Fourth and Fifth, was a French restaurant famous for its salad, but in the opinion of the gourmets who inhabited the lobby of the Tulane, it was vastly overrated. As a matter of fact, all food at hotels and restaurants throughout the South was hardly fit to eat, but the quantities were enormous. Southern fried chicken with white gravy was a greasy concoction that was only palatable with copious quantities of white corn whiskey. The price of whiskey was ridiculously cheap, and the menfolk, as a whole, drank it as if the supply were soon to be exhausted. I may be wrong in the next observation as I have no statistical evidence, but I believe the consumption of whiskey by the young was somewhat less than it is today. The inevitable cocktail before dinner was not as prevalent and, in our level of society among our friends, where today one could omit napkins with less comment than omitting liquor, in the early part of this century the serving of whiskey or gin before meals was almost unknown. We "heard" that one or two families in town did it, but they were obviously decadent. As a matter of fact, prior to World War I in the upper-middle-class Jewish group in which my family and I circulated, cocktails and highballs in the home were looked upon as something strictly for the goyim.

A Confetti of Papers

Journalism in those days was also quite different. First of all, the price of the newspaper was usually two cents. *The New York Times* was one cent, as were all the large metropolitan papers. Nashville had two papers: the morning paper, the *Nashville American,* and the evening *Banner.* The *Banner* was run by Jimmy Stahlman's grandfather, the major, who was of German descent and came from North Carolina.

In passing, I must include a brief reference to the recent social prestige status of different churches. I am not certain what denomination the Stahlmans originally attended, but I feel certain they were Lutherans. When Jimmy came in the chips, he became an Episcopalian and attended Christ Church. Christ Church had a series of rectors including Bishop Dandadge, Peyton Williams, and Ray Ferris, who started preaching a type of Christianity that was entirely too compassionate for the old reactionary Southerners. Stahlman was among those who established a new church, St. George's Episcopal, in Belle Meade but even that was too fellow-feeling for Jimmy, and he finally found in Walter Courtenay, the preacher of the First Presbyterian Church, a man who preached his type of religion and had the "right" people in his flock. With growing intelligence among the Protestant clergy, I feel that poor Jim eventually will have to become a Catholic as did his fellow traveler, Mister Ed Potter. But back to ancient history.

One distinguishing feature of the morning paper was that every day at the upper left- and right-hand corners of the front page Burk & Co. had its trademark, the cleverest advertising stunt I have ever seen. *The Tennessean* appeared as a competitor to the *American* about 1908, and Charley Gilbert could tell you of its rise with the subsequent disappearance of the *American.*

WHICH BRINGS ME to the judiciary. The distinguishing feature of our legislative and judiciary branches of the government was not their ethics or their costumes, weird as both were; the most outstanding feature of all forms of government in the early part of this century was the size of the cuspidors. They were beautiful brass, highly polished, and standing at least sixteen inches high. They were not meant to be hit, merely targets for the host of tobacco chewers that inhabited our courts and our legislative halls. No one but the lower classes and prostitutes smoked cigarettes. The only cigarettes available were of the Turkish variety: Murads, Fatimas, Sweet Caporals, etc. The mild cigarette, with a blend of Virginia tobacco, did not reach any degree of popularity until World War I. Chewing tobacco either in the plug or twist was used by many, whether they were ball players or judges. The more fastidious smoked cigars. An interesting debate could be raised as to which form of the weed is the more obnoxious to the non-smoker, cigars, chewing tobacco, or cigarettes.

No women smoked except prostitutes. This was the badge of their trade. A large number of women in the middle and lower classes used snuff, and I expect that two-thirds of the employees of the May Hosiery Mills in this period were snuff dippers. Quite a few men used snuff also, and the first governor of the local branch of the Federal Reserve always had a stream of snuff juice running down both sides of his chin after ten a.m. each day. Our courtrooms and legislative halls were without much decorum. Judges did not wear robes, and it was not unusual to see the bailiffs, the attorneys, and the hangers-on all in shirtsleeves arguing a case. I can't recall whether or not the judges themselves took off their coats. I doubt it. The picture of a Southern lawyer in a shirtsleeves shouting at the top of his voice to a jury of illiterates is fixed in my mind. Many of them had handlebar mustaches, chockablock with their chins, with a fine mixture of corn whiskey and chewing tobacco on their breath. Jurors were all professionals. No businessman would ever serve on a jury; I never knew a man who was ever even called to serve on a jury. A Negro was never referred to either in legislative halls or courtrooms by any other term than "nigger," and the adjective form used by the elite was "nigra," such as nigra schools, nigra churches, etc. Almost all people in the Deep South still persist in this pronunciation, and many do right here in Nashville, but in the early part of the century, it was universal.

Typical of Southern justice in this period was the Cooper case. The Coopers, father and son, lived at the Tulane and murdered Senator Carmack in front of where the YWCA now stands on Seventh Avenue. They were "avenging their honor" because Carmack had written an editorial in *The Tennessean* entitled "The Diplomat of the Zweibund."

"Zweibund" was a German phrase meaning a conspiracy of two, and Carmack intimated that the elder Cooper and the governor had been guilty of political skullduggery. I happened to be there within the block of the murder and arrived there in time to see the corpse being carried off. The Coopers were tried in our local criminal court, and the elder was acquitted while the younger received a twenty-year sentence. Within a few hours after he was found guilty, the selfsame governor, Ham Patterson, who had been the alleged co-conspirator in the *zweibund,* pardoned young Robin

The Score After Three Score

Cooper. Robin Cooper bought the home that Bernard Fensterwald lived in subsequently on Leake Avenue, and one day Cooper's body was found in Richland Creek near where it crosses Harding Road. Our supersleuth, Charles Gilbert, was then attached to the attorney general's office, but all his Sherlocks never uncovered the murderer.

Why I happened to be in the neighborhood was because my second home was the Carnegie Library, which, then as now, was just one block from Eighth and Church. We had few magazines and no books at the hotel, and all my reading was done at the library. I read the *Chicago Tribune* daily, especially because of my interest in humor. I was especially stimulated by two on their staff, one of whom I recognized as clever and the second as pure genius. B.L.T., Bert Leston Taylor, was America's first columnist, whose column "A Line O' Type or Two" was the forerunner of F.P.A.'s in the old *New York Mail.* The other was Ring Lardner, who rose from the sports pages of the *Tribune* to worldwide recognition as a great in literature. I read *Puck* and *Judge* weekly, both humorous magazines, and then there was the old *Life*, which in its heyday was an early twentieth century *New Yorker*. Unfortunately, in the 1910s some of its humor was anti-Negro and anti-Jewish, but that was typical of the era. In this magazine Bob Benchley first scored recognition as he did the drama reviews. (We have produced only two outstanding humorists in my lifetime, Mark Twain and Bob Benchley. Others may disagree but they were the only two men whose writing would produce not smiles but real belly laughs.)

When Carmack was shot, I was busily engaged in my reading pursuits. Unfortunately for posterity, I didn't hear the shots and reached the scene too late to be in on the big excitement.

Taxes were low but public services were lower. There were a few paved streets in Nashville. West End was paved to Twenty-first Avenue on the City's western border but Church Street was not paved even in 1910 beyond the viaduct. All downtown streets were paved with cobblestones about three inches wide. The roads outside the city were almost impassable. Up to 1920 automobile trips outside the city required as much preparation as going to the North Pole. To get to Chattanooga by automobile, the Automobile Blue Book recommended driving to Huntsville, which would take all day, and then putting the car on a riverboat up the Tennessee River. In 1914 there were only two paved pikes out of Nashville. Harding Pike was paved—and I am using the word "paving" loosely as the paving was equally loose—as far as Nine Mile Hill. The Dickerson Pike had some degree of pavement to a point beyond Goodlettsville. Between Nashville and Columbia even to about 1923 or 1924 there were five toll gates, at each of which you paid an elderly gentleman or his wife ten cents to proceed over a gravel road or water-logged macadam.

Education in those days was somewhat less than it should have been. Our superintendent of schools was a scholar named Weber who time and again would say that he preferred teachers who hadn't had too much education. He preferred teachers who had finished only two years of high school, as he thought they made the best instructors. Mister Weber was applauded in this idea by almost all the populace who, then as now, were suspicious of educated people.

We had a mayor for many years, a Mister Hillary Howse, a shrewd and unscrupulous politician whose education, like his honesty, was somewhat limited. The stories about Howse are legion; my two favorites are the ones about his speech at the Ryman Auditorium and the comment on local infant mortality. I heard the former; the second may be apocryphal. He was accused of dishonesty and neglect of the schools. He rose on his hind legs to several thousand cheering supporters in the old Ryman and said, "Ladies and gentlemen, I seen my duty and I done my duty." The other story involved a committee of women who went to see the mayor to ask him to help make pasteurization of milk compulsory to alleviate infant mortality. The mayor, with the urbanity that goes by the name of Southern courtesy, replied to the ladies, "I don't know much about this here milk business. I haven't drunk any milk in thirty years. As for the infant mortality, if it's a good thing, I will support it." As I said, the latter story, although supported by dozens of eyewitnesses, may be fictional, but the chances are that it is true.

THIS IS AN appropriate time to pass on to the practice of medicine in this period. Disease was rampant. Surely one-third of children died before they reached the age of ten. Refrigeration was very limited, and summer dysentery decimated last year's babies. Parents were urged to have their babies in the early spring for some dubious reason, possibly so that the mother could nurse the child close to the second summer, which was feared as we fear polio. Deaths during childbirth were very high, and no expectant mother would think of having a child in a hospital. All of our generation were born at home as the maternity death rate in homes was much lower than in hospitals. Puerperal fever claimed thousands annually, and the rate in some hospitals where the poor were forced to go was unbelievable. Hosts of diseases that we have almost forgotten claimed lives by the thousands. The Northwestern Insurance Company would not write anyone in Tennessee except in five or six counties as the other ninety had so high a death rate from malaria that no prudent underwriter wanted the risk. Pneumonia and the infections following influenza claimed thousands, and these diseases struck the young and, for some peculiar reason, seemed to be more lethal among the strong athletic type. Yellow fever also was prevalent in the South, though Nashville has had no epidemic in this century. I still remember that my father could not go to Birmingham or Montgomery because Nashville had a quarantine against travelers from those two cities. He could go but there was no assurance that he could be allowed to return because of the prevalence of Yellow Jack in Alabama. Syphilis was a horrible plague. Diagnosis was difficult, and Doctor Ehrlich had not yet discovered Salvarsan. The only treatment was bismuth and mercury with varying degrees of success. Almost every family in Nashville had at least one victim and could name four among our leading families who subsequently developed tabes or paresis.

We had a whole host of diseases that claimed children. Diphtheria killed hundreds. One could see many adults even up to a few years ago who still carried the scars of emergency tracheotomies, performed to save their lives. Scarlet fever with its subsequent heart involvements killed or maimed many. My own brother died of meningitis although the diagnosis was vague. Doctors' offices were crude places where one described one's symptoms, and actual physical examination by the physician was rare. Tuberculosis was the great white plague, and there were estimates saying that one-fourth of Nashville's population were victims. At least one-half of the population had or had had rickets to one degree or another. Another vitamin deficiency disease, pellagra, was very common. My mother fortunately kept us on a constant dosage of Scott's emulsion. Although she knew nothing of vitamins, she surely had the right medicine. On the other hand, the stress diseases were not as prevalent. Stomach ulcers were relatively rare, and I have a feeling that there were fewer psychosomatic disorders. Heart disease and cancer, of course, were less prevalent, for the obvious reason that few people ever lived long enough to get them. Hospitals then were like high schools; they were scarce and poor. We had three high schools in Davidson County, Fogg on Eighth and Broadway, Central, and Pearl. Pearl was perhaps the most inappropriately named school in America as it was a filthy frame building located just off of Black Bottom. We also had three hospitals in town, Saint Thomas, City, and Vanderbilt, all small and dirty. We had also several "infirmaries" run by surgeons. The most famous of these was that run by Doctor Dixie Douglas, located at Second and Peabody. Others were Doctor McGannon's, situated where the new Federal Reserve Building is presently located, and Doctor Eve's and another one, Doctor Fort's, I believe, at the site of the parking garage back of the Bennie Dillon Building. These infirmaries were crude and septic but run by men possibly even more dedicated to their profession than the current crop of doctors and surgeons. Possibly because of the smallness of the city and possibly because of the hopelessness of such medicine, the doctor/patient relationship was more wholesome and personal.

Office calls were one dollar and house calls were two dollars. A "complete" physical examination, and advisedly I have placed complete in quotes, cost usually five dollars, but I doubt if it was worth that much. It consisted of having one's weight and height taken, a "urinalysis" run immediately by the M.D., consisting of a Benedicts that required one minute to run and heating about 2cc of the specimen in a test tube for albumin. A stethoscope would be applied to one's chest and rales noted, and, if there were any loud heart murmurs, they too were noted and then one's blood pressure would be taken, and that was a complete physical. Oh, I forgot. There was also the cough test for hernia and a knowing glance at your tongue. No written record was kept. The electrocardiogram, blood chemistry, and routine X-rays were all to come as was our knowledge of vitamins, enzymes, hormones. The whole subject of the ductless glands, blood chemistry, etc., was terra incognito.

Two other diseases should be mentioned as they were constant threats. Typhoid fever was rampant in all age groups. Those who recovered spent weeks in bed with high fever, and there were many deaths. A whole host of parasitic diseases plagued the population, especially the poor, and the Rockefellers gave millions to investigate one, hookworm, which many thought by itself had kept the South lazy and inefficient.

And then there were "blood poisoning" tetanus, mastoiditis, gonorrhea, and a whole raft of diseases produced by bacteria that have disappeared completely or are relatively rare. And diabetes. Any young person who developed this disease had his death warrant. Older people could then as now with luck prolong life by diet, but many doctors and more laymen advocated visits to certain spas. Europe was full of them, and each spa was earmarked for one specific disorder. I was always amused by some of these European spas whose waters were so potent that they were good for all diseases, and these would be known as luft spas. Nashvillians of means would go to Waukesha, Wisconsin, and my mother, Mortimer, and I would leave Nashville every year without exception the day after school was closed and stay usually in Wisconsin or Michigan until Labor Day. I spent two summers in Europe before I was fifteen years old and visited spas there such as Baden-Baden and Wiesbaden.

No paper of this type would be complete without talking about Nashville water. This was before chlorine treatment and other filtrating methods. Tap water in Nashville was pure mud and tasted like clay. We had a large stone filter, and my mother filtered every drop of water that we drank. We were prohibited from drinking water in the Tulane dining room or anywhere else. Many rich people in town drank spring water from such springs as Horn and Lockland, and there was a large sale in distilled water. When chlorination came in, many still stuck to their spring water until one typhoid epidemic was traced to one of the "pure" springs.

With the passing of these plagues, minor and major, we have developed a race that is bigger and healthier. When I first started working in the hosiery mill, men's socks were made in sizes from 9 to 11½" long. Today we make no 9 or 9½ except a few for customers selling to Mexicans in Texas. Very few 10's are sold, and the average size now was almost the maximum in 1920, that is, size 11. Men's socks are now made up to 12, 12½, 13, 14, and occasionally we get calls for 15's and 16's.

SO MUCH FOR the state of medicine in my youth; I will devote less space to business. Today all manufactured goods are better, and this statement can be made without much fear of contradiction. Today low-priced goods may lack some of the glamour of the more-expensive, but intrinsic quality is taken for granted in everything that is sold. The principle of business that prevailed throughout my youth of caveat emptor, let the buyer beware, has been replaced almost one hundred percent by the principle of caveat vendor, let the seller beware. All one has to do is to look through a Sears or Ward's catalog of the twenties and compare it with one published today. The lowest-priced automobile is supposed to run almost as well as the best. The cheaper sock must have the same wearing qualities as the best. Mass production and a change of the political and economic climate has assured better production for less cost. Of course, prices have gone up, but if one would convert the number of hours that the average working man has to work to get a pair of shoes or an automobile, it can be demonstrated that he works fewer hours now and gets a better product than he did forty years ago. This is true for almost all merchandise; it may not be true for what the economists call non-goods, namely services, as I doubt if one gets one's money's worth in this area in 1961.

Grocery stores were really unbelievably poor in the good old days. Good meat was absolutely unobtainable in Nashville, and the quality and choice of groceries was very limited. The market house was located in the square on the first floor of the City Hall, perhaps the ugliest city hall in all America and indescribably filthy. Refrigeration was almost nil, and the passing of this public market was mourned by no one except the undertakers.

The chief change in merchandising is that, with the growth of national chains simultaneously with the growth of cities, distribution is no longer personal. In 1910 I doubt if there was a single publicly owned chain store in Nashville. Kress was the only five cent-ten cent store, and this was their Store #2, #1 being in Memphis. A&P had a small store on the north side of Union Street between Fourth and Fifth, but both of these companies were then privately owned. Hill's had quite a few branches but it was, as it still is to this day, a family company. All business was done with one's neighbor and, if this was a plus value, it was more than offset by a whole host of negative values. The ladies in the family bought their dresses from Rich-Schwartz, which claims to have invented the word ready-to-wear, Loveman's, Armstrong's, Busy Bee (later Cain-Sloan), Timothy's, Lebeck Bros., all located in the downtown area. My clothing came from Burk & Company. Burk was located in an L-shaped building on the northeast corner of Fourth and Union where the main branch of the First American Bank is now situated. The Nashville Bank and Trust Company occupied the corner, and Burk surrounded the bank, with the boys' clothing on the Fourth Avenue entrance and the men's on Union. Joe Fensterwald's merchandising philosophy was completely personal. It was strictly not a one-price house, and Joe Fensterwald gave away hundreds of suits to people who were in financial embarrassment. If you paid the full price for a suit, you were surely entitled to a free pair of suspenders or a belt

A Confetti of Papers

or a pair of socks, and a good pair of socks was worth fifteen cents.

Manufacturing was all done on what would now be considered a sweatshop basis. It was shortly after World War I in 1919 when Henry Ford astounded the world by increasing wages to five dollars a day. Prior to that date Ford was paying twenty-four cents an hour for his mechanics on a ten-hour day. Manufacturing locally was done on a fifty-seven-hour week at wages ranging before World War I from three cents to twelve cents an hour. Child labor was rampant; kids ten years of age and even younger were working in industry. In 1933 NRA established a minimum wage in the South of 27½ cents an hour, representing almost one hundred percent increase in wages. My company was paying an average of seventeen cents an hour prior to NRA, and I knew of two other textile companies in Nashville that were paying twelve cents and fifteen cents respectively. We gave all of our employees a physical examination in 1933 and discovered that over half of them were suffering from inanition, a fancy medical phrase for undernourishment. What a contrast with 1961 when a similar examination would disclose that obesity and over-eating complicate the health record of over half of our employees.

For the benefit of J.C. Bradford Steine, one paragraph must be devoted to finance. There wasn't a single member house located in Nashville. There were several with telegraph connections but none with tickers. Goulding Marr and the Platers were two names I remember. There were also always one or two McCoy bucket shops here. I remember one was in what used to be the old Exchange Building. Even in those days, bucket-shopping was illegal, but every house in town was suspected of indulging in this intriguing business, even some of the most respected bankers. Our first member house was Wagner & Company, which bankrupted right after World War I. They were located on the ground floor of the Stahlman Building, and from about 1910 to World War II there was always one member wire house on the second floor of that building. Almost all of the local brokers eventually went busted in the crash of either 1907, 1920, or 1932. Of course, the record of the New York Stock Exchange members has been amazingly good, as only two have bankrupted since 1928 and, in neither case, did any customer lose a dollar, and that was true even in the outrageous bankruptcy of Richard Whitney. But that happy state of affairs did not exist when I as a boy. My father always traded in the market, and for one of my early birthdays, I received ten shares of Pacific Mail common. Remember this was about 1908 and, although I cannot attribute this gift to my later interest in mathematics and finance, I am certain that it didn't hurt any.

Banking was cold, impersonal, and difficult. Loans were hard to come by, and the small businessmen who ran the wholesale houses on the Public Square and Market Street was the source of most of the wealth as this was one field in which they might prosper. Herman Brothers, Lindauer, Bogatzy Bros., Harris Solinsky, Eskind and Greenspan, Sam Levy, and on the corner of the square in retailing, Gilbert's, along with Neely-Harwell, Lyles Black, and J.S. Reeves were the backbone of Nashville business. Almost all of them had accounts of people in town who left money with them, and the gossip was Sam Levy had over one hundred thousand dollars in money that recent immigrants had given him for safekeeping, and it was well kept. The bankruptcy of one firm, Weinbaum Bros., was a major scandal as it had accepted much money just prior to its insolvency.

I HAVE COVERED the occupations of all the members of the club to some degree with the exception of the ministry. Every politician is told to avoid this subject, but not being too good a politician and now that the councilmanic election is over by two hours, I shall plunge into this field too. Of course, my church was the Vine Street Temple.

I believe my wife's grandfather was its first president. He was a Forty-niner who had just returned from California, and I presume he found a need for religion. The Gay Street congregation was located on one of the most appropriately named streets in the whole world. Gay Street was one of the prominent streets in the local red light district, and it and Crawford and the adjoining side streets made a thriving area in an old occupation that subsequently, for the first time in several thousand years, has disappeared thanks to the automobile and the amateurs.

A third congregation was formed on Fifth Avenue next to the Ryman. The three congregations in those days represented nationalities as much or more than they did religious differences. The Vine Street was started by the German immigrants. The Gay Street was started by Russians, Polish, Rumanian, and other Eastern Europeans, and the Fifth Avenue by Hungarians. I still remember with great amusement the fact that my father lent the Gay Street group six thousand dollars to build their building. As I said above, folks didn't go to banks for such loans but to other individuals. This was an arm's length transaction, and I can still remember shortly after my mother's death in 1911 when I started assisting my father in his personal bookkeeping, coming upon a mortgage that he held as collateral on the Gay Street Building. Whatever humor I have must have been inherited from my mother as my father saw nothing humorous about his holding a mortgage on a synagogue. For my amusement, I could picture my father with a long Simon Legree whip running the congregants out of the church on a wintry night because of their failure to pay the interest. But he was not amused by my speculation. To him, it was a routine piece of business, and the six percent interest was just correct. His charitable contributions had nothing to do with this loan.

Subsequently membership in the three congregations changed from country of origin mainly to finance. All individuals, with few exceptions whose rating in Dun's was approximately C-1½ or better or who had nubile daughters for whom they were ambitious, became members of Vine Street. This was especially true in the period immediately following World War I. Every year the confirmation class would consist of a large majority of daughters over sons, and parents with daughters peculiarly were more liberal in their religious outlook than parents with sons. The usual routine was to have the sons of the eastern European immigrants go to Gay Street to be bar mitzvahed while the daughters would go to Vine Street to be confirmed.

My father, although brought up extremely Orthodox, was a poor church-goer. My mother was somewhat more religious, but I never attended any Sunday School in Nashville. Quite incidentally, I did go to kindergarten at Mrs. Jonnard's, which was located between the Vine Street Temple and the Vine Street Christian Church, but I didn't enjoy it. I complained constantly that it was too childish and, even at six, I was far more interested, unfortunately, in politics, a completely misspent childhood that I was careful to avoid for my own children. Promotion and exploitation of religion with brotherhoods, clubs, study groups, socials, etc., was virtually unknown. These fringe benefits in all churches, irrespective of denomination, is a by-product of Madison Avenue methods applied to religion. (Note that Walter Courtenay has his name in BOLD BLACK capitals in the current phone directory.)

Transportation was a constant problem. We had a horse and buggy that we kept at Bennett's Livery Stable, and for the sake of permanent record, Bennett's telephone number was 9. My first telephone call was made when I was about seven, and I would call 9 and get the horse and buggy sent over. A colored boy would ride back on his horse that he had tied onto the back of the buggy. And once in a great while, I would be allowed to ride around the block on his horse, a thrill indeed. If you forgot the telephone number, you could ask the operator for the number as there were few subscribers and the operator, who was then known as Central, would know most of them by heart. I have often wondered what happened to Central.

SO WHAT IS the score now? The best thing about the good old days was the fact that I was younger. In almost every other respect, the good old days were not so good. Of course, we had a greater peace of mind because Russia wasn't fourteen minutes away via ICBM. Everything was farther away. My father and mother always wanted to see the Hermitage, and on two occasions we tried to get there by buggy but our mare, Jenny, couldn't make a twenty-five-mile trip. The only way to get to the Hermitage was to take the Tennessee Central, which was built when I was about eight, among much fanfare by Mister Jere Baxter, to Hermitage Station at which point one would have to rent a horse and buggy to go to Andrew Jackson's home. This had to be arranged in advance by mail as there were no long-distance telephones and, because of the train schedule, one most likely would have to spend the night at some private home. We never got to the Hermitage.

In spite of the menace of Russia and in spite of two World Wars, I still envy my grandchildren. The progress that we made economically, scientifically, yes, even morally, will be accelerated in the next fifty years at a geometric rate. My grandchildren, when they get to their seventh decade, will look upon Montgomery and Little Rock as we regard the witch trials at Salem. All deaths other than accidental deaths will be as a result of biological decay, pure and simple. With the awakening of the world and with the new educational opportunities, another sixty years should bring in an era of well-being, the likes of which this planet has never seen. True, the chart of our moral progress will be one of ups and downs, but each peak will be higher than the last.

Although much of the old was good, more was bad. I can think of but few areas in which the old was better than the new. One that disturbs me the most is the constant reduction in age of criminals. The criminal of my youth was usually a man over twenty-five. Today he is usually under twenty-five. In the same way, delinquency among women has definitely increased, but these losses are relatively minor when one considers the greater gains. Then, one-third of

A Confetti of Papers

Nashville's citizens could not read and write. Disease, ignorance, and poverty was the lot of almost all the population. Women were haggard and exhausted at thirty-five and dead at forty-five. No sector of our society has gained more than the female and, if there is anything to sociological and religious theories, this fact alone will eventually be productive of a better society.

I would be somewhat less than human if I did not regret the passing of a few things connected with my youth. One, believe it or not, was fires. Every fire alarm box in town was numbered, and every citizen had a list of these numbers in his pocket. Whenever a fire broke out, the bells in the City Hall tower and Tarbox School at Seventeenth and Broad would toll the box number, and the citizenry would hie it on foot. No automobile ever will have the glamour of the three horses pulling the old-time fire engine. The pumpers were steam engines, and under each engine a kerosene pilot flame burned continuously. This flame, under the boiler, was ready to be touched off at an instant's notice, and, while the engines galloped down the cobblestone streets, the engineer could be seen shoveling coal into the fire box with great frenzy so that he would have adequate pressure by the time he reached the fire. Preceding the engine would be the hose reel, which was literally a hose reel. Behind the engine would come the hook and ladder. As I remember, the hose reel had two horses and the others three. In all, it was quite a performance unmatched since the chariot race of Ben Hur's. There was an engine company consisting of all three wagons back of Christ Church on Ninth Avenue, and any uptown fire guaranteed their passing down Church Street, as Commerce Street was yet to be built. What a thrill for seven-year-old Danny.

I also bemoan the passage of the steam locomotive. No diesel, however efficient, will ever have the glamour and the excitement of the steam engine. I notice that the Reading Railroad still has a few steam locomotives, and they run excursions about three times a year for the railroad buffs and their children to re-create the excitement of the steam locomotives.

Finally, I am saddened by the passage of the legitimate theatre. We had two legitimate houses in Nashville, the Vendome, where Loew's is currently, and the Bijou on Fourth Avenue north of Charlotte that was just recently torn down after having been a Negro movie house for some forty years. The Bijou would have a new show every week with six night performances and two matinees. My mother took me every Saturday afternoon unless the show was a tragic melodrama, which might excite me to the point of insomnia. There at the Bijou I saw Fred Stone in *The Wizard of Oz* at least four times, George M. Cohan in *The Four Cohans* at least twice. It was a low-priced house appealing to the masses. The Vendome ran the better New York productions with the name stars, and they would stay here one or two nights, but I never was taken to them. I can't remember what the box office price was at the Bijou, but I somehow have a feeling that matinees were either fifty cents or seventy-five cents. One particular show came back a dozen times called *Busy Izzy,* which used to tickle the risibilities of the Tulane Jewry, although the stereotype derby-hatted Jew was resented by me then as it would be today.

But with these rare exceptions, there is not much of the past that I would try to recover if I were God.

We might have for our subject of discussion tonight,

since this paper is not very controversial, the question of whether there ever were any good old days. I am certain that there will be more than one opinion on that question.

On another subject, however, I am certain there is only one opinion, and that is the Shamus Club should stick to its schedules. My paper was due in September and if Mister E and others had not been derelict, I might have written something of more importance and surely not so rambling and lengthy as this one. I pray your forgiveness.

And we didn't have central heating or air-conditioning. Good Old Days. Hah.

Another generation heard from. I detect some improvement.

Solyman Brown

by Andrew May (1959–)

Read to the Old Oak Club in April 2008

WHEN I APPLIED to Yale College in the fall of 1976, I listed my father and older brother in the section marked "Alumni Relatives." My mother, reviewing the application, remarked, "You forgot about Solyman Brown; I think he was in the class of 1812."

"Who was Solyman Brown?" I asked with some surprise.

"Oh, he was my Grandma Brown's great-grandfather," she replied. "A Swedenborgian minister, a poet, and a pioneering dentist."

So I listed old Solyman on the application, half-thinking that my mother was pulling my leg, but it seemed to do the trick—I got into the college despite a variety of serious academic deficiencies. That conversation prompted an interest that I have revived from time to time.

A Confetti of Papers

Family history is dangerous ground for speakers. What seems engrossing to the writer is often pure tedium to the listener—no one really cares what I may have found in the Goshen, Connecticut, cemetery records or the Ellis Island ship manifests, or that my grandmother's mother married her sister's husband after the sister died, etc., etc. So I take a risk here that I may commit that greatest sin, to bore the audience. But I think I have found, in my obscure ancestor Solyman Brown, a life worth recounting—both for the variety and eccentricity of Solyman's undertakings and for his interactions with some of the great characters and ideas of America in the first half of the nineteenth century.

Many of you know a little something of the May family, a pretty conventional German-Jewish commercial grouping who came to Nashville by way of New England and Cincinnati, but this Solyman comes from my mother's mother's side—a bunch of eccentric families, mostly near-extinct, of Dutch and British extraction, including some seventeenth-century arrivals.

Solyman Brown (named for Suleiman the Magnificent) began life in Litchfield, Connecticut, in 1790. Litchfield, in the northwest hills, was an important colonial town, with a population of over three thousand (compared to about thirteen hundred today) at the time Solyman was born. The Litchfield Law School, founded by Tapping Reeve, numbered both John C. Calhoun and Aaron Burr among its graduates. Solyman's father was the son of a Scots-Irish immigrant with a land grant in the area, while his mother Thankful Woodruff came from very old Connecticut stock—descended from a Matthew Woodruff, who came to America sometime before 1642 when records show he married in Farmington,

Connecticut. (There is still a Woodruff Street in Litchfield today.)

The Brown family were Presbyterians, typical of the Scots-Irish, and Solyman was baptized and received into the church in 1797.

A distant relative saw promise in the young man and paid for an education. Solyman trained at Yale to be a minister, receiving his B.A. in 1812 and his M.A. a year later. He apparently suffered some setback of health following his graduation that prevented his immediately beginning a career of preaching, so he did farm work in upstate New York for a year or so before apprenticing with an experienced preacher in Goshen, Connecticut. After a year, he received a four-year license to preach in Connecticut—and immediately began to have conflicts with some of the most notable characters in New England. His application to preach was apparently opposed by Lyman Beecher (the father of Harriet Beecher Stowe) on account of Solyman's brief apprenticeship.

During four years of preaching and teaching, Solyman also began to write both poetry and criticism. (More later about his poetical achievement.) His "Essay on American Poetry" attracted the attention of William Cullen Bryant, almost certainly the greatest poet in America in the early years of the century. Bryant wrote, in the *North American Review*,

> *Mr. Brown has fallen into a great mistake of thinking himself qualified to write a book. In the present instance, with talents of a very humble order, he has assumed a very pompous tone and made a great parade of small acquisitions.*

Brown was offered a pulpit in Ellsworth, Connecticut, in 1817, about the time his first preaching license expired. He now came into open conflict with Lyman Beecher, who opposed his re-licensure, citing Brown's "constitutional levity, which led him into various impertinences." While some Connecticut clerics and reporters took Brown's side in the matter, the great Judge Tapping Reeve, founder of the law school in Litchfield, thunderously agreed with Beecher, and the preaching license was not issued—essentially ending Solyman's association with the Congregationalists. He preached in upstate New York for a short time before experiencing "hemorrhage of the lung" that forced him from the pulpit.

Bereft of his chosen vocation, Brown moved to the city of New York, where he taught school and indulged his literary enthusiasms. Brown taught at a variety of private schools during this period, some of the best in the city—and as a result mixed with some of the social and literary elite. He wrote serious essays on educational theories of people like the Swiss theorist Pestalozzi. He did some preaching at Presbyterian and Congregationalist churches and became the religion editor for the newly established *New York Mirror*, a literary paper most famous for introducing the poetry of Edgar Allen Poe. When the *Mirror* sent him to do a refutation of the Swedenborgian theology, he immersed himself in the topic by attending services, reading Swedenborg's writings, and interviewing a pastor named Mister Doughty. Instead of completing his reportorial assignment, old Solyman instead resigned from the paper, began to attend Doughty's church, and was soon ordained in the New Church, as the Swedenborgian schism called itself.

Just a word about the improbable Swedenborgian

religion and its inspiration, the work of Emanuel Swedenborg, the Swedish scientist turned spiritual wanderer.

Swedenborg (1688–1772) had a prolific career as an inventor and scientist. He was internationally famous for his practical mastery of the smelting of non-ferrous metals. At the age of fifty-six he entered into a spiritual phase, in which he experienced dreams and visions. This culminated in a spiritual awakening, where he felt he was appointed by the Lord to write a heavenly doctrine based on a reformed Christianity. He claimed that the Lord had opened his eyes, so that from then on he could freely visit heaven and hell and talk with angels, devils, and other spirits. For the remaining twenty-eight years of his life, he wrote fourteen theological works, of which the best known was *Heaven and Hell* (1758).

Swed's theological views were unconventional: He rejected the notion of the Trinity, believing that God was indivisible, and that the Father, Son, and Holy Spirit were aspects of a single person, Jesus Christ. He believed that salvation was available to believers of all religions who were sincere in their faith and particularly sympathized with Muslim theology in its rejection of the notion of Trinity. A lifetime bachelor, he believed that marriages continued into the afterlife. (Some of us will have trouble with the notion that the old ball and chain will follow us into paradise.)

Above all, Swed rejected the core Lutheran doctrine that only by faith can a person achieve salvation. Related to his syncretistic notion that non-Christians might find their way to paradise, he believed that faith and charity were jointly required for a man to be saved; in fact, that the sole practical reason for faith was to inspire the conduct of the believer. It was this last notion that so inspired our hero Solyman

Brown, a rock-ribbed believer in right conduct as the measure of a man.

Swed never started a religion, but within a few years of his death, a church inspired by his extensive theological writings had emerged in England—the only place where many of his palpably heretical ideas could be freely published. The church spread to America by the second decade of the nineteenth century and was merely a seedling called "the New Church" when it found Solyman Brown.

Solyman became a leading figure in this fledgling movement. His sermons were reported to have been attended by large audiences and were published by the church.

In 1834, at the age of forty-four, Solyman married Elizabeth Butler, a girl half his age with whom he had initially become acquainted when she was thirteen and he was her schoolmaster. Solyman and his new bride were sent by the Officials of the New Church on a honeymoon preaching tour that lasted over a year. Astonishingly, this adventure took them into western Virginia, where they visited the Natural Bridge, and west to Mammoth Cave. Of course Jackson was President at the time of the trip, and Kentucky was hardly the frontier anymore, but I suspect that central Kentucky was really the Third World to this sophisticated New Yorker and his patrician bride. Their trip took them north as well, into the Canadian Maritimes where they journeyed as far as Cape Breton Island.

By this time, Solyman had become fast friends with a fellow named Eleazar Parmly, a friendship that would change the course of Brown's life. Brown and Parmly were acquainted socially, and Solyman had been the teacher of some of his friend's children. Parmly was a dentist, but in the

1830s anyone could say that he was a dentist. There was no licensure, no dental school, no professional societies or scientific or technical publications. Parmly was among a group of New York dentists who were attempting to professionalize the craft. Solyman, inhibited in his preaching by continuing health problems, began to learn dentistry by observing Parmly at work. They lived in adjacent homes on Park Place in lower Manhattan, and Parmly maintained his office at home.

The two dentists became part of the movement in New York City to professionalize dentistry. The proximate cause for the effort was a business rivalry with foreign charlatans, the Crawcours.

In 1833, two opportunists from England, the Crawcour brothers, brought amalgam fillings to America. They opened their office in New York and advertised their cheap, easily placed "new" filling containing a mixture of silver and mercury. They called them "silver" fillings, because silver sounds like jewelry. The Crawcour brothers were ruthless competitors and were soon considered a threat to American dentists. Amalgams were denounced not only as an inferior filling material but also as a harmful, toxic mixture causing gum disease, mercury poisoning, and fractured, painful teeth. The Crawcour brothers were eventually expelled from America.

In 1834, fifteen dentists formed the Society of Dental Surgeons of the City and State of New York. Horace Hayden was the first president, and the secretary was Solyman Brown, now two years into his first glimmer of interest in the profession. By 1839, Solyman was the president of this, the first professional dental society in the United States. In 1840, meeting at Solyman's home, the leadership of the New York group formed the American Society of Dental Surgeons, the first national dental organization in the world. Solyman was its first secretary.

None of this should suggest that Doctor Brown's personal practice of dentistry was going particularly well, or that his life was easy. Marrying at the age of forty-four, Brown had eight children with Elizabeth over the course of the next twenty years; there were many mouths to feed. His practice partnerships always seemed to be short-lived and very modestly remunerative. But he was a man of great intellectual energy and ambition.

Flush with enthusiasm for the profession he was learning from Parmly, Brown undertook a startling project—he penned a five-canto epic poem about dental hygiene, which he entitled "Dentalogia." It goes on for about eight hundred lines, but I'll limit my recitation to just a few.

> *Let every fair one shun Urilla's fate,*
> *And wake to action, ere it be late;*
> *Let each successive day unfailing bring*
> *The brush, the dentifrice, and, from the spring,*
> *The cleansing flood: the labor will be small,*
> *And blooming health will soon reward it all.*
> *Or, if her past neglect preclude relief,*
> *By gentle means like these, assuage her grief;*
> *The dental art can remedy the ill,*
> *Restore her hopes, and make her lovelier still.*

Is this poem remembered? Is it anthologized? Yes, it is! I found excerpts in the *The Stuffed Owl: An Anthology of Bad Verse* and in *In Search of the World's Worst Poets*. More promisingly, I found the entire poem on the practice website of Doctor Mark Ryan, a Washington, D.C., dentist with apparently refined literary tastes. With this achievement, my ancestor became "The Poet Laureate of Dentistry."

Brown and his colleagues, also in the mid-1830s, began to publish the first dental journal in the world, the *American Journal of Dental Science*, which Solyman edited for several years. He was a prolific contributor to this journal and the leading proponent—very controversially—that dentists should share their advances in technique with their professional peers. He wrote a paper entitled "Remarks on Professional Morality," the first writing on dental ethics and filled with the Swedenborgian imperative to make oneself useful and charitable in this world. Herewith a few lines:

> *Rules:*
>
> *(a) Realize that since the relief of pain is equally for rich and poor, dentists often must do good without reward.*
>
> *(b) Make your fees neither extortionate (thus keeping services available to all) nor degrading (thus keeping the proper class of practitioner in dentistry).*
>
> *(c) Do the best work for all.*
>
> *(d) Do only needed work.*
>
> *(e) "Perform the duties of our profession in every instance as we would wish them performed were the case our own."*
>
> *(f) Do not allow the feeling of rivalry or jealousy toward other practitioners, but have a neighborly feeling.*
>
> *(g) Do not cherish professional secrets; we are after a community of truth.*

BY THE MIDDLE of the 1840s, however, Solyman had ceased to practice dentistry at all. While some of my sources describe a hand tremor as the cause, my guess is that he simply found it dull. Whatever the reason, his idealism now led him down a bad dead-end. Brown had become fascinated with the utopian socialist ideals of Charles Fourier, who believed that all human beings should live in communities of 1,620 persons called phalanxes built around communal crafts and agriculture. There was a generous helping of promiscuity tossed in: There were to be no fixed couplings. Brown had seen the first of these experiments at work in the Brook Farm community in West Roxbury just outside Boston, a Fourierist Community organized by Transcendentalist clerics of the other main branch of anti-Trinitarians, the Unitarians.

Brown sold his practice and moved with his wife and five children to the incipient North American Phalanx at LeRaysville, Pennsylvania, in Bradford County near Elmira, New York. (LeRaysville still appears on the map, but the county, in the Endless Mountains, has a population similar to that in 1840.) Brown apparently invested a significant amount of his personal capital in this utopian venture. The Phalanx lasted only a few years, and Solyman left within a year of his arrival for unspecified reasons. If the bizarre sexual mores embraced by Fourier in his writings were being employed at the Phalanx, Solyman may have . . . well, one can only speculate. Suffice it to say that my ancestor—Solyman's third son, Eleazar Parmly Brown—was born at LeRaysville, raising some doubt about whether Solyman is really my great-great-great-granddaddy after all.

The adventure at the Phalanx was a financial disaster for

a minister with a large brood of offspring. The family moved to Ithaca, New York, for a time, where Solyman had a series of pulpits in the New Church congregations in the area and put food on the table by gardening. His ministerial salary from his tiny church in Ithaca was $274 per year. The family was desperately poor, and Solyman, at least, was used to a city life with intellectual stimulation, so they moved back to New York, where Solyman began a series of ventures in the manufacturing and sale of false teeth, becoming, against all odds, an industrialist of sorts.

The Italian inventor Fonzi had first developed ceramic teeth in 1807, and they were made by craftsmen in the U.S. as early 1820. But the industrial manufacture of teeth in quantity was not undertaken until Stockton of Philadelphia began his production facility in the 1840s. Solyman was first a New York rep for the Stockton Company, then, with partners, capitalized the New York Teeth Manufacturing Company.

Eleazor Parmly Brown

Early in the history of the enterprise, they were exhibitors at the first American World's Fair, one of the thousands of vendors of industrial products with space at the Crystal Palace (in what would become Bryant Park, named for the very same W.C. Bryant whose doubts about Brown's literary talent we heard earlier). New York Teeth was still exhibiting in the Crystal Palace when it burned in 1857—a conflagration from which Brown personally saved the company's display. A financial panic in 1860 ended the enterprise and left the family broke again, reduced to taking in boarders at their modest home in Brooklyn.

By this time old Solyman was seventy, though he still had a seven-year-old daughter in the house. He had returned to preaching in the New Church and turned his considerable remaining oratorical strength to the fight for abolition. On the eve of the Civil War, he preached a sermon that was published and apparently widely quoted and praised.

> *Spiritual liberty can never be enjoyed by any people who willingly subject either themselves or other to civil and political oppression . . . transforms and exalts every effort for the overthrow of . . . oppression into a noble endeavor. . . . Members of the New Church must everywhere hail the progress of social reformation and civil freedom. . . . Man must love to see his neighbor free as well as himself, before he can be a true freeman. . . . [The national purpose is] to bear the blessings of Liberty, of Civilization and Christianity on its "banner of stars" to every people on the earth. . . .*

Solyman lived late in life with his children, sometimes

near New York City and sometimes near Ithaca. He never experienced any financial success or security but continued to write poetry and garden. A letter to a friend from 1868 finds him bitterly denouncing the candidacy of Seymour and Blair in their attempt to unseat the incumbent Grant for the Presidency. Finally, in 1875 he moved west to Minnesota to be with a daughter who had followed a husband to the northern plains. He died and is buried in Dodge Center, Minnesota.

SOLYMAN BROWN'S LIFE begins in the first year of Washington's presidency with the ink scarcely dry on the new United States Constitution and ends with the United States as a continental power with global ambition. It begins in an era when men and information moved at the same speed as they had moved in Caesar's time—powered only by muscle or wind—and ends when the telegraph and the steam engine had revolutionized both.

Solyman was directly involved (at least in a small way) in the major social trends that roiled the century:

- The rise of the professional class and the formalization of its structure and governance. Solyman was there.
- The rise of the Unitarians, Transcendentalists, and other anti-trinitarian Protestant denominations. Solyman was there.
- The embrace of pre-Marxist utopian experiments in communal living. Solyman was there.
- The Industrial and scientific revolutions—there was Solyman at the Crystal Palace.
- Finally, westward expansion. Solyman's grave in Minnesota was dug when there were fewer than half a million

people living in the state, up from about one hundred thousand people just fifteen years prior.

I guess that Solyman was pretty ineffectual as a manager of a church, a dental practice, or a business. He was too stiff-necked to compromise on matters of principle and probably lost interest in the details of any enterprise. His catholic interests probably made him a delightful companion, but his mercurial enthusiasms probably made him a frustrating business associate. His enormously productive pen and his dedication to "doing right" made him tremendously valuable to the fledgling organization of the dental profession. Much of his writing is pompous and long-winded, but he did get the words down on paper—and for that reason he is remembered, and his career can be documented in detail.

Solyman's descendants have been less consequential than he. Only one son survived to adulthood—he was a dentist of moderate accomplishment, most notably receiving a patent for developing the notion of putting flavor in dental floss. His war experiences in Virginia were formative, and he dressed in his blue uniform on occasion, even as an old man. One of Solyman's grandchildren, Judge Enu Brown, according to family lore, invented the single-serving cereal box that could be cut open to serve as its own bowl. He introduced the idea at the General Mills Corporation by storming up to a receptionist and demanding to see the General. Enu, part of a large brood, was named by his father Eleazar Parmly Brown, as a result of three successive tosses of an alphabet block—it came down E-N-U. My own great-grandfather, H.C. Brown, seems never to have exerted himself at all, relying entirely upon the efforts of a highly industrious farm wife, Maria.

Solyman Brown

When my father, as he often does, tells me I look like the Browns, I know he doesn't mean to bestow an unalloyed compliment.

Solyman was a ferocious patriot and Union man. I'll close with some lines from his 1822 poem, *The Birth of Washington*, which speak perhaps to the American condition today:

Then, blest Americans! with such a clime,
Transmit your glories to the latest time;
If War impend—dismiss all coward fear:—
Some other WASHINGTON shall then appear;
Shall call around him many a Warrior brave,
And lead them on, to Glory—or the Grave!—

The Shamus Club in 1964. Back row: Bernard Werthan, Albert Werthan, Herbert Kohn, Randy Falk, Lou Silberman, and Sylvan Schwartzman. Front row: Charles Gilbert, Jacques Back, Bob Teitlebaum, Robert Eisenstein, Dan May, and Manuel Eskind.

An excellent thesis, even if not proven here below. Much support for this can be found in classmate Peter Braestrup's book, *The Big Story*.

Draft Riots of the '60s: Tet and the Battle of Nashville

Read to the Shamus Club December 16, 1987

WHY SHOULD ANYONE fight to kill or be killed? Let's say he is a nineteen-year-old farm boy off his father's farm raising corn in central Ohio. Why should he fight to stop the slaughter of Jews in the gas chambers or to free the enslaved black man of the Southern plantation or to ensure capitalism in South Korea or anti-communism in Southeast Asia or to stop the spread of radical Moslems in the Middle East? Why, my friends, should he fight at all, or if some causes are just and worth the fighting, how is he to distinguish them? While I read, have this question in mind. I will proceed to refresh our recollections of two of these wars, which did indeed take place.

I will give you the answer; you give me the question. The answer is "SMU, MIT, UCLA." The correct question for this answer is, "How do you spell smumitucla?" Having done well with that one, the next group of answers is, "The Massachusetts Institute of Technology, Vassar, La Salle, Bates, Swarthmore, and the University of Maine and Cornell." The correct question here is, "Name some of the fifteen colleges that were founded in the North during the Civil War." During the years of 1861 through 1865, college enrollment in the North declined only very slightly. During the period of the late 1960s, a little over one hundred years later, college enrollment while a war was being fought actually increased. During both wars, higher education flourished—exactly what that says, I don't know. But it is the study of such comparisons that I would like to undertake this evening. Historical parallels are often ephemeral and often wrongly interpreted. Nevertheless, they are a source of fascination for the dabbler, and historical dabble is what we have in this evening's paper.

TO THOSE OF us around this room, Tet and Vietnam seems as but yesterday, while the Civil War and its battles seems as remote as Homeric legend. Only one hundred four years separate Tet and the Battle of Nashville—not really long at all. All of us in this room know people who were alive at the end of the Civil War, or at least know people who knew such people. My own grandfather, when an infant, probably heard the cannon at the Battle of Nashville. Surely he did, but so what? The gulf seems enormous. Vietnam was modern, the Civil War ancient. Somehow, the Civil War days are monochromatic, while the Vietnam memories are in vivid Technicolor. Nevertheless, difficult as it may be to believe, the people were quite similar in both instances, and the trees were just as green in 1864.

I will take a look at the comparative stance and attitude of the two centuries with regard to the two wars as they involved the following: morality, strategy, tactics, politics, the press, public support, the draft, draft riots, Canada, and a short look at the two decisive battles of Tet and Nashville.

Tet and Nashville

To begin, let's examine Tet and Nashville. In both cases, the Federal troops of the United States won smashing victories. It was the perception, however, of the Southeast Asian victory that the battle, if not won, was at least not going to be the last one. With Nashville, the perception was the reverse. One wonders if John Bell Hood had, rather than leading his armies directly toward the entrenched enemy, retreated into the countryside *à la* General Giap and had units operating on the land in Kentucky, Indiana, Pennsylvania, whether or not he could have prevailed to at least a negotiated peace. The Battle of Nashville should be well known to us all. After all, we live upon its dark and bloody ground where about thirteen thousand people bled and died in two days of battle and because of the additional six thousand who just bled. The battlefield is marked now by only a few random and largely unintelligible historical markers. The battlefield itself is gone—paved over by a new civilization. I wonder if even the ghosts of those two terrible days in December have the resolve to mix with the Green Hills traffic of a Saturday afternoon.

A Confetti of Papers

We remember that after the disastrous losses and the fall of Atlanta in the summer of 1864, Jeff Davis, together with his pet general, John Bell Hood, hatched a plan. It was the Federals' concept to sweep across Georgia to the sea and then northward into South Carolina, leaving behind a path of destruction that would leave the South economically abject. To counter this, Davis had Hood march northward.

It might have been a more conventional concept to retreat and set up a smaller perimeter in the deepest portion of the South as was done at Pusan eight-five years later. However, the South chose not to shorten its lines, but to spread out northward and westward with a plan that just might have worked. As the Northern armies swept southward, the western regions were left less protected. If Hood could have managed to use this weakness to get across Tennessee into Kentucky and into the central North, the Southern armies might have obtained a strategic advantage at the eleventh hour. When it became apparent to the Federal general staff that this was Hood's intention, General Schofield was sent in pursuit of Hood across northern Georgia and Alabama and into Tennessee. It was Schofield's hope to reach Nashville in time to reinforce General Thomas for defensive purposes.

Schofield succeeded at Spring Hill by having the Northern army pass the Southern army in one night at amazingly close range. A matter of yards, not miles. The story hardly seems credible. John Bell Hood was an extremely sick man, a double amputee having lost one arm and one leg, and had to be strapped upon his horse. He likely treated the pain of these amputations with laudanum, an opium derivative, and maybe alcohol, which may have dulled his sensibilities.

In any event, on finding that he had been passed at

Spring Hill by Schofield, Hood made a frontal assault the next day at Franklin. He lost six thousand men and six of his best generals. General Schofield, having won at Franklin, retreated to reinforce Thomas in Nashville.

The promotion of Hood is the Civil War's confirmation of the Peter Principle. While he had served as a young officer with great courage and tactical skill in every battle, once he was promoted to general, he failed in every battle thereafter. At Nashville he was thirty-one years old.

Two weeks later Hood, having failed in his frontal assault at Franklin, tried to lay siege to Nashville. In doing so, he broke the cardinal rule of warfare—in order to lay siege, one must have superior strength. Hood did not. He had vastly inferior strength, and when Thomas chose to attack, the two-day battle ensued with disastrous results. The hardships of that battle need a little repetition. Men had no sleep and little food for as long as seventy-two hours at a stretch. There were no blankets and no shoes, just bloody tracks through the snow and the mud. As December 16, 1864, ended, Hood was in agonizing retreat southward down Granny White Pike, having left thirteen thousand dead in Franklin and Nashville.

He passed south of the Tennessee border to lick his wounds during the winter and was never again a factor. One can only speculate on the course of the war had he used the tactics of General Giap by breaking his army into small units. Here he had some excellent guerrilla activists, as exemplified by Nathan Bedford Forrest. Had he been able to get around Nashville, rather than taking it head-on, had he been able to reach Kentucky, Ohio, Pennsylvania, and had he been able to disrupt the countryside, would not the American people have lost their will and sued for peace? We have the example of Vietnam to suggest that it is not an unlikely scenario.

Tet

Tet is the celebration of the Chinese New Year. In 1968, on January 30, the South Vietnamese guerrilla armies known at the Viet Cong simultaneously attacked all major cities, towns, and military bases in South Vietnam. These attacks reached right into the heart of Saigon and into the grounds of the U.S. Embassy there. The battle, which took place at over a hundred different sites, lasted for one month. In some cases, towns and installations were won and overrun, but by and large the attacks were repulsed and held at bay until the cessation of activities about thirty days later. In Saigon, battles were carried on by handfuls of guerrillas who infiltrated the city by commercial busses. The attacks on the U.S. installations there were largely suicidal, but for the first time in the war were within the full view of the press.

A more conventional attack was undertaken on the Marine installation at Khe Sanh, only a few miles below the border separating North and South Vietnam and hundreds of miles north of the capital in Saigon. It was presumed that the U.S. Marine installation there would fall first and early. It did not fall, however, and survived Tet intact, contrary to the conventional wisdom of the time. A third city attacked was the provincial capital at Hue. This loveliest of all Vietnamese cities was torched and captured by the Communist forces. During the two weeks of their occupation, the bloodiest of atrocities in the war took place. Some three thousand men, women, and children, including American forces, missionaries, and babies, were tortured, executed, and put into a mass grave. By the end of the month of February, however, the town had been regained by the Vietnamese government forces.

Khe Sanh, Hue, and Saigon were diversely typical of the hundreds of battles that occurred in this short period. What were the results? It is clear that the attacking forces of the indigenous Viet Cong that did most of the incursive fighting suffered a grievous military setback. Tens of thousands of their most dedicated and experienced men emerged from the jungles and the countryside, only to meet a deadly rain of gunfire within the towns and cities. They lost the best of their generation of resistance fighters. After the Tet offensive, these Viet Cong troops had to be replaced by North Vietnamese regulars, who thereafter carried the war. The insurgency aspects diminished, and more conventional battles were carried on thereafter. The South Vietnamese did not rise up against their government. They gave little or no support to the attacking guerrillas. The Communist claim for popular moral and political authenticity in South Vietnam suffered a serious blow. The South Vietnam government itself was stressed, but did not falter. After Tet, Saigon leadership nearly doubled its military strength and became a much more effective government. The Viet Cong losses were staggering. It is not clear what their leadership had hoped to accomplish. Certainly no decisive victory such as the Dien Bien Phu victory of 1954 with the French could have seemed likely, but if the Viet Cong lost the battle, and lost decisively, it was at Tet that they won the war.

Morality

So much for military facts–what of morals and the spirit? Morality has set a tone for all American wars. The moral high ground of the abolitionist and the end of an odious system of human slavery may not have been the only reason for the Civil War, but certainly gave the United States an undergirding fiber. In Vietnam, the moral undergirding also involved a type of enslavement. We sought the prevention of absolute state slavery, rather than private individual slavery. Kennedy and Johnson sought to prevent the imposition of a dictatorship and potential for a holocaust, which in time did come. Whether either of these two moral stances were communicated or were important to the public, one cannot know. It seems that the fervor against communism never reached a moral level as high as did the fervor against slavery. However, even there it may be that the moral outrage was never a generally held view across the population. The removal of the conflict in both cases must have impacted the view of morality. The distances in the two wars, if not in geography, were in time similar. It took about twenty-four hours to reach Vietnam from Washington by military plane, and it would have taken the same twenty-four hours to arrive from Washington in Nashville by train. It is not clear that the man in the street cared much whether two million Southeast Asians were slaughtered or not, or if black people (and many in the North had never seen a black person) were held in bondage in a remote area. But the Civil Was seemed the more justified. Maybe there is more rectitude in a rifle shot than sprayed napalm.

Strategy

The strategy of the military in each war was not dissimilar. The U.S. in both cases sought to use its superior industrial machinery, its superior science, and superior navy to crush the opposition. In both cases, blockades were imposed. In both cases, the allegiance of allies in Europe proved to be an uncertain variable.

Tactics

The tactics of the Civil War were largely determined by officer corps of both sides who trained together at West Point. The North hoped to use large units to split the South. This was eventually accomplished by driving from Fort Donelson to Nashville to Chattanooga to Atlanta to Savannah and the sea. The South hoped to defeat armies by superior generalship and higher motivation. It sought to win battles, not territory. In Vietnam, America's general corps also trained at West Point and were prepared by the grand-scaled battles of World War II. To that end, the generals used the technology and weapons that had been developed in the years since World War II to fight that war again. The Vietnamese soldiers under General Giap did not come from this tradition. They fought with small units capable of enormous sacrifice and staying power while harassing the enemy troops and demoralizing the civil population. As we have said, such tactics were not unknown to the South in the Civil War. Nathan Bedford Forrest of our own region led small cavalry incursions and was most effective in harassing the Northern armies. My estimation is that had Lee put more faith in these roving bands and less in grand armies, popular demoralization of the Northern civilian population would have been more likely. The prospect of a long extension of the war past 1865 could have produced demoralization among the Northern population and the possibility of a negotiated peace.

Politics

The years 1864 and 1968, Tet and Nashville, were presidential election years. A new Republican party elected Lincoln in 1860 and, with his reelection in 1864, the fate of the South was substantially sealed. With the war *seeming* to go badly after the Tet offensive in 1968, Lyndon Johnson declined to run. After the assassination of Robert Kennedy and the rise of Gene McCarthy, the Democrats nominated Hubert Humphrey. The electorate returned to the Republicans in that year, and it elected Richard Nixon. Nixon, in each of the five years that he was in office, reduced our soldiers in Vietnam by approximately one hundred thousand per year. The disappearance of Lyndon Johnson foreshadowed loss as much as the reelection of Lincoln foreshadowed victory.

The substantial Northern peace movement coalesced in the Democratic Party in 1864. A platform plank was adopted, drafted by a Copperhead, that stated, "After four years of failure to restore the Union by the experiment of war, justice demands an immediate cessation of hostilities that peace may be restored." General McClellan was nominated along with his Vice President Gentlemen George Pendleton of Ohio, a real Lincoln-hater. The Republicans won over this ticket in November by a landslide in the electoral vote only. The popular vote found forty-five percent voting for the peace Democrats. In the three states of New York, Pennsylvania, and Ohio, the combined plurality for Lincoln was only eighty-six thousand votes.

The election was watched in the South with bated breath. It was assumed that if McClellan and the Democrats won, the war was over. A Democrat would broker peace.

When this hope was dashed, the war did end six months later, but on their terms of surrender.

The press in the North in the 1860s ran a wide spectrum of viewpoints. Horace Greeley at *The New York Tribune* was vehement in his condemnation of slavery, but not as vehement in his support of Lincoln. There was much forceful press opposition to the war in the North and strong peace editorial policies. The prevailing sentiment was support for the war. Though Lincoln was much deified in the press, he also vilified. *The Catholic Weekly* of New York opined that "Abe Lincoln, passing the question of his taint of Negro blood, is altogether an imbecile. He is brutal in all his habits. He is filthy. He is obscene. He is an animal." *The New York World* said of the 1864 Republican ticket of Lincoln and Andrew Johnson: "They have nominated two ignorant, boorish, third-rate backwoods lawyers. It is an insult to common sense." No such diversity appeared in the press of the 1960s. The opposition to war among the media establishment was general. Walter Cronkite lost faith in the war and, save the exception of perhaps the *Wall Street Journal*, none of the news magazines, the networks, nor *The New York Times* nor *Washington Post* had anything but unrelieved opposition thereto after the time of Tet. The press was near-unanimous in its opposition, and it subsequently has been as unanimous in its amnesia of its own role in promulgating a defeat that was followed by the killing fields and the death of two million gentle Cambodians. The boat people are mentioned but casually. There is no memory of one hundred thousand political executions nor the deaths from malnutrition, the reeducation camps nor the sale of slave laborers to build the Eastern European pipelines. The forgetting of this holocaust remains an unexamined, yet vital, fact of our generation.

My own classmate Peter Braestrup details much of this in his acclaimed book, *The Big Story*.

Public Support

The public support for both wars was ambiguous at best. In the case of Vietnam it was clear that the college population *did* support the war. This was particularly true if the college was an Eastern Michigan or a Middle Tennessee college. There are many more students at these than there at the Ivy schools. But it is the elite schools' opposition that seemed to pervade. There was a notion that the "young people" were against the war. Certainly, they were at these prestigious institutions. I was on the Harvard campus for several months in 1968. The campus leaders, who in gentler times would be running for student organization presidents or planning proms, were making pronouncements on geopolitics with red bandannas around their foreheads. These students' statements thereon were immediately reported in column one of *The New York Times*. This is pretty heady stuff for a twenty year old. I will never forget the rallies of that era. The white columns of the congregational church in the Harvard yard were smeared with red spray paint of peace symbols, and from the choir lofts that once gave forth Bach and Handel now blared the cacophony of acid rock. My own estimation is that the public in any war would rather not think about such things and occupy themselves with the day-to-day routine of life. As noted initially, time was found to start fifteen universities while the Civil War was in progress. The transcontinental railroad was authorized and neared completion while the war was in progress.

Who went to war and who didn't

The rich evaded the Civil War; the bright evaded the Vietnam War. In both cases, conscription led to cynicism. In the Civil War, soldiers were needed. The number required was divided among the states in proportion to their population and further subdivided into districts. Each district could reduce its quota by volunteers, and the balance was obtained by drafting men by lots from a registered list. There was no attempt then to first levy on young men or bachelors. Instead, exempted classes were ministers, family heads, and most of all, those with money. One could commute service by the payment of three hundred dollars, or evade service for the entire war by procuring a substitute to enlist for three years. It was no matter if the substitute died or deserted the next day. In our own day, one could avoid the draft by remaining in institutions of higher education. Such deferment made a class-split along elite and non-elite lines and in a popular democracy makes a travesty of equality of commitment. Graduate schools in these years swelled. Many young men attended seminaries in the late '60s. One wonders whether it was the call of Jehovah in their ear or the odor of nitrate in their nostrils that motivated their footsteps to the cloister.

Canada

Interestingly, one outlet for both wars was Canada, with an underground railway of sorts that led young men in both conflicts to wander across the border. No statistics can be found on how many crossed the border, but the numbers in both cases were substantial. During the Civil War, Union draft dodgers, called "skedaddlers," took refuge in Canada.

Also, it provided an outlet for escape for fugitive prisoners of war. Thus, the Canadian border remained for one hundred years an outlet valve for the disaffected.

The Draft

During the 1960s, the protest of the draft ran from ubiquitous peace signs and campus demonstrations to draft card burnings. Some violence took place, with bombs going off at ROTC armories and draft headquarters. These instances were recent and well remembered. However, for real draft disaffection, one must turn to Manhattan in 1863. In the week following the Union victory at the Battle of Gettysburg, the island of Manhattan erupted into an insurrection that left some two thousand dead and probably cost the Union the fruits of its great victory in southern Pennsylvania. Among one great subgroup of Americans, the Northern Irish Catholics immigrants, the war was immensely unpopular. These recent, tough immigrants were generally employed in low-skill manual labor jobs. The companies so employing them used black labor to diffuse the power that such a cohesive labor force might develop. Along the New York wharves, the longshoremen had already engaged in battles with blacks for jobs. Archbishop John Hughes of New York warned the European clergy that his flock was "willing to fight to the death" for the support of the Constitution, of the government, and of the laws of the country, but in no way for the abolition of slavery. It was thus that the Emancipation Proclamation and importation of Negroes to break the stevedore strike caused Irish resentment to well up into insurrection. The downtown area of Manhattan near the present-day City Hall was the rallying ground for the Irish toughs. On July 13,

Draft Riots of the '60s: Tet and the Battle of Nashville

1863, while the names of draftees were being drawn from urns, the Provost Marshal of the city was driven from his office by the mob and beaten to death. For the next four days rioters controlled the streets of Manhattan. The Irishmen sacked and looted shops, including then-downtown Brooks Brothers. They burned the homes of antislavery leaders and looted saloons of money and liquor. They burned assorted mansions and, most grievously, a colored orphan asylum. Any Negro who could be located was fair game for torture and lynching. The mob, over the course of the day, swept northward up Manhattan's west side. It was only the pleas of the priests that dissuaded them from burning Columbia College and the home of its President. When the mob could no longer find blacks, they vented their rage on Chinese and Germans or anyone else who would not go along with them. The priests and police, who were of course mostly Irish, did their best. It was not until troops poured into the city that order was restored. Property damage ran into the millions. It is not clear how many perished in this insurrection, but the number of dead has been put at two thousand. This four-day rampage was the equivalent of a battle victory for the Confederates. Meade, the hero of Gettysburg, had to dispatch detachments for guard duty in New York and in other Northern cities and was unable to pursue the wrecked Confederate army retreating after the victory at Gettysburg.

The drafts continued throughout 1864, but were never successful in raising significant manpower. Every new draft brought competition between districts to reduce their quotas and fill them with bounty-bought volunteers. The troops in the North were obtained by scouring occupied portions of the South for blacks, and men were even obtained from the poorhouses of Belgium and the slums of Europe. Federal officials through the three-hundred-dollar bounty were bribed to admit cripples, mental defectives, and even criminals as recruits. It is not difficult to imagine the effect on morale of a veteran regiment when it received replacements of this sort. It is significant that the news reporting of these riots was generally suppressed in the North, and the effect on the morale of the troops was therefore localized and insulated.

Not so in 1968. After Tet, it became clear that the Vietnam War was not simple in concept, nor would it be quick in military resolution. This realization, drummed home by a hostile and eager press, led to the withdrawal as a candidate of Lyndon Johnson in March, only one month after the end of the Tet offensive. And in time the war ended. The American people would not stand for it. Would the same thing have happened if Hood had passed Nashville? One suspects that the press in 1865 eventually would have seen to it. Once united, the press in our country, even more so now with the electronic media, is a force that may not be resistible.

The My Lai massacre involved about two percent of the victims that the Hue massacre did. But it was *New York Times* reporter Seymour Hersh, who himself never set foot in Vietnam, who won a Pulitzer Prize for reporting concerning My Lai. There were fifteen Congressional Medal of Honor winners for valor during Tet in the American forces. If their bravery and heroism was ever brought to the attention of the American people, it was not evident in my research or memory.

If the press was ill-equipped and ill-informed to cover the Vietnam War, and if it eventually got off the team, perhaps it was because the country itself was not on the team. It may that the newsmen represented and reflected the American society, which too bore no deep commitment or enthusiasm for the war. But, in the chicken-and-egg view of the press mood and the public mood, I feel the press came first and influenced public perceptions rather than the other way around.

Finally, the United States and Vietnam are about as far removed geographically as any two nations. There are enormous differences in the language, national character, way of life, and way of thought. Tet involved an intelligence failure, but it was not so much the lack of information as the lack of understanding. The United States never really understood its formidable foe nor its inadequate ally in Saigon.

Contrariwise, the North and the South in the Civil War had a common language, a common ethnic background, a common religion, and a common history, and yet the horrible war still took place. In the final analysis, then, why do men fight? I do not know, but it is not over differences. It is over the perception of differences. I would argue that it is those perceptions that won one war and lost the other. The thinness, subtlety and fragility of these perceptions in a large nation made random results probable. These two wars could have ended otherwise. What do you think? And what of our original question, "Why do young men fight?" Why? There are reasons.

The Shamus Club, c. 1950. Back row: Bernard Werthan, Albert Weinstein, Julius Mark, Dan May, and Lawrence Goodman. Front row: Herman Spitz, Stanley Rich, Jacques Back, Charles Gilbert, Bernard Fensterwald, and Alf Levine.

This and the following three papers tell of four disparate, extraordinary Jews (Rothschild, Marx, Monroe, Berg). They are biblical only in their diversity and magnitude. Enjoy!

What a Berg!

*Read in honor of Fred Russell, who knew him,
to Old Oak Club in June 2002*

"*GENUG*, ENOUGH," I told our esteemed secretary at the beginning of this, our one hundred fourteenth year. After reflection and nine meetings later, I've decided that my judgment at that time was good. I know nothing of club membership that brings immunity from either senility or mortality, so enough, *genug*. I have been in Old Oak for thirty-five years, more than a third of a century. That is three hundred papers. Most I heard, and some I missed. I have squeezed ten papers out of my brain to inflict upon our gentle and kind membership. That membership belongs to a unique, astonishing, and wonderful institution. To sit down every three-plus years to collect one's thoughts on some subject of general interest and organize those thoughts on paper to present to this distinguished group is a privilege. In exchange for this, all that is required is the reciprocal opportunity to hear the same from one's colleagues. To repeat, this is a wonderful organization. Nashville has several others similar to it. I have often wondered whether counterparts exist in other American cities. I have never heard of such. And we have survived now for some one hundred fourteen years without a publicity committee. As far as I know, we've never had any committee. Our tiny fellowship has included a Federal Supreme Court Justice (James C. McReynolds) and a federal fugitive (Tupper Saussy). Could you name them? Surely no organization of our size can match that statistic. One old friend quit the club because he needed a job. Who? (John Nixon)

The quality of our papers has been pretty good, with the subject matter restricted to any topic of general interest. It seems to me that we have met that requirement. As I write this paragraph, I recall with pleasure a few of them. Rob Roy Purdy's masterful treatise on astrology converted this group of learned skeptics to superstition in one evening. George Cate described the largest oaks in Nashville, giving for each species its precise location. Ward DeWitt took us on a tour of every statue and monument in the county. Bill Harbison recalled the fascinating Buntin disappearance and subsequent court battles. Cliff Meador described the phenomena of invalids, both male and female, with delicious wit. Bob Collins told us how we could not beat the system as life expectancy has grown while lifespan has not. In Bob's subsequent and recent paper he provided an amazing amendment. George Paine described Vietnam, and Jack Allen described Rarotonga, both of which I visited subsequent to

What a Berg!

their papers. Tupper recounted the saga of the black plastic salmon. Bob McGaw researched the word "Harpeth," which occurs nowhere else other than our river. And on and on. These delectations and many others were savory morsels. I know—I've heard three hundred of them. I have been told that all of the papers are stored in the Tennessee Library and Archives. I have no factual proof of this, but I accept it along with the Easter Bunny and Tooth Fairy. I do know that our last cataloging of members' papers was published in 1938 on our fiftieth anniversary. Sixty-four years seems an appropriate length of time to get on with a supplement.

My own papers, soon to be ten, run a wide spectrum from e.e. cummings to Marilyn Monroe to the draft riots of the sixties in two centuries, from the first lines of dirty limericks to Meriwether Lewis's suicide in Middle Tennessee, from the heroism of Nathan Hale to the engravings of Albrecht Durer and the simple effectiveness of the one-time pad. So, at this point, I will make my last bow. An Old Oak paper is best if it is interesting, witty, and brief. However, of these three, brevity always wins. I will indulge myself tonight by taking up three subjects that have interested me: 1.) the Jewish immigrant experience, 2.) espionage, and 3.) baseball. Now let me get at it.

IN 1894 IN a tiny but all-Jewish village in the Kamenets-Podolski region of the Ukraine, there lived a restless young man named Bernard. He was young and knew two things well. One, he felt constricted by village life, and two, he was obsessively in love with Rose Tashker. The life of the village was governed by the tradition, law, and superstition that sustained most Eastern European Jews, but the pervasiveness of it was suffocating to Bernard, and he fled. He promised Rose that he would send for her when his travels ended.

First, he went to the United States and didn't like what he saw. He crossed the ocean back to England. He was told that he could get citizenship in London if he volunteered for the Boer War. When he arrived at the Citizenship Office, he found that this offer had been rescinded four days earlier. So with great courage and boundless energy, he again found a New York-bound vessel. This time it was a freighter, and he earned his way back by shoveling coal in the engine room. Once in New York, Bernard took a job ironing on the Lower East Side. It was New York, and the United States, but it was very familiar. Bernard had no intention of staying in a Jewish ghetto. He began saving his money. Rose was sent for and joined him in 1896. By this time Bernard was running a laundry and taking evening classes at the New York College of Pharmacy. During the day he would prop his textbook on a washboard and read as he pushed the heavy black iron across the shirts. Bernard learned without any apparent strain. In New York he taught himself to read English, French, and German to go with the Russian, Hebrew, and Yiddish that he brought from the Old Country. Once he learned to speak acceptable English he never spoke Yiddish again.

In the four years from 1898 to 1902 Rose and Bernard had three children: a son, Sam, a daughter, Ethel, and finally, a second son named Morris, born in 1902. In 1906, Bernard bought a pharmacy in West Newark. Four years later he bought a building with his savings and opened his final drugstore in the Roseville section of Newark not far from West Orange. Roseville had good schools, middle-class residents, and very few Jews. To Bernard's mind, this was perfection. He would work here, and the family would live in an apartment above the pharmacy, until he died. When Rose wasn't upstairs cooking, she was downstairs behind the counter making change and crocheting. Bernard worked fifteen hours a day, seven days a week. A pharmacist at this time was at once a chemist and a physician. Customers would come into the store, describe their symptoms, or those of their children. If it sounded serious, they were told to see a doctor. Otherwise, Bernard would treat the affliction himself. He always put his castor oil in root beer, and always included a candy with the prescription. This store, with its scales to weigh yourself, magazines, cosmetics, school supplies, and a wooden telephone booth puts me in mind of the Herbert Schwartz drug store at Thirty-second and West End of my youth. In any case, here Bernard and Rose's children grew up and in time, Sam, the oldest son, became a highly respected and important doctor. Their daughter, Ethel, took a degree in education and became a pioneer in preschool development. She taught in the public schools at the kindergarten level for fifty years. She broke new ground and was much beloved. The younger son, Morris, also went on to have an interesting career.

The story so far is not exceptional or unusual, but it speaks a history that bears re-telling. The next story, however, is unusual.

JUST BEFORE CHRISTMAS, 1938, Otto Hahn, a German radio chemist, was experimenting with uranium by bombarding it with neutrons and was getting results that were fantastic. He wrote of this to an Austrian physicist, Lise Meitner, in Sweden. Lise had left Germany a year earlier. She was Jewish, and earlier in 1938 had slipped out of Germany by train just ahead of the Gestapo. She wrote Hahn immediately on hearing of his news that the results were indeed amazing. It was Hahn who had discovered the transformation of uranium by neutron bombardment that we know as nuclear fission. Atomic physicists at this time were an intimate community of scientists for whom the implication of Hahn's discovery was immediately apparent. Enrico Fermi, sitting in his Columbia University office, made a small cup out of his hands and said, "With a little bomb like this, all this city would disappear."

Hahn had not simply split the atom; he had also split the international physics community. Between 1933 and 1941, more than one hundred prominent scientists, including Edward Teller, Hans Bethe, Fermi, and Leo Szilard had fled countries all over Europe to come to the United States. But there were others, including Hahn, Friedrich von Weizsacker, Max von Laue, and Werner Heisenberg, who remained in Germany. It was recognized that among all of the geniuses mentioned, Heisenberg was the greatest theoretical physicist in the world. He was a short man with a freckled, boyish face; he played the piano beautifully, doted on his children, and kept photographs of these scientific friends on his desk. Heisenberg had been offered several jobs in the U.S. during the 1930s but always refused, saying that Germany needed him. He knew that under Hitler, Germany had been contorted into something he hardly recognized. As painful as this was to him, the ground was still German, and Heisenberg remained loyal to it. This commitment recalls Robert E. Lee. To the American scientific community, the patriotism of Heisenberg was troubling. German scientists had supplied Hitler with some of the most lethal and most expensive military technology in world history, from tanks to submarines, and it was thought by our learned community that the Germans were way ahead of other nations in atomic research. Heisenberg was the man the U.S. physicists knew would be in charge of an atomic bomb project, and once Hitler got wind of its potential, he would have no choice but to pursue it. The refugees and American scientists did not share these concerns with many. Finally, however, Szilard badgered Albert Einstein into sending a letter to Roosevelt informing him of atomic potential and stating that the German scientific community had poured enormous amount of funds into this project. The result of this letter was the Manhattan Project, which began to be slowly built.

But the foreboding of the American physicists remained substantial. The Germans had a heavy water plant in Norway where uranium production had been increasing since 1941. The capture of Czechoslovakia brought them additional uranium reserves. A number of American scientists reported trouble sleeping, and were driven to making macabre bets as to when the atomic bomb would be developed under Werner Heisenberg's direction.

In June 1942, the Manhattan Project was put under the command of Colonel Leslie Groves. About the same time, the Office of Strategic Services, the OSS, was formed and put under the command of World War I hero Wild Bill Donovan. One of the priorities given at the beginning of the OSS was to find out if Germany was in pursuit of an atomic bomb, where this was being done, and under whose direction. It was assumed that the person was Werner Heisenberg.

If this were true, the OSS was tasked with either kidnapping or killing him.

After months of trying, incredibly contact was made with Heisenberg in 1944. On December 18 he arrived in Zurich, Switzerland, to give a lecture at the university. After careful intelligence work, the OSS did indeed have a man attend the lecture. He had posed variously as a French businessman and an Arab merchant, but here he passed himself as Swiss physics student. It was thus that one of that small audience at Werner Heisenberg's lecture in Zurich was an OSS agent. During the lecture, the agent took copious notes on the arcane equations of theoretical physics. Following the lecture, the agent attended a small dinner with Heisenberg. Afterward they walked out together into the cold winter night of Zurich. It was an ideal moment for murder. The agent fingered his gun nervously and then did not use it. He coldly calculated that if Heisenberg were supervising a bomb project, it was unlikely that Hitler would have permitted him a long public visit to Switzerland. Besides, only a large dose of OSS wishful thinking would have Heisenberg with his bomb nearly built, telling a lecture hall full of foreigners about it.

And then there was the matter of timing. It might have made sense to steal or shoot Heisenberg in 1942, when it was first suggested to Bill Donovan. But it was now December 1944, and it was simply too late. The agent thought that he could have killed him but that probably it would have made no difference. You could have shot Fermi in 1944, and it would have made no difference. By that time, the year before the use of the bomb, no fewer than one hundred thousand people were working on it. By 1944, Heisenberg was simply no longer valuable. The agent had made a cold decision. He did not shoot him. This story is an exercise in anti-climax.

Four months later on April 12 in Paris, the same agent was having lunch with the Director of the OSS, William Donovan. They were interrupted with the news that F.D.R. had died. Both men were stunned. Wild Bill's first words were, "Roosevelt knew what you were doing." Years later Morris copied this quote into his notebook with the comment, "And what I was doing was known to very few."

AND NOW FOR another unusual tale. In the first three decades of this century, when baseball was truly the national pastime, the team rosters were filled with hayseeds from the deep South, Great Plains farm boys, and rubes from mid-Atlantic mill towns. For different reasons, there were no blacks or Jews, and few college men. Those few college men who played the game professionally did not come out of the eastern Ivy League schools. Exceptions might include Bowdoin's Christy Mathewson and Columbia's Lou Gehrig. Another glaring exception was an intellectual Jew from Princeton. He had played shortstop brilliantly for three years as an undergraduate, and as a senior, after winning the Ivy League championship against Yale in Yankee Stadium, signed for five thousand dollars to play for Wilbert Robinson's Brooklyn Dodgers. The year that he changed his black and orange Princeton jersey for the blue and white flannel of Brooklyn was 1923. In entering the major leagues without minor-league experience, he had much to learn, but manager Robinson said that he had one of the best arms he had ever seen. He was a straight overhand thrower.

"Moe Berg Griff's catcher talks with Walter Stewart before opening game in Wash" (written on the back of this picture) This was in 1933 after Walter Stewart came over from the St Louis Browns. He had won 20 games in 1932 and of the 6 games against Washington, had beaten them 5 times. That's the reason Griffith, who owned Washington, bought Walter's contract and several others. Walter went on to win the game that cinched the pennant that year for Washington. He opened the World Series against the New York Giants and got knocked out of the box in the 3rd inning and they lost. Mel Ott hit a homer and 3 singles and Washington just couldn't hit anything that day and went on to win the Series.

This picture and comment are from my good Nashville friend Bryan Stanley, who himself got to play with Walter Stewart after he returned to Crossville, Tennessee, in 1947, '48, and '49.

He got the ball away fast. His aim was true and his speed terrific. In his first year with the Dodgers he played forty-seven games and did not miss a major league season for the next eighteen years. Although he was a typical good-field,

What a Berg!

no-hit player, his vast knowledge of the game was enough to make him valuable for a long career when most others would have left early. Along the way he made a switch from shortstop to catcher, and from the National to the American League. He played for Charlie Comiskey in Chicago, then the Washington Senators, and eventually ended up with the Red Sox in Boston. For the last several years of his long career, he became that apotheosis of mediocrity—a third-string catcher. Nevertheless, he was a fixture in the game. This Ivy League infielder was in the thick of baseball during its greatest decades.

In 1913, and again in 1922, professional American players visited Japan. Tris Speaker and John McGraw were part of the first entourage. By the early 1930s two powerful trends were developing in Japan. One was a national craze for baseball. The game combined both individual discipline and team interdependence, which fit the Japanese psyche. At the same time as baseball was on the ascendancy, anti-foreign sentiments were also widespread. Japanese militarism was starting, and a national paranoia had set in. No cameras were allowed to be carried by foreigners. The assumption was that any pictures taken were to be used for purposes of espionage. At the invitation of promoters, the baseball impulse conquered the nationalist one, and American teams were invited in both 1932 and 1934. Because of his ability to catch Hall of Famer Ted Lyons, the Jewish catcher from Boston went on both trips. He took with him a new Bell & Howell movie camera.

Perhaps because of the celebrity of the visiting ball players, he was able to take a lot of pictures. On one occasion he slipped to the roof of a hospital where an American friend's daughter was having a baby. He took a three-hundred-sixty-degree picture of Tokyo. He brazenly photographed everything, and although on a number of occasions the film was confiscated, he came back with a chest full of footage. At the end of the 1934 tour, with the film in tow, he left his teammates and took the Siberian Railroad across Russia to get home. His teammates took a more direct route. They included Babe Ruth, Jimmy Foxx, Lou Gehrig, Earl Averill, Charlie Gehringer, and Lefty Gomez, among others.

As the 1930s progressed, the Jewish catcher was more relied on for his experience than his reflexes. He spent more and more time in the bullpen, and played only a few games, retiring in 1941 with a lifetime batting average of .243 and the record for consecutive errorless games at shortstop.

It seems amazing now in the age of satellite photography to know that we once had no pictures of Tokyo, just as in 1943 we had no intelligence organization. When time came for Jimmy Doolittle to make his B-25 bombing raid on Tokyo, the organization to which the government had to turn was not the intelligence service, but the Boston Red Sox. The squadron of bombers had to use movies taken by a catcher in 1934 from atop St. Luke's Hospital in Tokyo. So, as Morris had a hand in the European theater of World War II, he also had a finger in the Far East.

ROSE BERG'S THIRD child weighed twelve pounds at birth. She named him Morris, but she called him "Moe" from babyhood. Moe always loved to play with balls. As a baby he would roll them across the floor, and as a toddler he would attempt to play catch with the beat patrolman. He followed sports actively from the time he could read, and was always on a sandlot playing basketball or baseball. This would have distressed his old-world parents, but they had little to complain about. Moe was a gifted student. His teachers loved him, and knowledge came easily. Moe had a photographic memory. When confronted by an unresponsive class, Moe's teachers would sometimes have him stand up and hold forth on whatever subject the class was studying. He retained everything. Physically, he had a large head with thick black hair and soft olive complexion. His sad and wistful eyes were the accent of a very serious face.

He was skipped ahead and finished high school at age sixteen. He had made headlines as an all-star infielder as well as for winning medals in Latin, Greek, and French. He was a recognized star, but kept to himself. It was possibly his Jewishness that set him apart. I think it is more likely that it was his personality. Moe always liked to be alone, and he often wandered off to do so. He had never had any formal Jewish upbringing and lived in a half-Protestant, half-Catholic neighborhood. In summer he played baseball on the Methodist Church team. His best friend was a Catholic, and occasionally Moe would attend Mass with him. There was never any indication there was a stirring of Christian faith. It was more likely that he liked the new experience, and it was a chance to use his Latin. At home his father and mother taught him Hebrew at Moe's request. Moe said he did not want to learn it from a rabbi who wanted to talk religion. He was simply interested in the language.

Being so young, he took an interim year at NYU where

he played baseball and basketball. His academic performance must have sparkled because there was no evidence of any problem in getting admitted to Princeton.

His Princeton career was a repeat of high school—brilliant in academics and brilliant in athletics but, although admitted to an eating club, he was always outside the larger social scene. Again this could have been because he was Jewish. We have the fictionalized case of Robert Cohn in Hemingway's *The Sun Also Rises,* who always felt his difference. But my read on it is that that it was temperament. Moe just never liked to be close to people. He was a superior student. Foreign languages were what interested him. He graduated *magna cum laude,* and in the process he learned seven languages: Latin, Greek, French, Spanish, Italian, German, and Sanskrit. To these seven, he added another seven or eight languages during the course of his lifetime. These included tongues of the Near East, Far East, and Eastern Europe. He also, while at Princeton, developed his lifelong zest for eclectic knowledge. He studied everything: mathematics, philosophy, biology, the sonnets of Patriarch, and the satires of Juvenal. His was a unique intellect, and he loved scholarship. He spent the winter after his first season with the Dodgers enrolled at the Sorbonne. He said that this Paris time was the happiest of his life. He was at home in the foreign culture, in the foreign language. He was forever after at home in any cosmopolitan center from Rome to Tokyo. He never experienced any language barrier.

His lifelong habits had by this time begun to develop. He was addicted to newspapers. Every day of his life he read eight to ten papers. The language made no difference. He would drink his coffee and read the papers for an hour after breakfast. I wonder how he would manage to do this today. I somehow can't imagine him watching *The Today Show* as a replacement.

In the middle 1920s, Moe completed his formal education by getting a law degree at Columbia, worked in between baseball seasons. He graduated from Columbia Law in 1929 and passed the bar on his first try. In 1930 he went to work as a lawyer at a fine, white-shoe Wall Street firm. That he got such a plum appointment speaks to his academic record, but not to his temperament. He never worked as a lawyer more than a few months, and found that the work left him restless and bored. By the time he had finished law school, he was about halfway through his baseball career, and decided he would limp along with the old rather than apply himself to a new profession.

He continued in all respects the intellectual loner. He was never impressed with his own intellectuality nor his own Jewishness, but used both traits as a way to set himself apart when it was convenient to do so. The ball players, as was true with many others, liked him but realized he was different. As one of his teammates remarked, he can speak fifteen languages but he can't hit a curve ball in any of them.

He did have a great affinity for the marvelous sports writers of that golden era. There were such famous names as Damon Runyon, Ring Lardner, and later Fred Russell, Shirley Povich, Red Smith, and John Kieran. It was particularly Kieran with whom he developed a friendship—an affinity that lasted their lifetime. Both were intellectual sports fans, and they got along very well. You will remember that Kieran was one of the regulars, with Oscar Levant and Franklin P. Adams, on the radio program, *Information Please*. Kieran saw to it that his savant catcher was a guest on *Information Please*. His first appearance on the show was brilliant. He answered obscure questions on the Dreyfus affair and Willie/Nicky correspondence, and he correctly identified poi, oy, and soy. He also identified three presidents who had been ex-athletes, as well as answering a question or two on comets. He received a call from Judge Kennesaw Mountain Landis saying that he had done more for baseball in thirty minutes on *Information Please* than Landis had done in his lifetime. It was clear to all that Moe's brilliance was genuine.

VERY EARLY IN his baseball career, Moe adopted a number of habits for a lifetime. These habits included high-living with fancy foods, sponging off friends, both famous and otherwise, disappearing for no reason only to reappear after weeks or months, and not the least, his choice of clothing.

For almost all his adult life, he wore a dark grey three-button suit with a white shirt and a black tie. When he was well off he had eight such outfits; when poor he had but one. He had bad feet in spite of being a graceful athlete, and wore shoes that were oversized and looked like those that policemen wear. His white shirts were nylon after the war. He rarely traveled with luggage, having only a few toilet articles in a bag. He would wash out his nylon underwear and shirt at night before going to bed. He also would bathe often, sometimes three times per day. His company was always sought. He could always find a companion to buy him dinner or to put him up for a night or for a month, but he would disappear without saying "goodbye," and his whereabouts were often unknown.

All of this made him an ideal OSS operator. OSS looked for eccentric, brilliant characters who, after getting minimum training, would be turned loose with their assignments. It is precisely the free-wheeling habits that made Moe such a good OSS man that made it impossible for him to exist in the CIA.

The CIA wanted something else. It quickly became a bureaucracy in which everything was budgeted, and everyone was at the end of a communication channel to someone above at all times. Accounting for money and his time were foreign to Moe, and he left the CIA in 1948.

For the rest of his life he did mostly nothing. This twenty-five-year period one biographer calls "a life without a calendar." It was a life without a daily structure or an annual rhythm. If pressed for a place to live, he would stay with his brother or sister at one of their places in Newark. Otherwise, he lived off the kindness of his many friends and acquaintances. The list of his acquaintances is quite astounding. It included Chico Marx, Nelson Rockefeller, Albert Einstein, Joe DiMaggio, and dozens of others, both great and small. He would arrive in someone's home with a toothbrush and would delight everybody with stories of his baseball days or his wartime adventures. He was welcome everywhere as a delightful raconteur. He would leave before his welcome wore out, and perhaps not see or talk to the host family for years. He also became a familiar figure around New York celebrity spots like Toots Shor's. Where he was, or how he supported himself, was always a mystery. His brother and sister would occasionally give him money, and he had myriad friends from whom he accepted kindness, but from no one ever to the extent of being a nuisance or a burden. He simply treaded water and drifted for twenty-five years without address, clock, or calendar.

When he did die of an aneurysm of the aorta at age seventy, he had had no address for many years. His brother and sister did not speak to each other, but both doted on their little brother. Doctor Sam had him cremated. Months later his sister had the ashes exhumed. Ethel took the ashes on a trip to Israel. In Jerusalem she asked a rabbi if he would select a site for her brother's ashes. The orthodox rabbi refused. Ethel is believed to have spread the ashes on Mount Scopus, but no one is sure. The final mystery of Moe's strange life is that, in death as with life, nobody knows where he is.

None of the three children of Rose and Bernard Berg ever married. The couple from the Ukraine, who had endured so much to get to this country, had no grandchildren. Over the years, Moe had dates with dozens of attractive women. He had short affairs with several, but none lasted more than a few weeks. At least one of the women to whom he felt close was his intellectual equal. The problem here could have been sexual, but I believe more likely it was his attraction to his own inner life, which made any other situation take a secondary role. There were some hints of homosexuality in his baseball days. He liked to throw his arm around his teammates in the locker room, and made on occasion ambiguous requests. Those who knew him best, however, scoffed at this thesis, because all through this time he was seeking female companionship on an ongoing basis both for dinners on the road and dates at home. On at least two occasions later in life when he was staying in the home of a friend who had daughters, they reported that he had touched them in unwanted ways. The girls were ages seven and nine. These facts were told by the women themselves when interviewed as adults. This may only show that Moe, as he aged and floated, may not have had full control of himself.

It appears that though Berg was a genius at learning and facile in superficial interpersonal matters, he was also emotionally bereft and starved for affection. Throughout his life Moe's father took no interest in his notoriety. He never once went to see him play baseball, and never gave him any praise for his accomplishments. His mother stayed in the father's shadow and did not assert herself. The three children accomplished greatly, but the relations between the three of them varied between distant and non-existent. When his sister and brother died, they had not spoken with each other for years. I can't explain this very strange, unusual, and wonderful life. In praise of Moe Berg, I would say that he lived life on his own terms and accomplished enough to make an Old Oak paper.

AND IN CONCLUSION, a strong epitaph. In the entrance hall of the Central Intelligence Agency in Langley, Virginia, above the pistol and silencer that belonged to Wild Bill Donovan, are two worn baseball cards. Beneath them is a plaque that says: "Moe Berg–Former catcher–Charged with learning all he could about Hitler's nuclear bomb project. To this end he undertook many missions." Thus ends the outline of the amazing life of Morris "Moe" Berg. At the outset of the paper I said that it would be about baseball, espionage, and the Jewish immigrant experience. All of these were subsumed in the life of one extraordinary and brilliant man. He lived his amazing life with the joys of elevated thought, with a depth of intellection, and within the huge variety that life in America can provide. Those three are enough.

Herewith I acknowledge much debt to Amos Elon's *Founder* and some to God. But of course if I were Rothschild I'd be richer than Rothschild—I'd do a little teaching on the side.

Some Rothschilds

*Read to the Shamus Club March 11, 1999,
at the home of Jim Blumstein*

I REMEMBER IN an aside from Sam Sandmel when once revisiting Shamus, he said, "It is a wonder to contemplate the amount of talent that was crammed into the ghettos of Europe." I have thought of this often. *It is a wonder to contemplate the amount of talent that was crammed into the ghettos of Europe.* At the time, were the Jews themselves aware of it? If so, did the talent ensure survival? Did it also make them arrogant, stiff-necked, aloof, and impossible to deal with? But that that compacted talent blossomed with the oxygen of freedom cannot be denied. Just look around. America is witness.

Now let's talk about one such blossoming.

This paper is the illegitimate child of Bob Eisenstein's

paper on John D. Rockefeller and Harris Gilbert's paper on the Gift of the Jews. Rockefeller, by foresight, industry, and luck, created vast wealth, and he engaged in massive philanthropies, and his progeny have achieved mightily. In the case of Cahill's book, you will recall that he reviewed the life of Abraham who founded a religion and gave civilization direction. He then covered the moral imperatives given by God to Moses at Sinai and followed the prophets who created a social conscience for the world. Harris asked the question, "Are these gifts in and of themselves enough for the survival of the Jew?" From Harris and the Shami, answer came there none. Perhaps they were chosen.

Tonight I would like to examine another family—the Rothschilds. Their story is even more remarkable than that of the Rockefellers and may shed some light on Harris's question. I will hand out a somewhat abridged family tree of the Rothschild family covering roughly five centuries. As you can see, it is ancient and wide. For the purpose of simplifying a subject too vast for any one book or evening, I picked three men whom I have circled on their tree, and will take a look at their lives. Coincidentally, all have the same three names, Meyer Amschel Rothschild. We can examine them in their own environments—one in the late eighteenth century, another in the mid-nineteenth century, and finally one in the late twentieth century. The tradition in naming called for the father's first name to become the son's middle name. Thus in our three men, two of them had a father named Amschel, and one had a father named Meyer. The name Rothschild itself comes from a red shield on the front of the home on Jew Street in Frankfurt Ghetto. It was the house of the red shield, or Rothschild.

Some Rothschilds

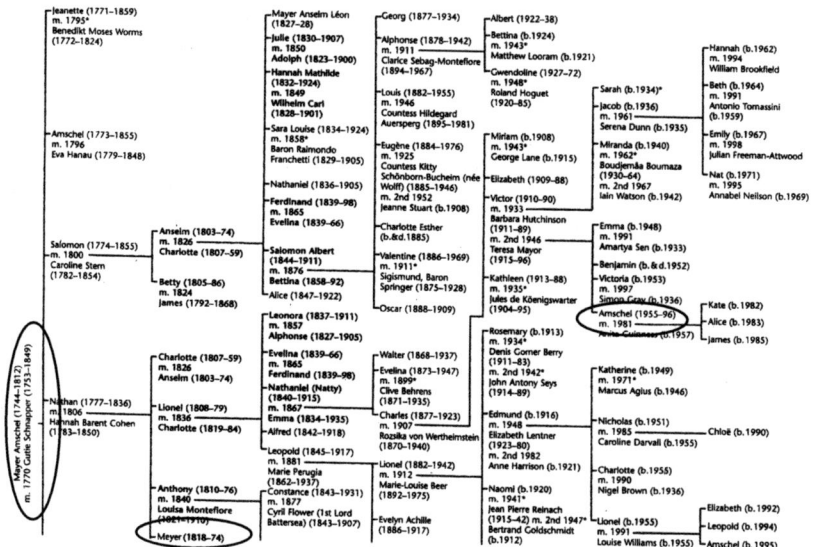

A part of the extensive family tree. Circled are the three Rothscilds discussed herein.

The family, in the two and one-half centuries since Meyer Amschel, has achieved mythic reputation. Just for instance, the family loved the pleasures of the table. Their name is now bestowed on a French soufflé made of fruit, brandy, and vanilla, and a seafood dish of prawns, cognac, and Gruyère on toast. In Israel there are towns and numerous streets named after members of the Rothschild family. There are two owned vineyards, Mouton and Lafite, of the standard fine wine drunk the world over. There is a Rothschild Island in the Antarctic. Pieces of music have been dedicated to the Rothschilds by Chopin and Rossini, as have books by Balzac and Heine. The family is famous in the art world for its many collections and in horse racing circles for its Derby winners. Thanks to a family-wide interest in zoology and horticulture, there are no fewer than one hundred fifty-three species or subspecies of insects that bear the name Rothschild, as well as fifty-eight birds, eighteen mammals, including a giraffe, and fourteen plants, to say nothing of three fish, three spiders, and two reptiles. The family had interactions with the leaders of Europe for two centuries, including Napoleon, Gladstone, Bismarck, and even Adolph Hitler. It was said that in the nineteenth century no country could consider going to war without the blessing of the Rothschild family. How did all this come about?

The Rothschilds were bankers. Not in the sense of a neighborhood savings and loan, but more in the sense of the Federal Reserve. They were in effect the nineteenth-century version of Alan Greenspan. Governments can only finance their deficits three ways: through greater taxation, depreciation of the currency, or through borrowing. Borrowing was the most expedient of these, and it was to the Rothschilds that governments sold their debt. The Rothschild family spread out across Europe to every capital and maintained contacts with governments at the highest levels. This not only meant a widespread family apparatus of trustworthy people, but it gave them an intelligence organization second to none at the time. They used carrier pigeons and private couriers. They used the knowledge gained thus to reap enormous profits.

One anecdote on the use of intelligence to reap enormous profits occurred after the Battle of Waterloo. The Rothschild courier reached London one boat ahead of Wellington's envoy. Knowing that he had an intelligence coup, Nathan Rothschild took his position by the Rothschild post on the London stock exchange and began to sell British bonds. The market assumed that Rothschild knew that Waterloo was lost, and the market in British bonds collapsed

Some Rothschilds

in a matter of hours. Enormous fortunes were lost. Then at the last moment before the news got back to London via the official envoy, Rothschild bought all of the British bonds and made in one afternoon another fortune.

They were always both unscrupulous and trustworthy, and so they prospered. There is a new book on the subject of the House of Rothschild that examines only the banking and financial strategies employed to build their great wealth. It makes fascinating reading, and our financial types will find it worth the study. But for tonight it may be more accessible just to look at the personalities.

MEYER AMSCHEL ROTHSCHILD was born in 1743. He was the patriarch of all I have described. When he was eleven years old his father took him out of the cheder in the Frankfurt ghetto and sent him away to complete his education in a Jewish seminary. Why he was shipped out of town is unknown. A few months after he had left Frankfurt, an epidemic of smallpox swept through the town. His father died in 1755, and his mother nine months later. He was not yet twelve when he returned to Frankfurt as an orphan. He returned to a little-changed Jew Street, which was the Frankfurt ghetto. Let me describe it. Here three thousand Jews lived on a narrow street that the sunshine pierced only at high noon. It was so foul-smelling that it was never necessary for a stranger to ask to locate it. Here the odor of cooking merged with that of refuse and sewage. It was a closed town, shut off from the rest of the city by high walls and three heavy gates. The gates were guarded at all times by soldiers and were locked at night, and all day on Sunday, on any Christian holiday, and from Good Friday until after

Easter. Jew Street at its widest was about twelve feet. As one crossed the river Main, the first thing a traveler came upon was the notorious Jews' sow. This was an obscene painted relief sculpture on the wall of the south bridgehead. It was put here not by some bigoted individuals, but by the city government itself. It was a caricature that depicted a fat sow holding up its tail for a Jew with its tongue hanging out to lick its excrement. Other Jews were suckling at the sow. All Jews were dressed in their obliged garb of round and pointed hats. After passing this visual abomination, one could enter the north end of the Jew Street. It was somber, humid, and filthy. The general gloom was enhanced by grim fire walls that were built between the crumbling tenements and reached high above their roofs. Parts of the street were unpaved. The air was rancid from the sewer, which ran through open and shallow ditches. The houses were mostly made of wood, cheap and

The notorious Judensau (Jews' sow) on the main city gate. Anonymous woodcut, c. 1470

available, but in a fire the entire street would burn down. The whole street was destroyed in 1711, 1719, 1721, 1774, and 1796. Each of these fires left much of the population destitute. The language of the ghetto was not Yiddish, but a dialect of Hebrew and Frankfurt German. Inside the ghetto were four synagogues, a public bath, and a communal bakery. The Jews were taxed at double the rate of the other citizens of Frankfurt. They could not go into the city itself for anything other than business. They could not use the public park, which had signs policing them, saying no Jews or dogs allowed. Jews were forbidden to linger in the public square or visit any inn or coffee house, and required always to step aside and bow low with hat removed at the demand of any citizen. Even children would say, "Jew, make your manners," at which demand they had to step aside and bow.

Local laws regulated everything. Dress, family size, and occupation. Men were required to wear a hat with two concentric yellow rings, women a striped veil. No man could marry until age twenty-five, and the population of the ghetto was to be kept at five hundred families. In order to enforce these and many other decrees, frequent police inspections ran through the ghetto. One might well ask how sanity was kept under these conditions. I would put it down to the very fact that they were Jewish. They had the Sabbath, and they had their learning, and they retreated into those institutions. They provided a *modus vivendi*.

Well, back to Meyer Amschel Rothschild. By the time he was in his early twenties, he was a tall young man with large, penetrating eyes and high forehead, sensuous lips and good-natured, and an ironic—though some might call it sly—smile. We get this description from the memoirs of contemporaries.

A Confetti of Papers

No portrait of this Rothschild has survived. Probably for religious reasons none was made, but there are many portraits of his descendants. Rothschild got ahead by making himself useful to powerful people. He was enormously energetic and enormously ambitious. He started out his career by selling coins. This could not possibly have made him rich, but it enabled him to establish contacts with the wealthy and important. The decisive man in this regard was crown Prince Wilhelm, who was to be the future landgrave of Hesse. He was well connected. King George III was his cousin, and his father was the richest man in Europe. He was married to the daughter of the King of Denmark. As crown Prince, he was already the absolute ruler of the little independent country of Hanau. The Prince's father had become enormously wealthy by selling his citizens as soldiers to foreign governments. Not only would he sell them alive, but if they were casualties he would get payment from the hiring government as well. One user of these mercenaries was his cousin George III. George had bought from Hesse the soldiers called "Hessians," which he sent to fight against George Washington. (Parenthetically, the only other entry of the United States into this saga of the Rothschilds was in 1944 when our bombers destroyed Frankfurt and with it the last remnants of Jew Street.) The Prince was about Rothschild's age and had similar temperaments. The young Prince was thrifty to the point of avarice, and was shrewd, able, and autocratic, and appreciated ability in others, especially in money matters. He had no particular prejudice against Jews. He himself was a Freemason. In selling his rare coins Meyer Amschel made a friend. He was helpful, trustworthy, and obsequious. I quote a letter that he wrote:

Some Rothschilds

> *It has been my particular high fortune to make several deliveries to your lofty princely serenity to your highest generous satisfaction. I now stand ready to exert all of my energies and my entire fortune to serve your lofty princely serenity whenever in the future it shall please you to command me. Etc., etc.*

It was in response to this petition that Wilhelm named Rothschild a court Jew. The title was not of much value, but it was of some. It was perhaps instrumental in arranging a marriage to a neighbor on Jew Street named Guttle. The two settled down, had their nine children, four girls and five boys who were to become famous. It is interesting to note that in forming the business the founder made many rules. One of them was that no daughter or son-in-law ever be included in the business. Only sons bearing the name Rothschild and their wives were privy to its operations. This technique is a variation on primogeniture, but it has been successful for eight generations. At forty-two, Wilhelm was said to be the richest man in Europe, and he had a friend in Rothschild. As a manager of his fund, a man named Buderus had most of the landgrave's business and turned to his friend Rothschild. With Rothschild's help, Buderus's private investment grew to huge profits, and Buderus interceded with the landgrave on his behalf. And it was here that Rothschild prospered greatly. Times were changing. Rothschild's sons were now in the business, and they were dealers in commodities such as wool, cotton, and flour. At this time, his son Nathan was sent to London to establish the family at a location called New Court. Throughout the Napoleonic wars, he dealt heavily in these commodities. As other sons came along they were sent

The Shamus Club in 1999. Eric Chazen, David Steine, Richard Eskind, Jack May, Bob Eisenstein, Herb Shayne, Jim Blumstein, Harris Gilbert, Sam Richmond, Fred Goldner, Bernard Werthan, and Randy Falk.

to other capitals until a network was established that was to last for a couple of centuries. The family became more and more prosperous, but Meyer Amschel never left the house of the Red Shield in Jew Street. When he died he was a man of enormous wealth, but never moved from his grim circumstances in the ghetto. It would have been possible to do; the winds of liberty and equality were sweeping across Europe with Napoleon. However, Rothschild pursued wealth only for itself with thrift and energy until he died in 1812.

Rich, yes, but entirely obscure. Mayer's name remained entirely inconspicuous, even in the Frankfurt ghetto itself. But in the family's ambition the aim was extremely high. Compared to the aim, their position was so low and their foothold so precarious and their resources so feeble that any alerted rival could have destroyed them with a single stroke. But three items caused Mayer's house to overwhelm the continent of Europe. One was its clientele, which was not other middle-class people but people in the highest positions of royalty. Secondly, their ability to give low prices, which earned them cooperation and foothold. But most of all, the strength of the family came from Mayer's five sons. Had he not been a father of sons, it would have been all a vain gesture. He would have died unknown, a feckless Jewish businessman. But he did have

Mayer Carl von Rothschild, by Hahnisch, 1844

sons, and he became a mover of mountains. In time, No. 1 son, Amschel, became treasurer of the German Federation. The No. 2 son, Solomon, achieved exactly the same exalted position in imperial Vienna. No. 3 son, Nathan, rose to more power than any man in England. No. 4, Caldman (who changed his name to Carl), wound the Italian peninsula around his hand, and No. 5, Jacob, was to lord it in France during the Republic and during the Empire. These sons achieved beyond all reasonable expectation. They became Lord Rothschild this, and Baron von Rothschild that, members of the peerage, and near-royalty across Europe. How they did it is the subject of a longer paper and another book. I recommend the *House of Rothschild* for the details of the banking successes, and how they financed theABC wars and railroads of the continent.

WE CAN NOW skip ahead to Meyer Amschel's grandchildren. Fifty years after the death of the founder, we find his grandchildren living in splendor. Lady Eastwick, a woman of high intelligence and wit, said, "The Medicis were never lodged in the height of their glory as were the Rothschilds." Nathan, who had come to England to deal in woolens, now had a wife who thought her boys were overworking themselves and should move out of the center of the city. Consequently this good Jewish mother bought hunting country in the vale of Aylesbury. Meyer, the youngest son, hired the architect who had created Prince Albert's crystal palace, and built a super villa called Mintmore Towers. It was filled with several museums' worth of inlaid furniture, tapestry, carpets, vases, and other objects. It was surrounded with gardens, parks, pastures, racing stables, and a stud farm.

This Meyer, out of a devotion to a worried mother, became not a pale, pavement-bound clerk but the huntingest, shootingest, ridingest, merriest baron in all of England, and one of the most hospitable as well. At dinner the editor of the *London Times* would volley brilliant conversation with Lady Eastwick, who would volley right back. At dinner parties Prime Minister Gladstone would moderate, Matthew Arnold would make interjections, and William Makepeace Thackery would stand by silently as writers will, making an occasional *bon mot*. Thackery said at a Rothschild dinner party that current female dress is often like a winter's day. It begins too late and ends too soon. Long house parties would attract poet Robert Browning and Lord Tennyson, Disraeli and Gladstone. In Thackery's novel *Pendennis*, he describes Baron Rothschild's wife and daughter as follows: "I saw a Jewish lady only yesterday with a child at her knee, and from whose face toward the child there shone such sweetness so angelic that it seemed to form a sort of halo around them both. I protest I could have knelt before her too and adored her in divine beneficence." Imagine all of this just a few years after Jew Street. At each stage of this development to Lord Rothschild and Baron von Rothschild, etc., they were beset by classic European anti-Semitism, but what in the end would confirm the Rothschild supremacy was not any gestures they made to majority faith. Rather than fighting, the opposite-way process turned the trick. An Israelite family claimed preeminence in a Christian world by becoming more Jewish than most Jews.

A side anecdote has to do with one of the Rothschilds' dinner parties. Disraeli would regularly eat at the Rothschilds while he was Prime Minister. One evening a telegram arrived, which the butler presented to the table on a silver tray. The intelligence therein was that the Khedive of Egypt was in financial straits and was desperate to sell his shares of the Suez Canal Company. Two things were imperative: speed and secrecy. An enormous amount of money must be raised and quietly. Within one week the Rothschilds had done it, and Disraeli was able to write to the Queen saying, "Madam, it is settled. You have it. The French have been out-maneuvered."

Now, OUT OF a need to end this abridgment of a long and complex history, I will skip ahead to the mysterious year that I am sure all of us can muster memory—1996. The story begins with the son of Victor Lord Rothschild. His name was Amschel Meyer James Rothschild. He benefited from the advantages of a younger sibling in a Rothschild generation. He was not expected to man the business ramparts and could enjoy the outdoors in lordly seclusion. He became a country gentleman of near-ducal status. He oversaw the family estates that spread across the Suffolk hills of England. He manufactured a brand of apple juice, made his mark as a cricketeer on many exclusive lawns, and his trophies made silver the shelves of his den. The trophies came from, of all things, auto racing. He was a playboy. He went to London's chic night spots, like the Club Zanzibar. It was here that he noticed Anita Guinness, of the banking Guinnesses, and found romance. There was congruence in the rich lineages. Anita stood at the Club salad bar mixing greens. He asked for a taste, she offered a bowl, and they were married not long after in 1981. In four years they produced two little girls and a handsome little boy. Because he was a Rothschild, this last life seemed to set on a fairy tale course, but alas they did not live happily ever after. When he was just thirty-two his father, Lord Victor, asked him to enter the family bank. After a brief breaking-in period as a silver trader, they put him in charge of Rothschild Asset Management. It was a spectacular promotion. He had at his disposal eight mutual funds, handling under the Rothschild umbrella many international holdings. The entire portfolios added up to about twenty billion dollars, far less than Fidelity in Boston, but serious money. Amschel planned to consolidate these international funds into one fund that would have a global reach. Even for a seasoned Rothschild of toughest vintage, this would have been a thorny task. It involved long-distance strategizing, the creation of a Dutch holding company, harnessing of a cousin's branch in Paris, and integrating various and sundry transoceanic executive teams. Amschel poured dogged work and unstinted expense into the project. In 1995 it still did not pay off. RAM reportedly lost nine million dollars. A deficit of a different sort was suffered by Amschel's private life. No more rustic ease around an ample hearth at supper. His schedule now had harsher imperatives than the cricket league or breeding exquisite apples. Chronic travel weakened a close-knit family. There was always a limousine waiting at some airport to dash him to another meeting. He tried to be a good father in absentia but of course this would be difficult under any circumstances. He turned into an absentee husband. After fifteen years of marriage, rumors floated around London of his rows with Anita. Friends worried over the emptiness in his eyes. Then in 1996 it appeared his labors might find some reward. The ink at RAM turned from red to black, and in mid-summer there was a small family triumph. Amschel and his son were to play a big cricket match together the weekend of July 13. On the Monday before, July 8, he chaired a long and worrisome meeting on RAM matters in Paris at the family bank. Its agenda, while not sunny, was not particularly grim, and when the conference ended at five in the afternoon, none of the participants shaking hands with Amschel suspected that anything might be amiss.

Neither did the chambermaid at the Hotel Bristol around the corner, where he lodged in a nine-hundred-dollar-a-night room under bronze chandeliers. At 7:30 that same evening she knocked at the door to turn down his bed. Nobody answered. She entered with her pass key and found Amschel dead. He had hung himself from the towel rack in the bathroom. There was no note—no explanation of the suicide has ever been provided. It was stress, which may be the ruling spirit of our time. All of us are acquainted with stress, and perhaps that of managing a company with a worldwide network was simply too much. But it does leave one to wonder about the prospering of his namesake two hundred years before in the terrible depredations of Jew Street and his ultimate and great triumph. It is easy to make pronouncements in these contrasts, but I will leave that to my fellow Shamuses, who are wiser than I. Perhaps it was the weight of his ancestry that was too much to bear. Perhaps it is the hollowness of modern life. Perhaps it is the lack of certainty that the founder, Meyer Amschel, learned in the cheder. But to predict the survival and success of an individual, of a family, of a country, or a religion is a tricky business at best. There are many morals to be learned from an ambitious Jew of the ghetto and his five talented and greedy sons, but I am not sure that I can describe them for you.

Some Rothschilds

A S FOR THE Jews themselves, we have survived remarkably for thirty-five hundred years. But the Manichaeans, themselves a remarkable religion, survived for over a thousand years until they did disappear around A.D. 1200. I don't know how we have done it or if we will be able to continue to do so. It is surely not a clear prognosis. My own guess is that history, early childhood education, and abstinence in matters of intermarriage will not be enough. If we are to stay with God, He must stay with us in this non-religious, non-spiritual world. Christians, Jews, and Muslims in total don't make up fifty percent of the world today, so I can't guess the future, but I will ask you other eleven to try.

Again a look at the homicide vs. suicide riddle. With M. Monroe, as with M. Lewis, suicide is the likely answer.

Marilyn Monroe

*Read to the Shamus Club May 27, 1992,
and to the Old Oak Club January 26, 1995*

MARILYN MONROE WAS born under the sign of Gemini. It is a constellation that signifies duality. In her short life, these stars brought her both fabulous good fortune and hideous disaster. The date of her birth was June 1, 1926; the place, Los Angeles. Had she lived, she would be sixty-eight and a half years old. That age is not too far from the age of many of us. She is a person whose times are likewise familiar. She was, during her life, and maybe even still today, the most recognizable woman on the planet. She died thirty-two years ago at the age of thirty-six on August 5, 1962.

I did not know much of her life story other than her stardom and her marriages to the international celebrities, Joe DiMaggio and Arthur Miller. My interest in the subject was kindled a few years ago by an article in *Vanity Fair* in

Jack May presents his paper on Marilyn Monroe to the Shamus Club at Fred Goldner's home on May 27, 1992, his sixty-third birthday. Front row: Eric Chazen, Jack May, and Sam Richmond. Back row: Bernard Werthan, Harris Gilbert, Jim Blumstein, Herb Shayne, Joe Kraft, Richard Eskind, Randy Falk, Bob Eisenstein, and Fred Goldner.

May 1991. The article itself was sensational. It dealt with her probable suicide or possible murder, as a result of her association with the Kennedy family, both Jack and Bobby.

I have an aversion to conspiracy theories. They are too easily conjured up and are too easily received by something in the human spirit that seems to relish the arcane and the occult. I gave a paper to this group some twenty-five years ago about the death of Meriwether Lewis. That death was also a probable suicide and also generative of many theories. Those concerning his 1811 death in Middle Tennessee were still the subject of speculation in the Sunday newspapers until the turn of this century, almost ninety years after his death. The recent film *JFK*, which is apparently a tissue of lies, received serious reception in many popular and intellectual communities. I believe neither the Lewis nor the JFK theories, and it is hard to give much credence to a conspiracy in the death of Marilyn Monroe. Ultimately, I do not. I judge it an accidental though plausible suicide. However, you may judge otherwise.

Since Marilyn's death, there have been some forty biographies of her. They have been written by friends, confidants, journalists, lovers, and such intellectual types as Gloria Steinem and Norman Mailer. Although I did not when I started this paper, I now can understand the fascination both for writers and for the public of this complex human child. Each few months, another biography is published. I believe the reason this is so is that no one yet has gotten it quite right. With that daunting prospect, let me try.

MARILYN MONROE WAS illegitimate. Although her mother was married to a man named Martenson, he had deserted her more than a year prior to her birth. The birth certificate shows her name as Norma Jeane Baker. Baker was the name of her mother's first husband. But no one knows who her father was.

There is, however, a great deal known about her mother's side of the family. Her mother, born Gladys Monroe, was a product of a family tree of mental malfunction. Marilyn's maternal great-grandfather hanged himself at age eighty-two. Her grandfather, Otis Monroe, died in an institution of general paresis as a result of a life with syphilis. His wife, Marilyn's grandmother, died in an asylum one year after Marilyn's birth. The cause of her death was listed as manic depressive psychosis. Ultimately, Marilyn's mother, Gladys, was also institutionalized. She took up Christian Science, and she had other religious fixations such as a notion of atoning for unspecified sin. These symptoms are likely features of schizophrenia.

The little girl, Norma Jeane, had no family life whatsoever. Her mother's first husband had left with her two half-siblings. He rejected the disturbed mother entirely. Being unable to care for Norma Jeane, Gladys placed her in foster homes of either family acquaintances or those provided by Los Angeles County. There were some eight of those foster homes. Norma Jeane's childhood is marked by two clearly remembered traumas. One foster parent ran a boarding house. Apparently one of the elderly men invited eight-year-old Marilyn into his room and in some unspecified way molested her. The terrified little girl reported it to her foster parent and was beaten for the revelation. For a number of months after this, she reports developing a stammer. A year later at age nine, when she was living with a close friend of her mother's, the friend suddenly married and placed Norma Jeane in an orphanage for three years. At this time, her mother was in a state mental hospital. During the three years in the orphanage, young Norma Jeane would develop a spontaneous stutter. Eventually, the same aunt that confined her came back and reclaimed her and passed her on to yet another woman known as "Aunt" Ida. She was a kind and loving individual, but again a new husband made it essential that something be done with Norma Jeane. This time it was decided that at age sixteen, she should marry. Because of the dislocations of the many homes, Marilyn at age sixteen had completed only the eighth grade. This was all the formal education she was ever to have. The solution to finding a husband was accomplished by fixing her up with a twenty-one-year-old young man who lived on the same block. His name was Jim Dougherty.

Jim Dougherty was a good guy, perhaps of all of her husbands, the best mate for Norma Jeane. Marilyn later described the marriage as a real friendship but with sex privileges. The war was on then, and Jim went into the Merchant Marine. Norma Jeane went to work in an airplane factory. During Jim's long absences at sea, his wife apparently sat under the apple tree with numerous men, both for fun and for profit. During this period, she earned some extra money as a prostitute, working the local L.A. bars. Her day job was at the airplane factory. Here she was spotted by an army photographer attached to a motion picture unit of the armed forces. The photographer's commanding officer, a Captain Ronald Reagan, had assigned him the job of going to war plants to find pretty girls for morale shorts.

Marilyn's 35-22-35 figure made very pretty pictures

A Confetti of Papers

indeed. Some of the photos found their way to an L.A. modeling agency. Soon she was appearing in such girly magazines as *Sir, Swank,* and *Peek.* Her famous nude calendar was from this era. The photographers who sought her were better and better, and finally she ended up in *Life* magazine, photographed by Phillippe Halsman.

The modeling also led to being signed as a studio actress with Twentieth Century Fox. Once on the lot with a small contract, she managed by way of the casting couch and whatever else it took to advance her own career. This culminated in a small but memorable part in the movie *Asphalt Jungle.* All of this activity in hustling, modeling, and acting took place while her husband was in the Merchant Marine. On his return, she asked for a divorce and, reluctantly, Jim Dougherty granted it. They had been married almost five years, which is the longest of her three confirmed marriages. Parenthetically, Jim Dougherty went on to the elite LAPD swat team and was involved in the rescue of Patty Hearst. He eventually left California and went into politics. He is now a commissioner for a county in the state of Maine.

The biography written by Ted Jordan describes one version of the sordid period when she went from model to movie star. Jordan, whose real name was Friedman, was the nephew of the band leader Ted Lewis. This biography claims that Marilyn, while still the nephew's girlfriend, performed sexual favors for Ted Lewis and implies she also did for his friends, Damon Runyon and Walter Winchell. These contacts got her the first movie contract. The biography written by Anthony Summers describes this period with another set of characters. This line includes Charles Chaplin Jr. and a Joseph Schenck, a seventy-year-old mogul at Twentieth

Century Fox. According to her agent, James Bacon, who himself claims to have had a relationship with her: "It was Marilyn that looked after old man Schenck."

An acting coach was provided for her as she was ascending to stardom. This was Natasha Lytess, herself a former actress. It was while she was getting lessons from this instructor that she moved in with her and told some biographers that "it does not matter with whom you have sex as long as there is love in it." A second lesbian relationship is claimed by a woman who became her mentor as a sex goddess. This was the stripper, Lily St. Cyr. It was Lily who taught her the tricks of sexuality and the strategies for using males to mount a career.

There are literally hundreds of men in these biographies who have claimed to have slept with Marilyn. While there is obviously some truth-stretching in some of these stories, they all could not be wrong. All report of easy and frank sexuality. Marilyn apparently rarely wore underwear and delighted in her own body and the effect it had on others. One instance is recounted that she spilled something on her dress in a restaurant and went to the ladies' room, took off the dress, and stood naked in front of the sink while washing it. The restroom emptied out in panic and left her alone in the nude. Most women of her own age found Marilyn a threat or simply not an interesting person. On the other hand, her relationships when childlike or with girls as playmates and equals were rich. It is interesting that among her many husbands, she maintained relationships with Joe DiMaggio's son, with Arthur Miller's parents, and with the parents and children of many of the boyfriends and mentors that she had over the years.

The marriage to Joe DiMaggio was a brief and flaring disaster. The only thing the couple had in common was their celebrity. Joe DiMaggio was an Italian's Italian. He was one of nine children born to a Sicilian couple. He was a man of great discipline and with skills honed through hard work and a sense of place. To his dark Mediterranean side came this blonde California free spirit. It was not going to work. Joe had been married once before for about four years to Dorothy Arnold. She divorced him, pleading cruelty. In any case, to the mutual benefit of both Joe and Marilyn, a marriage was arranged. Joe had hoped that he would get a wife. Marilyn had no intention of foregoing her career, which was, at this time, just beginning to ascend. They were married for only nine months in 1954. Perhaps the precipitating incident for the divorce was the famous publicity shot for *The Seven Year Itch* with Marilyn's dress blowing up around her shoulders. This publicity photo was put into a huge display in Times Square. It is not clear either that Marilyn was altogether faithful. Joe simply could not stand this kind of loose behavior, immodest and flaunting. He agreed to a divorce, but to the end of his life, professed his love for this sex pixie.

Her next marriage was two years later to an entirely different type. She married Arthur Miller in June 1956. They remained married until January 1961. She divorced him only eighteen months before her death. She was then thirty-four years old.

When they asked late in life in an interview as to what was her religion, she replied, "I'm a Jewish atheist." She was converted to Judaism by a reform rabbi prior to her marriage to Miller. It does not seem to have been much of a conversion. Rabbi Robert Goldburg explained the basic tenets of Judaism. Marilyn promised that she would raise any children in the Jewish faith.

At this stage of her life, her closest relationships seemed to have been with Jews. They were the acting coaches, the Strasbergs, the poet Norman Rosten. She had by now taken to eating bagels and gefilte fish with Eli Wallach, and celebrated Passover with Milton Greene during the filming of *Bus Stop*. During her early years, she was trying to get ahead in the studio, and she was given to a rudimentary Jewish stereotyping. She would tease her Jewish associates about their stinginess and the like. There seemed to have been no malice in this. As she reached this period of her life, she felt most comfortable around people, often Jews, with a strong sense of self and with secure family ties.

I have already alluded to Marilyn's sunny nymphomania. There are some other continuing habits of her adulthood that are as ingrained as they are destructive. One of these is the use of sleeping pills to rest at night. She developed a high tolerance after many years of addiction to phenobarbital and chloral hydrate. She found early in life that she enjoyed alcohol. While married to Arthur Miller it was almost a daily routine to have a Bloody Mary at breakfast and to sip wine, usually champagne, throughout the day. Another lifestyle pattern is a history of gynecological problems. It is estimated that she had had as many as eight abortions. A tubal ligation had been reversed. She had an ectopic pregnancy, and for years had regular, painful menstrual cramps. Further, as best can be determined, she on two occasions seriously attempted drug overdoses to commit suicide. On a lesser note, she was more and more tardy. Her chronic non-punctuality was expensive and a headache to her studio and to her fellow stars. Clark Gable's heart attack came after being kept waiting hours on the set by Marilyn.

Thus, we find her married to perhaps the greatest playwright of his era, Arthur Miller. He had met her years before when he was in Hollywood working with Elia Kazan. Kazan, himself, was one of her long list of lovers. After the sad ending to her marriage to Joe DiMaggio she moved to New York to study acting. It was here that she renewed her friendship with Miller. After a long courtship, they married. The courtship including much intellectual tutoring by Miller. He recommended books that she seemed to read avidly and apparently absorbed. They lived in Manhattan, had a summer beach cottage on Long Island, and, with mostly Marilyn's money, moved to a farm in Connecticut. Miller was writing, which forced Marilyn to be alone and isolated in a rural environment. Miller became more emotionally distant, and life was very dull and difficult for her. She coped with the aid of alcohol and psychiatrists. It may have been the beginning of mental illness. Her psychiatrist, Ralph Greenson, advised Miller that she needed unconditional love and devotion. Miller was either too cold or too selfish to provide these. When she could get away from the farm, she probably had affairs.

One of these that lasted longer than most was with Yves Montand. As was her lifetime habit, she used sex as a way of getting childlike nurturing. But there was an inability on her part to find much adult pleasure or sexual satisfaction for long in these affairs or during the courtships and marriage with both famous husbands. She did, I think, love them, but she continued affairs with numerous others in an attempt to exchange sex for kindness and friendship.

Marilyn Monroe enters Madison Square Garden for the gala birthday celebration of President John F. Kennedy in 1962.

After four years, the marriage to the brooding New York Jewish intellectual became as unsustainable as it was unlikely in the first place. A divorce was obtained. Unfortunately, her acting career had by now become repetitive and unrewarding. She was a thirty-four-year-old woman without much future. It was in that condition of emotional distress and professional decline that she faced the glamour and strength of the Kennedy men.

J ACK KENNEDY AND Marilyn Monroe had met long before his election as President. As early as 1951, there are those who remember the young senator and the starlet attending Hollywood parties given by Charles Feldman, who was Kennedy's frequent host and Marilyn's agent. During the waning days of her marriage to DiMaggio, people had seen them together at a Malibu bar. It is not clear that these early dates were sexual. The promising young politician, though recently married, had a reputation for being sexually, but only sexually, interested in other women. As Nancy Dickerson said, "Sex to Jack Kennedy is like another cup of coffee, or maybe dessert." In this respect, Jack and Marilyn may have been mirror images of one another. They both seemed to enjoy sex on a superficial, noncommittal basis.

In later days, it is clear that Jack's go-between was his brother-in-law, Peter Lawford. Peter arranged dates with Marilyn and offered the use of his home. This was both before Kennedy's election as President in 1960 and afterwards. In Marilyn's life, it was after the divorce from Arthur Miller and her rejection at the end of her affair with Yves Montand. It was at exactly this time that the Kennedy campaign was getting underway. He was a powerful, handsome young man who had connections both in Hollywood and New York and stood for the many liberal causes that her friends in Hollywood and she instinctively cared about.

Rumors of her affair were widespread around the time of the Democratic convention. She met Jack after his New Frontier speech at the end of the convention. Although there were many rumors about Kennedy and other women during this time, Marilyn clearly was involved. One humorous article by Art Buchwald was full of double entendre. The title of this piece was "Let's Be Firm on the Monroe Doctrine." Amazingly, after Jack went into the White House, the affair apparently continued at the Carlisle Hotel in New York or Peter Lawford's beach house in Santa Monica. There are even witnesses who claim to have seen her coming in and out of the back door of the White House. Whatever else may or may not have been going on, one can imagine that the two made a good pair—she making Kennedy laugh and he making her feel serious and important. The exchange, however, was far from equal. Her life was coming apart, and she was very needy and insecure. Whatever charm she brought to his life, she was far more replaceable for the Kennedys than they were for her. Without a call from Peter to come to dinner, she was left out in the cold.

Then in the fall of 1961, Marilyn's friend and neighbor, Jean Carmen, went to the door of Marilyn's Hollywood apartment and was surprised to find Robert Kennedy. Whatever went on at the cabinet level to engender this switch, one can only speculate. Bobby was certainly different from his brother. He had a shy awkwardness and a sympathy for the underdog that made him seem far more protective and appealing to Marilyn. Bobby, however, had been married for more than ten years and had seven children. That he did do some womanizing was confirmed by his biographer, Arthur Schlesinger, who said, "Bobby was human; he liked to drink and he liked young women and indulged that liking when he traveled, and he traveled a great deal." In any case, it was Bobby, not Jack, who became the focus of Marilyn's fantasies. That Bobby was far more interested in her as a person made him far more desirable than the arm's-length sexual attraction with his brother Jack.

Marilyn, who was always looking for a family, may have mistaken the Kennedys' easy ways as a possibility that might eventually lead to another marriage. Certainly she was looking for a new man to anchor her drifting life. Friends with whom she shared this desire were stunned by her lack of both discretion and realism. Further, from Schlesinger's biography, Marilyn began calling Bobby at his Attorney General's office in the Justice Department. Police notes confirm this. They show that Marilyn had been using a private line directly to Bobby, but that after June 25, 1962, when he quit taking her calls, she began calling the general switchboard at the Justice Department. The discontinuing of his private line is testimony of Bobby's eagerness to end the relationship, and the continuing calls to the regular number are an evidence of Marilyn's desperate efforts to hang on. That the affair lasted for as long as it did is itself amazing. There was historical precedent for the Kennedys to feel that they could get away with this sort of thing. Roosevelt's long affair with Lucy Mercer wasn't written about until after death. When Eisenhower brought his mistress, Kay Summersby, from London, he relied on the self-restraint of the press. As yet, there had been no scandal, and there may not have been one ever. The important question is, why did the affair end so abruptly? One answer might include Marilyn's own extreme vulnerability. She was getting insistent,

A Confetti of Papers

"Happy Birthday, Mr. President," May 19, 1962, with Bobby, Jack, and Arthur M. Schlesinger Jr.

irrational, and crazy. Maybe the sexual flavor had just run out for Bobby as it perhaps had for Jack. Perhaps it was pressure from key Mafia figures who were angry at Bobby's Justice Department for the campaign against them. During the month of June, Jimmy Hoffa had been indicted for extortion. It is not unlikely that he had Marilyn's phone tapped. He did have ample motive for destroying Bobby's reputation. Mafia boss Sam Giancana was literally threatening to tell all. He was a close friend of Marilyn's sometime-lover Frank Sinatra. She may have been seen as a threat by Bobby just for her own indiscreet and out-of-control presence.

Whatever the real reason, Bobby seems to have tried

to meet with Marilyn and explain the break-off personally. On June 26, one day after he changed his private telephone number, Bobby flew to Los Angeles and joined with Marilyn at the Lawfords. The next day, June 27, he drove to Marilyn's house. Marilyn's housekeeper reports that she was deeply depressed after the visit.

During the month of July, Marilyn's mood was more cheerful. She still tried desperately and unsuccessfully to reach Bobby. She was making her plans for future movies and posing for the photographs that appear in the Steinem biography. She would still use alcohol. Once she was seen at Lake Tahoe on a late July weekend extremely drunk or perhaps even drugged.

Finally, July 1962 closed and the first weekend of August came and was tropically hot. Marilyn tried unsuccessfully to reach Robert Kennedy in San Francisco where he was on a political trip and staying with Ethel and four of the kids. On August 4, the day of her death, she spent the morning with her good friend and neighbor Pat Newcomb. She spent much of the day on the phone to friends, some of it with Doctor Greenson, her psychiatrist. She talked to Joe DiMaggio's son, to ex-lover Marlon Brando, to Sidney Skolsky the journalist, to her friend Jeane Carmen. Apparently throughout the day, she was taking phenobarbital and chloral hydrate in amounts close to fifteen times the recommended dosage. This fact was one solid thing that did come out of the autopsy. As the day went on, the telephone partners reported that she had become more and more slurred in speech. The last phone call she made, she did not hang up. The phone was found dangling by her bed, and sometime during the evening of Saturday night, she died alone.

A Confetti of Papers

WHILE THERE ARE theories that she was may have been murdered, these do not seem particularly convincing to me. She had, during her life, tried to commit suicide before. She was certainly on a path to do it again. It is also likely that it was not intentional, but rather a slow suicidal course. Not so slow as smoking unfiltered Camels nor as fast as a bullet through the head, but as surely suicidal as either. What transpired after the death is a source of much conjecture. My interest in this subject started with, and much of the above is from, the article in *Vanity Fair*. It tells in detail the chronology of the last day. In sum, Peter Lawford was keenly aware of Marilyn's distress. It seems from airport filings that there was plane and helicopter traffic involving Robert Kennedy. One theory was that he came in the afternoon, again trying to get Marilyn to be reasonable. Another theory is that he came from San Francisco to Los Angeles after her death to see about the details of a cover-up of Marilyn's relations with himself and his brother.

It is further likely that Peter Lawford employed a private detective to sweep the house to destroy any evidence that would be embarrassing to the Kennedys. No suicide note or unfinished letter was found.

It is possible that Marilyn was still alive when she was rushed to Santa Monica Hospital. It is most strange that after the trip to the hospital, she was returned to the house. One biographer speculates that the unsuccessful rescuers in this attempt were Bobby Kennedy and/or Peter Lawford in response to her last slurred phone call. In any case, there were some five or six hours between the time of Marilyn's probable death and the time the police arrived. There were a lot of comings and goings of helicopters. The housekeeper developed a late-night zeal for energetic cleaning. These may have given rise to a feeling that there may have been murder. On the other hand, there may be one simple rational reason of protecting the President and the Attorney General from sordid scandal. A more recent book by Donald Spoto takes a much less sensational view. He says that the fatal dosage of chloral hydrate was administered by an enema by Marilyn's nurse at the direction of her psychiatrist. This, in combination with the day-long taking of Nembutal, was fatal. In this sense the death was caused accidentally by miscommunication of internist and psychiatrist. Thus it was neither murder nor suicide. However, possibly not without culpability. Spoto, who seems to reject any conspiratorial complexity, dismisses the role of Peter Lawford and Bobby Kennedy as actors at the end. He finds evidence that indeed Jack Kennedy did have one, but only one, sexual encounter with Marilyn. This has a truthful ring. Jack Kennedy's biographers point to his early tendencies to seek out "names" in Hollywood for his adventures. Spoto dismisses Bobby's role in this, claiming that he was a family man and would not have taken the risk. However, even friendly biographers such as Arthur Schlesinger noted that on trips Bobby was not above Kennedy-ish shortcomings.

I have spoken about this to John Seigenthaler, who is, himself, a family friend of the Kennedys, particularly Bobby, and particularly during this period. John feels with sincerity that there is no evidence for any of the Kennedy involvement and, though he admits not knowing, does deny that there is any evidence that there ever were serious relationships between Marilyn and the Kennedys and certainly not serious entanglement.

A Confetti of Papers

So, then, what is to be made of it all? Let me speculate about some of the principals. First of all, the Kennedys. I am reminded of Scott Fitzgerald, who said in *The Great Gatsby,* "The rich are careless." With regard to Marilyn, this is probably their greatest sin. One woman I was dating during my widowerhood admonished me that if you keep fooling around with many partners, sooner or later you are going to find one who is crazy. So the Kennedys, rich and careless, powerful and secure, found a girl who was fragile and needing. They could not handle her, and she could not, indeed, handle herself. For them, she should have responded to reason. Her psyche by this time was too tender and her brain too addled to respond reasonably.

And then this whole fairy tale took place in Hollywood, California, a place without ancestors. A place without the usual societal structures and restraints. Someone observed that Watergate involved mostly Californians. People without a stern grandfather or uncle looking disapprovingly over destructive conduct. In a sense, Marilyn was a Cinderella. But in that story, there was a prince. In Hollywood, however, the princes are just as evanescent as Cinderella.

And what of Norma Jeane Baker, Marilyn Monroe? I do not believe that it was so much that she was used by the system. She was a shrewd cookie. She understood the uses of sex and was clever in manipulating powerful males to her own ends. I do not believe Marilyn was dumb, although she was blonde. But here, too, things are not what they seem. After the age of sixteen, she was blonde only by the use of peroxide. She was under-educated, but she surrounded herself with intellectuals. She was eager to read, and apparently she did so with great comprehension. But finally, she lacked the intellectual resources and mental toughness to handle her own amazing situation.

I think the ultimate word on Marilyn is love. Ironically, it is the lack of same that shaped this love goddess. Perhaps the greatest Hollywood movie, *Citizen Kane*, explores this through the rosebud theme, the ultimate shaping power of childhood rejection. If the loss of innocence comes too young, there is nothing that can be done to overcome the lack of secure nurturing. So, ultimately, the mystery of Marilyn Monroe, this national icon with already forty biographies to her name, can be best explained in one sentence. She was not loved as a child.

With plagiaristic gratitude to Paul Johnson, the indispensable, for *Intellectuals*.

Karl Marx

Read to the Shamus Club April 24, 1991

KARL MARX RESEARCHED the evils of British capitalists for years. He found many instances of abused workers and workers who were not paid a living wage. He was never able to unearth, however, a worker who was paid literally no wages at all. Yet such a worker did exist. She was to be found in his own household—his only employee in his lifetime. When Marx took his family on their formal Sunday walks, coming along behind and carrying the picnic basket and other items of the family, there was always to be seen a stumpy female figure. This was Helen Demuth.

Helen was known in the family as "Lenchen." She was born a peasant, and at age eight she joined the family of Marx's wife Jenny as a nursery maid. She got her keep, but was paid nothing. At the age of twenty-two, Karl Marx's mother-in-law felt sorrow and anxiety for her newly married daughter and gave Lenchen to Jenny Marx to help with her life with the intellectual. She remained with the Marx family until her death in 1890 at the age of sixty-eight. She was a very kind and tender person and maintained a stoic demeanor with regard to herself. She worked extremely hard. She did all of the cooking and scrubbing for the family and, in addition, she maintained the family budget, which Mrs. Marx (Jenny) was incapable of handling. Karl Marx never paid Lenchen a penny. When she was in her late twenties, when the financial fortunes of the family were at their lowest, Lenchen became Karl Marx's mistress and conceived a child. At the time of the conception, Mrs. Marx was also pregnant and, with the entire household living in two rooms, it was inevitable that Jenny Marx find out about it. It is likely that whatever affection there was between the two to that point ended with the revelation.

Lenchen's child was born in 1851, a son known as Henry Frederick Demuth. Marx refused to acknowledge any responsibility then or ever, and denied all gossip that he was the father. The servant Lenchen was a person of strong character. She insisted on acknowledging the boy as hers and put him out as a foster child to a working-class family. Occasionally the child, as he grew, visited the Marx household. He was, however, forbidden to use the front door and was obliged to see his mother only in the kitchen. Karl Marx was terrified that young Freddie's paternity would be discovered and would do him fatal damage as a leader. In an attempt to dissemble, he persuaded Engels to acknowledge Freddie as his own, which was a cover story for family consumption. However, Engels, on his deathbed and unable to speak, wrote upon a slate, "Freddie is Marx's son." It was a clear call. Freddie looked like Marx. Marx had a typically Jewish face and blue-black hair, and anyone who saw the two together would be struck by the resemblance.

Thus, Lenchen was the only employee Marx ever had, and his behavior in her regard was tantamount to slavery. In addition, he never really knew or met anyone in the working class. His own son Freddie might have been one, since he was brought up as a working-class youth and when he was thirty-six got a coveted certificate as a qualified steam fitter. He spent all of his life as a regular member of the Engineers Union, but Marx never knew him. They met once, presumably when Freddie was coming up the outside steps to the kitchen of his house. Freddie had no idea that the revolutionary philosopher Marx was his father. Freddie died in January 1929, about the time that I was being born. Marx's dream of the dictatorship of the proletariat was just beginning to take its terrifying form. Stalin, the ruler who achieved the absolute power for which Marx had yearned, was just beginning his holocaust of the Russian peasantry.

I START MY paper thus, because the dull writings of this intellectual are to a large extent impenetrable. We have had excellent papers from Eisenstein on Einstein and from Gilbert on Freud, two of the three great Jewish thinkers of the late nineteenth and early twentieth century. But in order not to make the third of the three too dull for the group, I start with this human story, which I would like to continue.

Marx lead a particularly unhealthy life. He took little exercise, ate highly spiced food, often in extra-large quantities. He smoked heavily, and he drank a lot. A result, he had constant trouble with his liver. He rarely took baths or washed much at all. This fact, plus his unsuitable diet, may explain the veritable plague of boils that he suffered for a quarter of a century. They increased his natural irritability and seemed to have been worse when he was writing *Das Kapital.* Whatever happens, he once wrote to Engels, "I hope the bourgeoise, as long as they exist, will have cause to remember my carbuncles." These boils varied in number, size, and intensity, but at one time or another they appeared on all parts of his body, including his cheeks, the bridge of his nose, his penis, and his bottom, which meant he could not write. Eventually, they brought a nervous, collapsed Marx trembling in bursts of rage.

His entire life was that of the Bohemian intellectual. He changed his clothes rarely. He didn't wash or groom himself, and he stayed drunk. He was dirty and lousy and full of fleas. He would loaf and be idle for days on end, then work night and day with tireless endurance when he had much work to do. His work habits included no fixed time for sleeping or waking. He often stayed up all night and lay down fully clothed on the sofa at midday to sleep until evening. In his home, there was not one clean or solid piece of furniture. Everything was broken, tattered, and torn, with a half-inch of dust over everything in great disorder everywhere. In the middle of his living room was a large table covered with an oil cloth, and on it lay manuscripts, books, and newspapers, as well as children's toys, rags, and the tatters of his wife's sewing basket. In a jumble about the room lay cups with broken rims, knives and forks, lamps, inkpots, dirty glasses, pipes, tobacco, ash. A junk shop owner would be ashamed of such a collection of odds and ends. When one entered the room where Marx worked, according to one observer, the smoke and tobacco fumes would make your eyes water. Everything was dirty, and even to sit down was hazardous business. There was a chair with three legs, and on another, the children had been playing at cooking. On this chair, which happened to have the requisite four legs, the visitor was offered a place to sit down. The children's cooking, however, was never wiped away and if you sat down at all, you risked ruining your trousers.

It was in this condition of disorder that Karl Marx wrote the documents that as much as any have shaped the modern age. Let us look a little further. With these particularly unattractive parts of Marx's personality, we now add anti-Semitism. His political and economic view of the world was rooted in the popular anti-Semitism of the 1840s. Marx was an intellectual and philosophical follower of Hegel. In general, Hegel's followers were all to some extent anti-Semitic. In 1843 one of these named Bruno Bauer, who was of the Hegelian left, published an essay demanding that Jews abandon Judaism completely. Marx replied to this in a published essay. He did not object to Bauer's anti-Semitism; indeed, he endorsed it. He did disagree with Bauer's solution. Bauer believed that the anti-social nature of the Jew was religious in origin and could be remedied by tearing the Jew away from his faith. However, in Marx's view, the Jews' problem was not religious but economic and social. He felt that the worldly cult of the Jew was huckstering and that the Jews' worldly God was money. Here is a quotation from this essay. "Money is the sufficient value of things, money is the alienated essence of man's work and existence, the God of the Jews has been secularized and become the God of the world." Further, Marx stated that the Jew had corrupted the condition of the world, and that he has no other destiny than to become richer than his neighbor. The world is a stock exchange. The world must emancipate itself.

The world could emancipate itself by leaving behind hucksterism and money and thus forswearing the real Judaism. So, having defined wealth as Jewish, Marx moves to expand money power from the Jews to the bourgeois class as a whole. Thereby, Marx proceeds from student café anti-Semitism to a picture of the economic situation in the world and from there proceeds to his view of the great crisis to come. I quote here the end of the key passage which expresses the Marxist political vision arising from his economic views.

> *The proletariat executes the sentence that private property pronounced on itself by begetting the proletariat, just as it carries out the sentence which wage labor pronounced for itself by bringing forth wealth for others and misery for itself. If the proletariat is victorious it does not at all mean that it becomes the absolute side of society, or it is victorious only by abolishing itself and its opposite. Then the proletariat and its determining opposite property, disappear.*

The passage is quoted both as Marx's own encapsulation of the end of the dialectic struggle and the withering away of the state but also to illustrate the academic nature of his writings and thought. All of this had no relation to the world at large, but only makes sense in the confines of the artificial universe of the university lecture room. It is worth reminding ourselves again at this point that Marx lived his entire life without ever meeting a working man or visiting inside a factory. It is ironic, I think, that his entire philosophy stems from his anti-Semitism while his style proceeds in the manner of Talmudic commentators who also used brilliant and microscopic examination of the works of their intellectual peers.

BIOGRAPHICALLY, MARX WAS born in 1818 in Trier, Prussia, and died in 1882 in London. Both his grandfathers were rabbis. His ancestors on both sides were of a rabbinic tradition, some of whom were famous. Marx's father, however, became a lawyer. The family was perfectly middle class and upward mobile. Heinrich Marx was a liberal and an intellectual. He knew his Voltaire and Rousseau inside out. Then a Prussian decree of 1816 banned Jews from the higher ranks of law and medicine. Heinrich Marx, being a pragmatist, became a Protestant immediately. Thus, Karl's father had been a Christian for two years when he was born. In 1824, Heinrich Marx had all of the six children baptized. Marx was confirmed and for some time probably was a passionate Christian. He attended the Jesuit high school and then Bonn University. From there, be went on to Berlin University, perhaps the finest in the world. He never received any Jewish education or attempted to acquire any, but it must be said that he developed traits and characteristics of the Talmudic scholar mentioned above. He went on in the university to achieve a doctorate in philosophy. He was particularly attracted to Hegel and his historic method of thesis, antithesis, and synthesis.

Aside from his academic pursuits, he was interested in poetry and, from an early age, wrote a great deal of it. Three manuscript volumes eventually were published, though most are lost. Most of the poems were pessimistic and savage. An example: "We are chained, shattered, empty, frightened, eternally chained to this marble rock of being. We are apes of a cold God."

He proclaimed in one poem, assuming the voice of God: "I shall hurl gigantic curses at mankind." His pessimism and anger mirrored the philosophy of the time, which held "that all that exists deserves to be destroyed."

He also wrote love poems to the girl next door, Jenny van Westphalen. She was a lovely child of Prussian-Scottish descent. He married her in 1841 at the age of twenty-three. Jenny was a red-headed, blue-eyed beauty. Marx was always proud of his wife's noble Scottish descent. It must be said that Jenny's life married to the revolutionary was miserable, mean, and embittering. Marx never worked and survived for his entire life living off his in-laws, his own relatives, including an uncle named Phillips in Amsterdam, who founded what eventually became Phillips Electric. As his life went on, he cadged money from his colleagues, including Engels, and ultimately from the Communist movement that he started. The irregularity of income meant that the family spent much of the time in poverty. Everything that Jenny owned, all of which she had obtained from her parents, was pawned. They were expelled from Belgium for revolutionary activities and took refuge in England.

They lived in poverty in Chelsea with their five children. Everything was sold, including beds, to pay the bills. In 1860 Jenny caught smallpox and lost the remainder of her looks, and from that point until her death in 1881 she faded slowly into the background of Marx's life, tired and disillusioned.

The two sons died in youth; the three daughters' lives ended tragically after their marriages. Marx always browbeat the sons-in-laws. His daughter Laura's husband, Paul LaFarge, came from Cuba and had some Negro blood. Marx always referred to him as the Negrillo Gorilla. He refused permission for his daughters to pursue careers. All three daughters died tragically: Jenny, about the time of Marx's own death, and Eleanor and Laura as a result of suicide pacts with their husbands. Only the abandoned step-son survived in this unrelieved tragedy.

FROM MARX, let's take a short look at Marxism. It starts with economic determinism. The belief is that all history is defined by economics. The basic tenet of this economics is the labor theory of value. This theory teaches that each product is worth only the amount of labor that it contains. From that, it follows that private property creates a class of capitalists who take the difference between the labor involved in a product, plus the labor involved in the capital, and sell products at a price higher than this total. This is profit. It enslaves the workers because it keeps them poor and makes what they purchase more expensive. This is a three-sentence reduction of the enormous work of *Das Kapital*. That volume is twenty-five hundred pages long, filled with the tiniest of technical matter. He dissects every economist with the pedantic and dramatic nature of an author whose main passion is to produce footnotes. Thus, I have spared Shamus Club tonight a lot of effort in my short explanation of Marxism. I will leave it for the discussion for exposition. It must be remembered, too, that Marx was not only an economist, but a political revolutionary. The two should not be mixed.

A Confetti of Papers

He called for a revolution of the workers against the capitalists, the establishment of a socialistic state run by wise planners who would provide for society by taking from each according to his ability and giving to each according to his needs. Eventually, the classes would become one, and there would be no longer a need for the state, which in time would wither away. Religion, "the opiate of the people," would be suppressed.

This view of the organization of government has been seductive. In the first half of this century, a long list of politicians, either the greedy or the idealistic, were persuaded. Among their number are Bernard Shaw, Ramsey MacDonald, Adolph Hitler, Mussolini, Pierre Laval, and many others, including the founders of the state of Israel. There are, of course, many others who were seduced by the socialist ideal.

One of the books I read in preparing this paper was a fine volume called *The Worldly Philosophers* by Robert Heilbroner. At the time he wrote this book in 1961, he credited Marx with shaping the modern world as evidenced by the two great powers of the Eurasian continent, China and Russia. Since that time, these two nations have collapsed economically, and the socialist economist Heilbroner has grown up. I recently saw a quotation from the magazine *Dissent.* It was a statement by Heilbroner as follows:

> *Capitalism has been as unmistakable a success as socialism has been a failure. . . . Here is the part that's hard to swallow. It has been the Friedmans, Hayeks, Von Miseses who have maintained that capitalism would flourish and that socialism would develop incurable*

ailments. All three have regarded capitalism as the "natural" system of free men; all have maintained that left to its own devices capitalism would achieve material growth more successfully than any other system. From this admittedly impressionistic and incomplete sampling I draw the following discomforting generalization: The farther to the right one looks, the more prescient has been the historical foresight; the farther to the left, the less so.

Most of this paper was taken from a twenty-five-page synopsis of Marx by Paul Johnson in his book *Intellectuals*. One of my favorite quotations of Johnson's is, "The Twentieth Century has seen the power of governments to do evil magnified and the power of governments to do good has moved forward slowly and ambiguously."

It seems to me that Joseph Goebbels knew his craft pretty well. "The big lie" will sell if packaged in jargon, pomp, and mystery. Marx said that with socialism, the worker would only lose his chains. He did not mention his freedom nor his future.

AND HERE I conclude. We have seen a man who was reprehensible and vile in his personal life and who retrospectively was wrong on every issue of his philosophy, both economic and political. Yet he was revered by generations for a century and a half. Is there anyone here who would like to explain this? Is there anyone here who on this basis is sanguine about the future of mankind?

The Shamus Club, November 30, 2004, at Jack May's home. Back row: Fred Goldner, Daniel Casse, Jack May, Eric Chazen, David Steine, Bernard Werthan, Louis Lavine, and Mike Schoenfeld. Front row: Harris Gilbert, Jim Blumstein, Gus Kuhn, and Daniel Cornfield.

In which a modest proposal is obliquely made. Religions (all of them) should be put aside or at least in the background as we really celebrate a pagan Saturnalia at the winter solstice and do it right with plenty of wassail, gifts, lights, and joy.

The House of Hasmon

Read to the Shamus Club in 1990

ONE OF LIFE'S great indulgences is to be a member of Shamus. The food aside, which is always prepared and consumed with restraint, there is no greater indulgence than that of being able to talk to an informed group of friends on nothing in particular. For that reason, my nothing in particular topic will be from Jewish history. It is a subject about which I am totally unqualified, but then, rabbis sermonize on business and politics.

In late November 1989 I attended Friday night services at The Temple. Rabbi Beth Davidson delivered a sermon on Thanksgiving, which set the train in motion for this paper.

Let me say at this point that I am a great fan of Rabbi Davidson. I recall that after she had been here only a few weeks I was sitting next to her on the bimah during the memorial service at 4:30 in the afternoon of Yom Kippur. I expect the reason for my being on the bimah at that time was due to an office error and that probably they had intended to call Leon. Nevertheless, there I was. I leaned over and asked Rabbi Davidson *sotto voce* how she was enjoying Nashville. She replied wistfully "I can't believe that I moved to a city without a National League franchise." Clearly, there was nothing she could have said that would have more quickly won my heart. And beyond her interest in the genuinely important things to life, I find her to be a serious, studious, and sensitive person. Well, back to Friday night of two months ago: The distaff rabbi chose to speak on Thanksgiving. She recounted that as the Pilgrims stepped ashore on Plymouth Rock in 1620 they gave thanks to God for that which had been provided. She remembered accurately that the Puritans, in search of religious freedom, offered none of the same themselves. They were "true believers" in establishing a colony; they provided themselves an opportunity to practice religion as they chose; however, they forbade that choice to others. Jews particularly were excluded from Massachusetts Bay. As time went on the colony grew more repressive and more restrictive. By 1692, it was a time of the horrors of witch trials in Salem and brandings with scarlet A's in the name of orthodoxy. Rabbi was pointing out that at the celebration of Thanksgiving Jews had more things to think about than the Pilgrims and the introduction of turkey and cranberries. I have some sympathy with Beth, but not completely. The story does not end in Massachusetts. Only fifteen years after the establishment of the Massachusetts colony, a man of great conscience named Roger Williams left the Puritans and established the liberal and religiously free colony of Rhode Island. Then in 1643 Anne Hutchinson, a woman of great courage, stood trial and was convicted of Religious Liberalism. She was banished and followed Williams to Rhode Island. Rhode Island did indeed welcome Jews (Truro Synagogue) and set the tone for religious toleration, which was eventually written into the founding documents of our country. A bad oversight, Beth. There is no basis either intellectually or emotionally that should prevent a Jew from the wholehearted celebration of the Thanksgiving holiday.

By the way, it strikes me that other than Passover, Thanksgiving is a singular holiday in that it is celebrated around a meal. What a magnificent thing the Seder is. It is a time of family togetherness in an atmosphere of holiness. I wonder if a more formalized and secular liturgical service could not be composed for Thanksgiving, as remembrance

Hanukah 1946 on Ellendale Drive in Nashville: Jack May, James Mark, Dorothy May, Peggy Mark, Betsy May, and the Rabbi.

of our deliverance into this land and a celebration of the law on which the nation is based. Would such a Hagadah be possible? Why not?

STILL, ON LEAVING the Temple that Thanksgiving Friday night, I felt that there had been something ungracious about Rabbi Davidson's final judgments on Thanksgiving. The next holiday up was Hanukkah, and I wondered if in telling the story of that miracle she would be as ungracious in depicting the sequel that followed the victory of Judas Maccabaeus. Since I doubt that she, in her Hanukkah sermons, preached on the excesses of the Hasmonians, I will so do. Perhaps we together can have a greater truth to discern than the simple guerrilla victory of Judas the Hammer. One man's freedom fighter is another man's terrorist.

The period of time from Plymouth Rock in 1620 to the present is about three hundred seventy years. In that same time frame, looking backward from the destruction of the Temple in A.D. 79, the Jews had a history stormy enough to make our own twentieth century seem tranquil. From the time of Alexander the Great's pushing out to Babylon through the rise under the Greeks of the Seleucids and the Ptolemies down to the times of Cleopatra, the Caesars, and Rome, the world was in constant churning and turmoil for the Jews of the Middle East. Nevertheless, at the heart of this period, roughly from 169 B.C. to 65 B.C. or roughly the time from Hanukkah to Herod, there existed a state under Jewish rule, a de facto autonomous kingdom with its own army and coinage. After the destruction of the Temple by the Romans, there was to be no such state there until 1948. In other words, between Alexander Jannaeus, called Yanni, and David Ben Gurion, a sovereignty hiatus of two thousand nine years existed. We know well of the modern state of Israel and of Judas Maccabee, but the real predecessors of modern Israel and the successors of the Maccabees were a line of three kings. John Hyrcanus ruled from 135 to 104, Aristobulus ruled from 104 to 103, and Alexander Jannaeus (Yanni) ruled from 103 to 76. Yanni was followed by his wife, Salome, who ruled until 68 B.C. Then with weak sons, Civil War broke out to be resolved by *force majeure*. The Romans had had enough and installed Herod.

But back to 175 B.C. At this time the Greeks were attempting to consolidate their colonies into one world. To a large extent, they succeeded in universalizing and liberalizing the diverse cultures of the classical world. They built schools, theaters, and gymnasiums in an attempt to bring the multi-tribal world under the Greek enlightenment. They even tried to rationalize their polytheistic religion with other old cultures such as Egypt, which had similar multiple gods. But this aspect of Greek culture could simply not be reconciled with Jewish monotheism. The pious Jews saw no difference between the new universalism with its statues of Zeus and the old Baal worship condemned so many times in the early scriptures. However, most other aspects of Greek culture found a welcoming audience among many, perhaps a majority, of the Jews. The reform-minded Jews of the period found that universalism was implicit in their monotheism. Isaiah had made this explicit. God is everywhere. In universal monotheism, the Jews had a new and tremendous idea to give the world. Now the Greeks also had a big general new idea, that of universalist culture. Many of the reformed pious and liberal Jews in the tradition of Ezra did not object to Greek rule in principle any more than they had objected to the Persians. They tended to accept Jeremiah's arguments that religion and piety flourished more when pagans had to conduct the corrupting business of government. They were quite willing to pay the conqueror's taxes, provided they were left to practice their religion in peace. It was from such policy that the movement of the Pharisees sprang. Most Jews in this period took Hellenic names and spoke Greek, particularly on journeys and in business.

The Greek policies of colonial rule were working pretty well. Had they not had the pressure of a rising Rome, which caused them to try to accelerate the process of Hellenization, the acceleration that brought the backlash might not have occurred.

Like most anti-colonial struggles, the Maccabaean revolt did not start with an assault on the occupier, but with the murder of one of their own, a Jewish reform collaborationist. A man named Abeles was superintending the opening of a new building at an official ceremony. The Hasidic Matthias Hasmon was so enraged by the perceived sacrilege that he stabbed Abeles to death. Matthias Hasmon was the head of a priestly family. He was an old man with five sons. One of these, Judas—nicknamed the Hammer—for the next two years conducted a guerrilla movement against the Greek Seleucid garrisons and against their Jewish supporters.

In two years from 166 to 164, they drove all of the Greeks out of the areas around Jerusalem and purged the temple of its sacrileges, including physical education. Its rededication to God was remembered in a solemn service in December of 164 B.C. We, of course, today still celebrate this with the feast of purification called Hanukkah. In many respects, the guerrilla warfare was civil warfare, with Jews on both sides. One has visions of the orthodox Jews of Nashville marching on the Jewish Center to purify the gymnasium of the desecration of Sabbath activities. We must remember that Hanukkah is the celebration of the victory, not over the Greeks, but over the universalist liberal co-religionists. Concerning our local disagreements with regard to Center practices, the conflicts are still civil. At the time of the Maccabees' revolt the issues were settled with bloodshed. The most apt modern parallel is not to be found in Nashville but in Beirut.

One might wonder why the powerful Greeks did not do better against the Maccabees and at least come back and squash them. The answer is that they were having troubles of their own elsewhere as the power of Rome was rising.

The House of Hasmon solidified its position, which lasted for over one hundred years. An alliance was made with Rome, and they were treated as the ruling power of an independent state. In the nationalistic enthusiasm that evolved from the rule of its own people, piety was generally pushed into the background. The last of Matthias's sons, Simon, ruled with an entrenched priesthood called Sadducees.

The Maccabees were strong, violent, fanatical, and brave men and saw themselves as reliving the book of Joshua and re-conquering the Promised Land. Most of them met violent ends. Simon was no exception and was treacherously murdered along with two of his sons. Simon's third son, John Hyrcanus, succeeded him and ruled for thirty years. He was imbued with a fundamentalist notion that it was God's will to restore the kingdom. Solomon was his model. He accepted the literal truth that the whole of Palestine was the divine inheritance of a Jewish nation. He created a modern army of mercenaries. In his conquest, like Joshua, he had to drive out the foreign cults and unorthodox sects. He was perfectly willing to murder any who clung to a diversity from the orthodoxy of the Sadducees. His army trampled all of Samaria and burned the Samaritans' temple. After years of siege, John demolished the city of Samaria entirely and brought streams to drown it so that no trace would remain. In the same way, he pillaged and burned a number of Greek cities. He was perfectly willing to massacre populations of cities whose only crime was that they spoke Greek. The province of Idumaea in the Sinai was conquered, and the inhabitants were slaughtered unless they were willing to convert to Judaism. John's son, Alexander Jannaeus (Yanni), took this policy of expansion and forceful conversion even further. He invaded the territory of Decopolous across the River of Jordan. He swept into Nabatia and took Petra, "the rose-colored city half as old as time." In becoming kings, rulers, and conquerors, the Hasmonians in two generations after Judas Maccabee suffered all the corruptions and the degenerations of power. Yanni, according to the evidence we have, turned into a despot and a monster. Among his victims were pious Jews from whom his family had once drawn strength. He became influenced by Greek ideas and changed some ancient ceremonies. At the time of Succus, he refused to perform the libation, and pious Jews pelted him with lemons. At this, Josephus writes, he went into a rage and slew about six thousand pious Jews. A civil war then proceeded and cost the lives of fifty thousand Jews. It was at this time that we first hear of the Pharisees, who separated themselves from

The House of Hasmon

the orthodox religious establishment. Their persecution was so great that they incredibly sought the protection of the Syrians from the zeal of the Sadducees. And so we come full circle from the Puritan separatists from the Church of England to the parasitic separatists from the church of the ruling Hasmonians. Yanni died after falling into a fit of distemper from hard drinking. The enormous dissipation sounds like nothing so much as perhaps Manuel Noriega.

After the Hasmonian rule, the strong and peculiar part-Roman, part-Jew, part-Arab leader Herod came to power. That, however, is beyond the scope of this meager paper. All I have tried to show is that there is nothing in our covenants with God that would shield us from the excesses of piety and power. At the close of this period, sects began to form in pockets of what is now Israel. The Dead Sea Scrolls recount one such group, the Essenes. Another reformist sect was founded and waxed under the genius and leadership of Saul of Tarsus.

MY STUDY OF this incredibly complex chapter of history is too shallow to allow for universal truth. Perhaps the only thing I can suggest is that when the rabbi gives a sermon, she might find within her congregants someone willing to think about it and write a Shamus paper. It seems to me that Hanukkah is a celebration of a violent victory by a conservative subset of Jews. Its equivalency to Christmas in modern times is convenient but not an analogy that bears comparison, Christmas being seminal to one faith and Hanukkah being a mere episode in one era in the astounding history of a people.

It is my profound hope, given my shallowness in

approaching the subject, that Randy will be out of town during this February meeting. If Randy shows up, we can all profit by hearing someone who knows something. I recall that the last time I tried a paper on a Jewish subject, it involved the Khazar. For that occasion, Lou Silverman suddenly appeared, not having been seen for several years before or since, and served as a mirror for my inadequacies.

Even so disclaiming, I would like to conclude this with four observations and suggestions.

1. Along with Purim, let's ease out the remembrance of the violent Hasmoneans from the celebration of our solstice festival of lights. I think I once heard the rabbi express some doubts about Purim. It is likely that this story is pagan. It was borrowed from the Persians during our brief exilic sojourn there. Anyway, hamantashen always makes me slightly queasy. If the rabbis approve, it would suit me to get rid of the whole megillah. But we do clearly need a deep winter holiday. Those of us in the northern hemisphere welcome a festival of lights. Particularly fine is one lasting for eight days at a time when the nights are the longest. I would suggest de-emphasizing rebellion and bloodshed even in the name of purification and put more emphasis on the cruse of oil. In the late twentieth century, oil and its conservation by miraculous means or otherwise has a new and enhanced meaning. In Genesis 1, God gave us dominion over the natural world. Maybe it is now time we paid some lip service to its preservation. We need our eight joyous nights of the family around the Menorah. An emphasis on God's world and our environment may be something more of substance to celebrate.

The House of Hasmon

2. Religions do evolve. Duality is always present in the human condition. The orthodox and the reform are always with us, as they are indeed ever-present in any body politic. There always remains the need to preserve the past, which got us here, and the need from here to adapt to the world, which will get us through to the next there. The Sadducees were in this period the establishment group. They represented the wealthy and the fixed in society. Their theological view came from a priesthood, which added its own tradition to the written law. The counter-force was the Pharisees, who were generally the poorer and more rural elements and who were theologically fundamentalists, harking back to the Torah as written. In modern times, to stretch an analogy, the Pharisees were the Church of Christ vis-à-vis the Episcopalian Sadducees. Throughout this period, as we have discussed, the constituencies and the doctrines of the two groups evolved, changed, and even exchanged. But the important thing was that there was always this duality. It remains with us, liberal/conservative, orthodox/reform, left/right.

However, religion did change and change fast. At the time of Herod, there were eight million Jews in the world. This fact is according to the Roman census as reported by Josephus. The Jews amounted to about ten percent of the Roman Empire. Polytheism was well-entrenched. The institutions of the Parthenon, the Pantheon, and the Pyramids seemed immutable. Nevertheless, within a few centuries, polytheism gave way almost totally to monotheism. The change was complete by A.D. 700 as the great Hebrew heresies, Christianity and Islam, spread across the globe. In our own time, non-theism spread around the world but seems to be receding as Marxism fails.

3. Military occupations are always difficult and, in the long run, impossible. The Maccabees were not all good, as we have discussed, and by a like token, the house of Antiochus was not all bad. The Seleucid Greeks had the dreadful dilemma of any occupying power. In general, their objective was to establish their Hellenistic culture throughout all of their lands. They tried both persuasion and repression. Neither really worked. It was, however, true that the magnificent culture of Greece was permeating, and the Jews were gradually assimilating. It was only when repressive measures were taken to increase the rapidity of this transition that they got their armed rebellion by zealots. Modern examples of these dilemmas are replete. See, for instance, the Japanese in Korea or the Israelis in the West Bank. At any rate, occupations are difficult and almost never successful. Perhaps the most successful in history is the MacArthur occupation of Japan from 1945 to 1952. It had two things going for it. As victors the Americans were generous and kind. The culture of the losers was that of the bamboo, not the oak. In the storm of loss they did not splinter; they bent. But the main thing about that occupation was that it was brief.

4. The final conclusion is that it is hard to run a country. It is particularly hard to run one when you are constrained both by the discipline of God's law and the exigencies of daily rule. Israel today has a special place in our hearts. That anything should befall it would devastate our universe. But just because we made our covenants and pacts with the Holy One, blessed be He, it does not follow that He will bless all of the actions of the new Zion. The last time we tried to run this country on the Mediterranean's eastern shore, it was

done shamefully. Yanni at a banquet in mid-reign, attended by many concubines and some friends, had eight hundred Greek-speaking Judeans crucified to decorate the banquet hall. Then, while the dying were still conscious, Yanni had their wives and children brought before them and had the throats of their loved ones slit.

We won't sink to that again, but righteousness in nationhood is a fragile attribute. To achieve it demands our vigilance and our prayers.

The Shamus Club, 1998. Back row: Randy Falk, Herb Shayne, Fred Goldner, Dick Eskind, Bob Eisenstein, Harris Gilbert, Eric Chazen, and Jim Blumstein. Front row: Sam Richmond, David Steine, Bernard Werthan, and Jack May.

Herein lies much but not all plagiaristic debt to James Reston Jr.'s *Collision at Home Plate,* which see. Also see *Sideways.* Paul would give his father Bart enormous *nachas.*

Angelo and Peter

A paper read to the Shamus Club May 24, 2000, at the home of Eric Chazen

I START TONIGHT with two quotations from the Apocrypha: "They were the honored of their generation; they were the glory of their times," and "Let us now praise famous men." This will be the tale of two giants, Angelo and Peter. They each achieved mightily, rose to positions of the highest esteem, and then collided and fell. At the pinnacle they wrestled like Jacob with the angel. They were dramatic analogs of Prospero and Caliban in *The Tempest.* One noble and one base, but both gigantic in their achievement. The seeds of the destruction of both Peter and Angelo started early in their lives. The men grew far beyond their families, but the seeds did not disappear. At their acme, they collided. After the collision, one would die early and the other would live disgraced. Let me tell you more of Peter and Angelo.

Their middle names were Edward and Bartlett. Not to continue this coyness, their last names were Rose, Pete Rose, and Giamatti, Bart Giamatti.

BART'S GRANDFATHER WAS an immigrant from Italy. He arrived in New Haven and worked as a laborer at New Haven Clock Company. His son, Bart's father, was named Valentine. When Val entered the first grade in New Haven he spoke no English. He was, however, a promising lad and eventually completed Hillhouse High and entered Yale College with a four-year scholarship, in a move that was very unusual in its day and is still an unlikely happening. The class differences between the Italian immigrant and the patrician Yalies of the 1930s was clear and searing. Nevertheless, Val excelled. He distinguished himself as a Phi Beta Kappa, then went on to Harvard to get a Ph.D. In one astonishing leap, the Giamatti family went from immigrant laborer to academic respectability. Then while studying abroad, Val met his future wife, Mary Claybaugh Walton, who was taking her junior year abroad from Smith College. Her forbearers had been colonial sea captains and shoe manufacturers from the industrial towns of New England. Their son, Angelo Bartlett Giamatti, was born in 1938 from a union of immigrant Italian and congregational Massachusettan. He joked that the two branches of his ancestors were united only in the two "T"s in Giamatti and the two "T"s in Bartlett. Bart's father taught at Mount Holyoke, a scholar of Dante. He taught well, but was never really confident enough in English to write the definitive book on the

Divine Comedy. For this insecurity the father compensated in the education of his children. He emphasized the wondrous possibilities of their native tongue, English.

In addition to elevated thought, smoking was one of Val's pleasures. He usually smoked four packs of cigarettes a day. At the age of fifty-one, he suffered a massive heart attack. As a consequence of the attack, he became crippled and walked with two canes.

So Bart was raised in a comfortable middle-class home full of love and of learning. Also, there was travel. After the war they spent much time as a family in Italy. Bart's Italian became fluent quickly. Bart often felt both the Italian and the American in his character. From Italy he got a sense of history and a concern for the fragility of institutions, which mixed with American optimism and a sense of possibility.

It was also in Italy that he got his first real baseball glove. It was one that had been left behind by an American GI. Back home again in Massachusetts, Bart became infused with a lifetime loyalty to the Boston Red Sox and more generally to baseball as a folk religion.

Starting in the fall of 1956, Bart followed his father and went to Yale, graduating in the Class of 1960. Though he had put in two final years at Andover, he arrived at New Haven feeling somewhat out of place. He and a close friend would wander down to the Italian section, which since my day has become a hostile area. I remember well having my first pizza there in 1947. I had never heard the word before. It occurred to me that this marvelous food should have wide national acceptance. Great foresight but no execution. Ah, me! After the uneasiness of freshman year, Bart had a wildly successful Yale career. He joined the Dramat, was a Pundit, and was active in the Elizabethan Club. Uncharacteristically he pledged DKE. It was a jock fraternity and, if he could not be one himself, he loved to be around the athletes. Then as a junior he entered the Aurelian Society and to cap off his career, he was tapped by Scroll and Key. His wit and eloquence made him popular. In his many associations he was considered a boon companion. Nevertheless, it was in academics that he made his mark. He was an English major and studied under Cleanth Brooks and Maynard Mack, who eventually became his lifelong mentor. His achievement through academics was so great he was accorded the high distinction of delivering the class oration at graduation. His speech was literate, scholarly, and heartfelt. It echoed his lifelong theme of acting on a unified body of belief. The modern man who has faced himself and found himself to be strong must then proceed to act.

Looking back on my own modest career in New Haven, Giamatti's record is astounding. He accepted the invitation to move directly to the Yale faculty as a junior professor. Then came a job at Princeton, interestingly not in comparative literature or English, but as an instructor in the Italian language. His doctoral dissertation, entitled *Earthly Paradise and the Renaissance Epic,* was published by the Princeton University Press. Bart's two great recreations in this period were Dante and baseball. Did Dante really love or have contempt for Virgil, his guide through hell and paradise? These discussions often took place as he accompanied his fellow professor friends to New York when the Red Sox were in town. Carl Yastrzemski v. Whitey Ford. Paradiso v. Inferno. A profound joy.

At Maynard Mack's urging, he returned to the belly of

mother Yale. He taught English 25, an advanced freshman course, which included Chaucer, Spenser, Donne, and Milton. Giamatti had great appeal to students. He could make Dante and Spenser fun and amusing, as well as profound and relevant. His particular gift was to make connections between the seemingly esoteric concerns of the Renaissance poets and the concerns of modern America: academia and baseball. Giamatti's tenure at Yale involved the turbulent times of the late sixties. These came to a peak in 1970 with the kidnapping and murder trial of Bobby Seale. This was when Kingman Brewster made a statement that he doubted any black revolutionary could get a fair trial anywhere in the U.S. This statement reached the ear of Vice President Spiro Agnew, who called for Brewster's resignation. Through this difficult period, Bart supported Brewster with both humor and eloquence, but the episode profoundly affected Giamatti. The role of the university and its need for order and rules, civilized discourse and manner, grace and restraint, were paramount values. These had been trampled by the entire hippie establishment, which had descended upon New Haven. Giamatti did stand up in public and was heard, and his voice caught the ear of the Yale establishment. Through it all shone Giamatti's sense of righteousness. He quoted from *The Fairy Queen:*

> *Made of iron mold, immovable, resistless without end*
> *Who in his hand the iron flail did hold*
> *With which he threshed out falsehood*
> *And did truth unfold.*

Through the 1970s Giamatti took various administrative

jobs in addition to his English teaching. He became master of Ezra Stiles College. Hannah Gray became provost during this time and found Bart generally useful. He spoke often of Machiavelli's view of politics as art. Machiavelli was a poet of power, and Hannah Grey used him in various mundane troubles with the food service crews.

Hannah Holborn Gray was appointed provost at the resignation of Kingman Brewster, who became ambassador to the Court of St. James. With the need for a new president, Cyrus Vance took the job as head of the search committee. In time the committee chose Henry Rosovsky, Dean of Arts and Sciences at one of the schools in the Boston area. In a dramatic weekend, Rosovsky was offered the job publicly and refused it publicly; the committee in bitterness turned to a Yale man. In embarrassed desperation they chose Angelo Bartlett Giamatti to become President of Yale. He became an overnight celebrity. He was interviewed by *The New York Times*. The reporter asked, "Some time ago you suggested Yale was waiting for someone to come in on a white horse to solve its financial and other problems. Do you have a white horse?"

"No," Giamatti smiled, "I have a yellow Volkswagen."

On Giamatti's first day in office he drafted a memo as follows:

> *To the Members of the University Community:*
> *In order to repair what Milton called the ruin of grandparents, I wish to announce that henceforth as a matter of University policy, evil will be abolished and paradise is restored. I trust that all of us will do whatever is possible to obtain this policy objective.*

This somewhat flip memo was widely published and commented on across the country. To me, it betrays wit, tongue-in-cheek humor, and above all, an innate idealism. Idealism is fine in the ivory tower, but this man was about to undertake the real world. Now in running a university and later in running the national pastime, he would have to see that the garbage was picked up. His erudition, wit, and charm were great, but garbage comes in big piles.

Angelo Bartlett Giamatti

Bart's administration had a number of controversies early on over appointments and reappointments. His provost choice of Abe Goldstein was controversial. The choice was complicated further by Goldstein's spending sixty-seven thousand dollars of university money on his own personal housing. In the aftermath of this revelation Goldstein resigned. Another issue was the reappointment of Robert Brustein as the head of the Drama School. He had made a national reputation for himself by putting on plays with Meryl Streep, Henry Winkler, etc., but had neglected the school's teaching role. Brustein too resigned. The controversies were continual. The fundamental difficulty at Yale was a very tight budget. Also there was a decaying physical plant, and a dreadful situation with his labor unions. Strikes occurred with regularity. Whatever idealism he brought to the job was dissipated in the daily grind of dealing with these problems. At the end of eight years of this, he was ready to move on, take a job in politics or in diplomacy as had his predecessor, or in some other service to society. It was in this vortex that the job of Major League Commissioner was offered to him, and it was with some relief that he accepted the job.

Bart's love of baseball had grown even more intense as an adult. He would spend afternoons, sometimes alone, watching the Yale baseball team. During his tenure Yale had a very good team built around a future major league pitcher, Ron Darling. This was probably the best Yale team since the heady days of Dick Tettelbach and Captain George Bush that sent four players to the major leagues, and in 1948 missed by a hair being national champions.

His tenure as commissioner was again haunted by difficulties with the umpires, players' unions, and, more particularly, with Dave Pallone. He handled each of these with success. He appeared to enjoy his role, although his weight had increased and his consumption of cigarettes had also escalated.

In 1988 a new problem came when his office had been notified that one of the league's stars had been gambling. The office of the Commissioner appointed an investigative prosecutor to dig into these charges, and six months later came the inevitable collision with Pete Rose.

PETE ROSE WAS born, grew up, lived his entire life, and still lives in the environs of Cincinnati, Ohio. He lived alongside the Ohio River in a tough workingman neighborhood. A river rat. He was small, often smaller than the girls in his grade school and junior high classes, but he had a small boy's cockiness with an intent to show that he could not be pushed around. He endlessly bounced a ball off the brick wall of a local tavern, and this was almost his entire life. He was fearless. Against his mother's warning, he would swim in the Ohio River, which was treacherous. Sometimes he would swim all the way across, ending up downstream on the Kentucky side, and would hop a freight train to get far enough upstream that he could re-cross it and return to where he started. His father, Harry Rose, was also a tough guy. He played semi-pro football in and around Cincinnati, and no one could call him anything other than tough. He played linebacker and fullback with enough enthusiasm to get a general local reputation. For pleasure he would take his boys, including Pete, across the river to the wicked Kentucky side. There he loved to play the horses and gamble in the wide-open city of Newport. Fun was playing dice and getting peeks of the strip shows that accompanied Newport gambling. This is the same father who taught Pete basketball. To improve in this sport, he made him shoot endlessly with his left hand. He hounded him from the sidelines in baseball. He taught him the game as well as he taught him of the low pleasures, but taught him he did. Throughout his Little League and Knothole years, and then into high school, Pete had good coaching. There was something poignant about the young little Pete. He was a determined boy who tried harder than anyone else but simply didn't have great talent. A professional future was not in the cards, his high school coach told him. He was compared to his teammate, Ed Brinkman, and his coach said it was like comparing a Cadillac to a Ford. He just didn't have it to make it in professional baseball. But Pete did have one thing going for him, and that was an uncle who was a scout. Uncle Buddy Bloebaum, fulfilling his family responsibility and using his baseball contacts, got Pete a seven-thousand-dollar signing contract with the Reds. Neither Pete nor his father and Uncle Buddy thought much of his prospects. He was slow, had a weak arm, and could not make the pivot, but somehow he was good enough to hold on. He played in minor leagues in Geneva, New York, for Johnny Vander Meer, and then went on to play in Macon, Georgia, for Davy Bristol. So it was with luck and energy that Pete at age twenty-two got his chance with Cincinnati in 1963. Through luck, having the right player injured, and energy, he was to be called Charlie Hustle. Pete made it immediately in the big leagues. He could always hit, and with experience learned to field well enough to be an asset. With a good batting eye and desire and focus, he was a major leaguer from the beginning.

Two instances in Pete Rose's career show the extent to which hustle can turn into recklessness and borderline cruelty. In trying to score from second on a single in the All-Star game of 1973, Rose crashed into catcher Ray Fosse, a twenty-three-year-old All Star from Cleveland. The ball had not yet reached Fosse, and yet Rose crashed into him with such force that he never again regained his career. It would have been comparatively easy for Rose simply to have slid into home safely. A similar instance occurred in a game between the Reds and the Mets, when on a double play Rose smashed into Bud Harrelson after making the pivot and getting the ball away. It was a clear late hit, and Rose's elbow broke Harrelson's nose.

On the other side of the ledger, Rose was achieving

Pete Rose in 1975

greatness. He was most valuable player on the Big Red Machine, one of the two or three best teams of the century. He won MVP twice, and made the All Star team year after year. In 1978 he set the National League record for hits in consecutive games at forty-four. He said he could have beaten Joe DiMaggio's record of fifty-six had he had as friendly scorers as had DiMaggio. Rose had a lifelong obsession with Ty Cobb and eventually broke Cobb's record of 4,174 base hits. This record is amazing. Rarely do the majors produce a two-hundred-hit season. Rose had to do it for twenty straight years to get to 4,000 and still had to get another 171 hits to break Cobb's record. He ended up by being a playing manager with the Reds in order to achieve the record of most lifetime total hits. I doubt this will ever be equaled given the nature of the modern ball player.

All this while, of course, Pete had a personal life. He had two wives, both of whom were strong women who shared a number of his traits. He also had three children and one paternity suit. At no time during any of his marriages did he stop his aggressive serial adulteries. He had a so-called Baseball Annie in every town. Often in Cincinnati he would flaunt them by bringing them right into the clubhouse. There is one instance that bears repeating as an insight into Pete's amoral nature.

Pete's second wife finally had had enough of the girlfriends and put a detective on her husband's tail. She followed Pete to an autographing show in Cleveland where he had checked into a motel with a driver and girlfriend. When Pete saw his wife Carol at the motel, he told the driver to take the blame for him. The driver wanted to take the girl to the airport. After a great amount of hysterics, the driver said, "You go down to the room where your wife is and I will take this girl to the airport." Pete said, "To hell with that. I didn't drive two hundred miles to sleep with my own wife!" There were more hysterics. Carol was in the hallway crying. When she finally got a room, Pete's driver went down to see her. She was in the room crying. The driver tried to explain to her that he was with this girl, not Pete. Pete at this time was up in his room having sex with the girlfriend while the driver was lying to his wife.

Pete's philandering was not always successful. He had one paternity suit, which he lost. He also had brushes with the U.S. Customs office for brazenly smuggling in great sums of cash and, on some occasions, drugs. He failed to report his six-figure income from baseball card and autographing shows, and eventually after his banishment from baseball served for about a year in a federal penitentiary for income tax evasion. But none of this low-lifery was what ultimately did him in. That fatal flaw was his lifetime addiction to gambling. His compulsion in this regard became self-destroying. To those of us who are not so addicted, it looks foolish and ultimately psychotic. Pete would bet on anything, beginning with the horses and then football and ultimately baseball. The amounts that he bet were enormous. He would bet ten thousand dollars a day on baseball games, including his own team, the Reds, which he was then managing. It was never finally established that he ever bet against his team, but those proofs were not conclusive. Because he bet enormous amounts, he lost enormous amounts. He would borrow heavily from his friends and simply not pay them back. He owed several of his friends debts of fifty thousand dollars or more. He owed Mafia types as much as a quarter of a million dollars. It was ultimately one of his friends who ratted him out and brought the problem to the attention of the Commissioner of Baseball.

GIAMATTI CHOSE FOR his investigator a Washington attorney named John Dowd. He was a Yale Law School graduate, tough ex-Marine, and ex-prosecutor. He had worked in the tax division of the Justice Department and, among others, had busted Meyer Lansky. Giamatti gave

Dowd his marching orders. He was not to pay for information, but he was to ferret out all of the small contours of the situation. It was not to be a noble investigation. The potential witnesses against Rose were small-time crooks, racetrack touts, leeches, Nautilus queens, artless dodgers, groupies, clubhouse flunkies, petty racketeers, tipsters, and con men. But do his job, Dowd did. The evidence against Rose was overwhelming. Dowd even had the betting slips in Pete's handwriting and with his fingerprints on the slips. In April 1987, Pete was betting huge sums on the NBA playoff and on the young baseball season. The sin here is egregious. A "don't gamble" clause is included in every baseball contract and printed in very large letters on signs in every dressing room in baseball. Gambling was a knife at the very heart of the game. Were it not thought that baseball was genuinely honest, it would in time mean its demise. Once before this century, in 1919, Judge Landis barred for life eight members of the Chicago White Sox who were thought to have bet upon the World Series with Cincinnati. That was the famous "Say it ain't so, Joe" episode. Rose's defense was simply to impugn the characters who had been witnesses against him. He also personally attacked Bart Giamatti as having hired the investigator and telling the investigator what to find. Rose's attorney, Robert Stachler, says there is no way given this situation that Giamatti could be an impartial, even-handed judge. He was, in fact, the prosecutor. Stachler was a rough, gravel-voiced litigator who relentlessly impugned Giamatti's impartiality and honesty.

Aside from the questions about the methods and procedures of the investigation, the entire process shriveled the soul of A. Bartlett Giamatti. He was profoundly and deeply and morally offended. This is not what he had entered the great game of baseball to do. He wanted to be a celebrant, its greatest romantic poet, its human bridge to its historical past. He wanted to hold the great players up to the American youth as icons. And instead of all this, he had upon his shoulders the mess of great mendacity.

But when ultimately Giamatti was faced with a decision, he made it and barred Pete Rose from baseball in any capacity whatsoever. What he did not do was bar him from applying for reinstatement, which he specifically said would be an option for Pete Rose. This is now eleven years later, and reinstatement has not come.

Immediately after Giamatti's wrenching pronouncement, he left for a vacation on Martha's Vineyard. For two days he simply took long walks on the beach to get the episode of Pete Rose behind him. The stress, however, was apparent. Since becoming Commissioner of Baseball, Giamatti had gained eighty pounds and continued to smoke his three packs a day.

Five days after the decision, Giamatti did take a phone call from George Steinbrenner. These two had maintained a jolly and bantering relationship. Steinbrenner was proud that he had majored in English literature at Williams and was capable of quoting Keats and Shelly. Bart would scoff at these as the outpourings of the minor "potted" Ivy League; Steinbrenner in turn took delight in citing a recent poll that showed Yale as merely the fourth-best school in the country. Steinbrenner did, however, have some serious things to talk to Giamatti about, and gave him his phone number at his horse farm in Ocala. Giamatti said he would be sure to call him, and Steinbrenner doubted that he would. "You doubt the chair," chided Giamatti, in an Elizabethan tone. "Only since you are sitting on it," Steinbrenner responded. Giamatti roared with laughter, and said: "Sir, you are a lout." Steinbrenner hung up in satisfaction. A few minutes later Giamatti was dead.

"BASEBALL BREAKS YOUR heart. It is designed to break your heart." So said Bart in one of his brilliant essays. He meant it in another sense, but the irony is direct. Or as one of Rose's bookies might say, and as my great friend Stanley Chernau does say, "Life is six to five against."

So what are we to conclude? Both men were done in by minor bad habits of their fathers. One given to eating and smoking, the other to horses and women. They were both enormous men who were felled by minor vices that became deadly sins. There is still great fervor today to bring Pete Rose back into the game. Rose was recently included on the All-Century Team. The percentage of people who believe that Pete never gambled on baseball has doubled since the time of his banning. He has recently stepped up efforts for reinstatement in the surge of public support. He has helped launch an Internet Hall of Fame petition on his own behalf that he be allowed into Cooperstown. I have no doubt with the passage of a little more time that he will be accepted in the Hall of Fame and be welcomed back into baseball.

So our mythic tale of Angelo and Peter is ended. If we were permitted to judge, it would be a case of yin and yang—of good and evil. But to judge in our day is considered presumptive, if not gauche. There is a huge movement to abolish capital punishment lest we judge, not necessarily wrongly, but at all. O.J. Simpson cut off his wife's head and was acquitted because one of the detectives was not politically correct. Our President has been forgiven for having used a junior employee for his own delight and then lying about it to a federal judge and to the nation. And what about integrity, anyway? The most popular sport on television is professional wrestling. Here there is no integrity, and the fact is well known. It does not affect the popularity of the show.

Was Giamatti's righteous outrage simply misplaced in these times? Bad things do happen to good people. Job dealt with this long ago. For me Job was hard to understand when I was young, and it remains hard to understand now. Dorothy Parker once quipped: "The good end happily, the bad unhappily; that's what fiction means." And what of Pete Rose, arguably the greatest player of the century when baseball was our national pastime, yet personally rotten to the core? Life, of course, does not balance out and is not fair. Many great men have been personally flawed. Does that really matter? What, dear Shamus, does matter?

The Shamus Club meets at Dan May's house in February 1950. Back row: Charles Gilbert, Dan May, Sam Sandmel, Albert Weinstein, Albert Werthan, Manuel Eskind, and Bernard Werthan Jr. Front row: Sylvan Schwartzman, Bernard Fensterwald, Stanley Rich, Jacques Back, Alf Levine, and Lawrence Goodman.

A redundant effort after the Tet paper, with apologies to those who know more and will find errors, and to those who know less and might be ashamed.

The Battle of Nashville, 1864

Read to the Shamus Club November 26, 2002

A T ALMOST ALL of the battlefields of the Civil War, the U.S. Department of the Interior has elaborate and scholarly facilities. These are well maintained and are much visited. Within an hour or two drive from here you can visit Fort Donelson, Stones River, and Shiloh. If you choose to, you will be rewarded with manicured grounds, libraries, panoramas, and movies. But at museum displays in Nashville, where was fought the last and decisive battle of the Civil War, there is naught save fifteen confusing and inadequate cast aluminum signs. The sensitive will be quick to ask why. I suggest three reasons. One, the battle was fought a long time ago by our near antecedents, and these are the "now and me" times. Secondly, the city of Nashville has prospered and grown over the very battlefield so forgotten. One-half of our membership sleeps each night without suspicion nor reverence upon that dark and bloody and frozen battlefield. And thirdly, the Southerners were decisively defeated in Nashville, and it may have been in earlier days a memory that did not stand reviving. There is no question of the decisiveness of the Battle of Nashville. It was the last battle of the war. There were no other major battles of any kind. There was certainly no battle at Appomattox. For all practical purposes, the war ended here. The North won at Nashville and thereby won the war. Had the South won at Nashville, I submit they would have won the war—at least the goal of secession.

In a broader view, the war itself is an unknown and a mystery to most of our generation. Of the six major battles in Tennessee (Clarksville, Chattanooga, Savannah, Franklin, Nashville, and Murfreesboro) I would doubt that one Nashvillian in one hundred can put them in the correct order in which they occurred. The Civil War, when viewed from our perspective, was a horribly bloody contest over issues that aren't perfectly understood even now. The intensity surrounding them is almost incomprehensible a century later. Nevertheless, one does not have to be a military buff to find fascination in the passion of this war, which swept across our own geography and which occupied so many men not too unlike ourselves. How the nation drifted into this war through the tortured decade of the 1850s is beyond the scope of this paper. It is apparently also beyond the scope of literally thousands of books on the subject. Let me only say that in the 1850s the American people generally believed

The Battle of Nashville, 1864

themselves to be the happiest and luckiest people on earth. They comprised a rural and self-sufficient culture with endless sandy roads winding leisurely through the country sides. The last thing that anyone needed was a war, especially one that would kill over six hundred thousand young men.

What I would like to do in this paper is generally stress the military history that lead to John Bell Hood's fateful march north through Tennessee and to try and reconstruct the Battle of Nashville. If I do it well, maybe some of you will pause a moment as you drive through the city and look differently at the few historical monuments inadequately and randomly scattered across the battlefield. Or perhaps some of you will pursue the subject in more depth with field trips, books, or a trip to the Nashville Room of the public library.

The Civil War was fought in two entirely separate areas. In the east the armies of the North and South fought

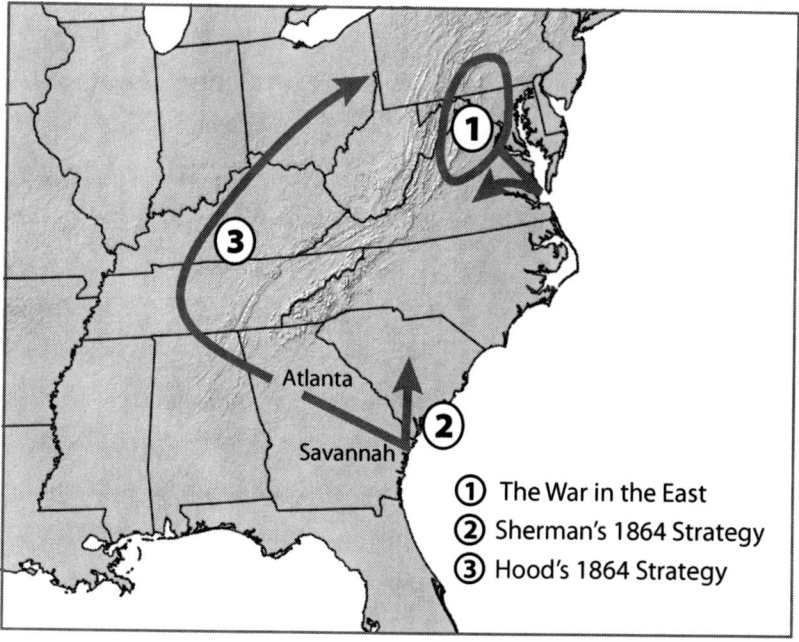

① The War in the East
② Sherman's 1864 Strategy
③ Hood's 1864 Strategy

battles of attrition in the narrow area of the Shenandoah Valley. The armies would fight to protect the flanks of the capitals of Richmond and Washington. These enormous battles involving armies of men were fought at such familiar places as Chancellorsville, Manassas or Bull Run, Gettysburg, and the Wilderness. However, the war in the west, which will occupy this evening, was a war of territory. The east was hundreds of thousands of men; the west was thousands of miles. The east was the old warfare of courage and slaughter. The west was modern warfare: mobility, interdiction, supply, and transportation. The eastern war was destroying the other side's men; the war in the west was capturing the other side's territory.

The Southern strategy at the start of the hostilities was to prepare a defensive line roughly coinciding with the southern border of Kentucky. The line was anchored on the Mississippi River at Columbus, Kentucky, thence across the state to Bowling Green, and then to Cumberland Gap. The Yankees sought to breech a point in this line. They found this breech in the north-flowing Tennessee and Cumberland rivers. The South, anticipating this, had positioned Fort Henry and Fort Donelson near the mouths of these waterways. The two forts were quickly conquered at the outset of the war by the Federal troops and gunboats under General U.S. Grant. It was at Fort Donelson that he gained the nickname "Unconditional Surrender" Grant. With its northern perimeter thus penetrated, the Southern troops fell back. Nashville could not be defended and so, almost at the outset of the hostilities, the Tennessee capital was abandoned to the Yankees. The Southern troops then collapsed back into Alabama, and the bloody battle of Shiloh was fought. The following spring in 1863, the North thrust southwest toward Vicksburg and southeast toward Atlanta. The indecisive but bloody Battle of Murfreesboro was followed by a Southern victory at Chickamauga. Then came a series of Northern victories at Chattanooga, across Georgia, culminating in the taking of Atlanta.

After the Battle of Atlanta, it was strange to find the Southern troops under General Hood retreating northward, whereas the Northern troops proceeded southward in General Sherman's famous land-burning march to the sea, across southern Georgia to Savannah. By this point the South had substantially lost the war. It would last only seven months more. The Southerners had few options. The one they concocted and carried out was the last desperate gamble of the South. It was the plan of General Hood and President Davis. In mirror-like counter ploys, both the North and the South hoped to favorably impact the Eastern War. By huge land sweeps from the south and west, each side hoped to attack the rear of the enemy in the east. General Sherman, after destroying the Southern breadbasket, planned to cross the Carolinas and complete the surrounding of Robert E. Lee's Army of Virginia. It was a sure but ultimately unnecessary plan for ending the war.

In a parallel conception, John Bell Hood and Jefferson Davis hatched a strategy of pressing northward into Kentucky, Ohio, and thence through Pennsylvania to encircle the rear of General Grant's Army of the Potomac. It was a long shot for complete victory, but if it were even partially or perhaps even potentially successful, there was a real likelihood of a negotiated settlement with a war-exhausted enemy.

This Southern plan of desperation was viewed with real

anxiety by Lincoln and his staff in Washington. After Atlanta they directed Sherman to dispatch General Schofield and his troops to head off the northward-marching Hood. This detachment could help, but all that really stood between the desperately wounded tiger of the South and the unprotected western jugular of the North was a garrison of troops under General George Thomas in Nashville.

Nashville in 1860 was the eighth largest city in the South. It had a population of seventeen thousand. Lebanon's population in 2002 is seventeen thousand. Nashville had never been eager for the war. The general mood at the beginning of the 1860s would have probably reflected a support for the practice of slavery, but not a general willingness to secede from the Union or to go to war for it. Not many locals, one supposes, were opposed to slavery. What few did, discreetly kept their views to themselves. The number of slaveholders in Nashville was a very small minority of the white population. Those well-to-do slave owners likely were not eager to go to war themselves to preserve the institution. The town was economically well off. It was a turbulent river town, a rising and rapidly expanding center of commerce and industry. There was much money to be made and much power to be attained. The fact of history is that people in pursuit of money are not those likely to be in the pursuit of wealth's destruction by way of warfare. Nashville was a frontier town as it faced the 1860s. There was opulence, but on every hand there was the turmoil that comes with fast growth. The streets were muddy. The water was dirty. There were no fewer than sixty-nine houses of prostitution in the downtown area. One can suppose the city needed some refinement, but it did not need war.

The Battle of Nashville, 1864

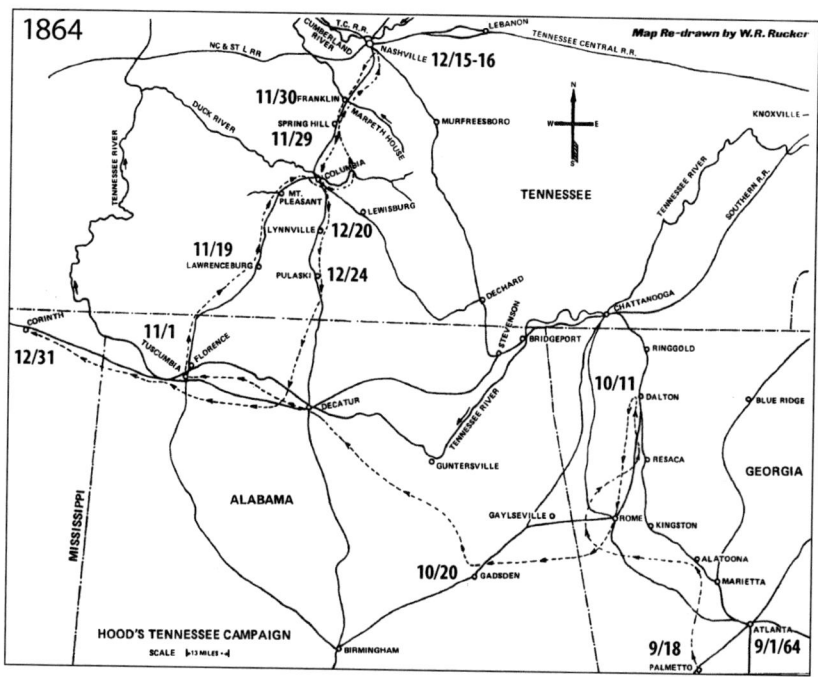

As we have seen, Nashville fell quickly and quietly to the Yankees without a battle in the city. Although it was harassed and worried by the guerrilla activities of the brilliant Nathan Bedford Forrest, the town was generally secure. The seventeen thousand citizens in 1860 had grown to eighty thousand by 1864. One of those who came into Nashville at about this time was my mother's grandfather, Morris Fishel. He was the first president of a reform Congregation in Nashville. My grandfather, Jacob Fishel, was born in the city while it was under Yankee occupation in 1864.

The occupied city was heavily fortified. As with any service city, prostitution, crime, and drunkenness were widespread. A local newspaper commented in 1864 that Nashville was filled with "thugs, highwaymen, robbers, assassins." Murder stalked the streets nightly. There were over three hundred in 1864. However, those Nashvillians who did not flee in many cases became rich. The merchants had an enormous market into which to sell. Those who were able speculated in commodities, such as corn, wheat, coffee, and sorghum. Those who were successful laid the foundation for the growth of Nashville that would last well into the next century. In time Nashville became a financial center for the South in no small degree based on the fortunes made during the Federal occupation of 1862 to 1865. One of the amenities that remained intact during this time was the theater on Charlotte that gave nightly performances. These included in the weeks before the battle a series of thirteen different plays in fourteen days by the greatest actor of the time, John Wilkes Booth. It was toward this rough and roaring occupied city that Hood approached from the South. The stage is set for the Battle of Nashville.

MEANWHILE BACK TO General Hood and his Army of Tennessee. After the much-storied Battle of Atlanta, the Southerners regrouped and marched north. Northerners, except Schofield's men, regrouped and marched south. For about forty days, like Moses, the Southern troops under John Bell Hood wandered through the southern wilderness. Eventually they ended up in Tuscumbia, Alabama, and then in late November they crossed into Tennessee. Sherman had dispatched an appreciable part of his army to go, not with him to the sea, but into the interior to Nashville to reinforce the Federal army under General George Thomas. These troops under Schofield moved quickly to southern Middle Tennessee and waited in Pulaski. Hood's urgent need was to get north of them and destroy them before they could consolidate with the substantial Federal troops in Nashville.

Hood accomplished the entrapment at the little town of Spring Hill, fifteen miles south of Franklin. As the day came to an end on November 29, he had surrounded the Federal troops and was on the threshold of making a major victory. As the night went on, however, Hood lost the Yankees. The Federals silently, sometimes within a few yards of the Southern troops, slipped through their lines. They got north of Hood's men and were well into Franklin by daybreak.

There has been much speculation in the literature about how this escape took place. The command post knew the Yanks were moving, but no orders for response came forth. It seems clear that if Hood had been able to communicate with his subordinates, the entrapment could have been completed. He did not. Much of the conjecture as to why no orders were communicated generally comes out with a question mark. The best informed opinion, however, concludes that after the sun went down, General Hood got drunk.

How can this be? The commanding general of one of the two Southern armies at the climax of his great plan, drunk? Who was Hood? A West Point graduate, he started the war with the rank of lieutenant. In three years he was a general. He fought through the various Virginia campaigns. He was gradually promoted through the ranks under James "Pete" Longstreet. After Antietam he was promoted to major general and participated in the Battle of Gettysburg. Here he was wounded in the arm and was deprived of the use of it. Though only partially recovered, he went with Longstreet to serve under General Bragg in the battles of Chattanooga. In the Battle of Chickamauga, on the first day of the battle, he mounted his horse with one arm in a sling and placed himself at the head of his command. On the second day of the battle, while leading a brilliant charge, he was shot in the upper part of his leg and had to be carried from the field. His leg was then amputated. About four months later after convalescence with a shriveled arm and minus one leg, he was yet able to mount his horse, be strapped on, and ride about. It was during the period of his convalescence that he came to know President Jefferson Davis. Davis was attracted to him though Hood's congenial personality and his brilliant record for bravery. This no doubt impressed Davis extremely favorably. In spite of his youth (he was just past thirty) he was then promoted to lieutenant general and succeeded General Joseph E. Johnston in command of the Army of Tennessee, then stationed in Dalton. This is the Civil War's confirmation of the Peter Principle. Although he had served with courage and great tactical skill in every battle in which he served, when he was promoted to general he failed in every battle thereafter. No doubt by the time he reached Spring Hill, fifteen miles south of Franklin, he was in great pain, without the use of two of his four limbs. One could hardly deny him the use of the bottle. There is no other solid explanation of how the Yankees got through his lines and established themselves in fine defensive positions in Franklin. The war was as good as over.

On the morning of November 30, Hood awoke to find his entrapment a failure. In a rage, he led his men on a forced march the fifteen miles to Franklin, where late in the afternoon he charged the entrenched Federal troops across the plains just south of town. It is said that the Federal troops knew they were coming because all the rats, rabbits, gophers, and small game charged out of the woods ahead of them, being beaten forward by the onrushing Confederate troops.

In direct disregard for the advice of Nathan Forrest, who had scouted the Federal positions, Hood mounted a direct frontal assault. Hood had been consumed with raging impatience for combat and was determined to attack and attack immediately. The frontal assault was as bloody as it was futile. The Confederates suffered losses of six thousand killed, while the Federals, operating behind barriers constructed during the day, had serious, but not substantial, losses. In addition to the six thousand troops Hood lost six of his finest generals. This was to cost him dearly in the coming Battle for Nashville. Schofield, the Yankee general, retreated the next morning to Nashville to join forces with Thomas. Hood then found himself in possession of the Franklin battlefield, which had netted him nothing but the blood of his generals and loss of his manpower.

A trip to Franklin's Carter House is well worth a Sunday afternoon. In this regard the other Civil War battlefields, most within an easy ride, are located in Fort Donelson, near Clarksville, Stones River in Murfreesboro, and Shiloh in Savannah. Any of these are well worth the trip. The National Park Service has done a marvelous job in these preservations and reconstructions.

Hood's troops were not only decimated by war and disease, they were also suffering from lack of supplies. Food was scarce. A meal of hardtack and molasses was all that many of the troops had had for literally months. Perhaps the greatest hardship was the lack of shoes and blankets. Nashville in December meant it could be either mild or cold. In December 1864, it was bitterly cold. Troops without shoes left paths

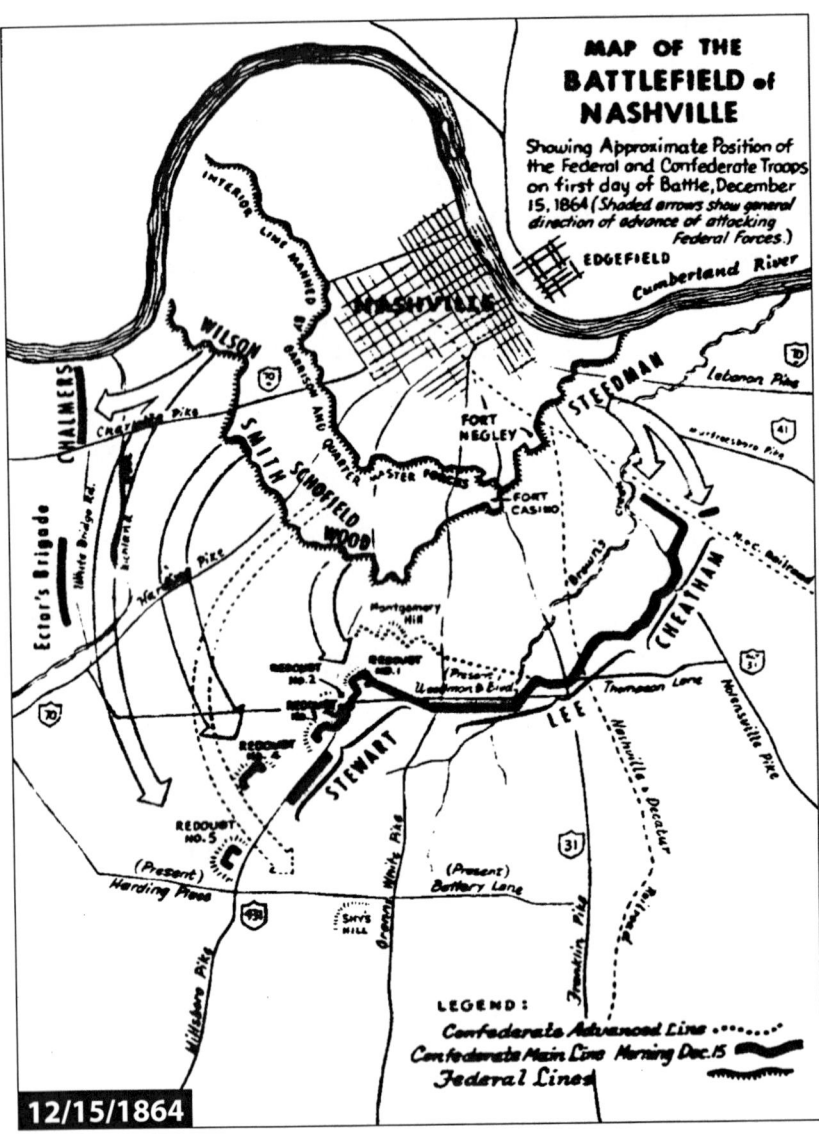

of bloody footprints in the snow. The Northern troops, on the other hand, had more than twice as many men as Hood and had had months to prepare. Now reinforced with the remnants of Sherman's army that had marched north, they were in an overwhelming position. There was enormous impatience in Washington with General Thomas. They wanted

The Battle of Nashville, 1864

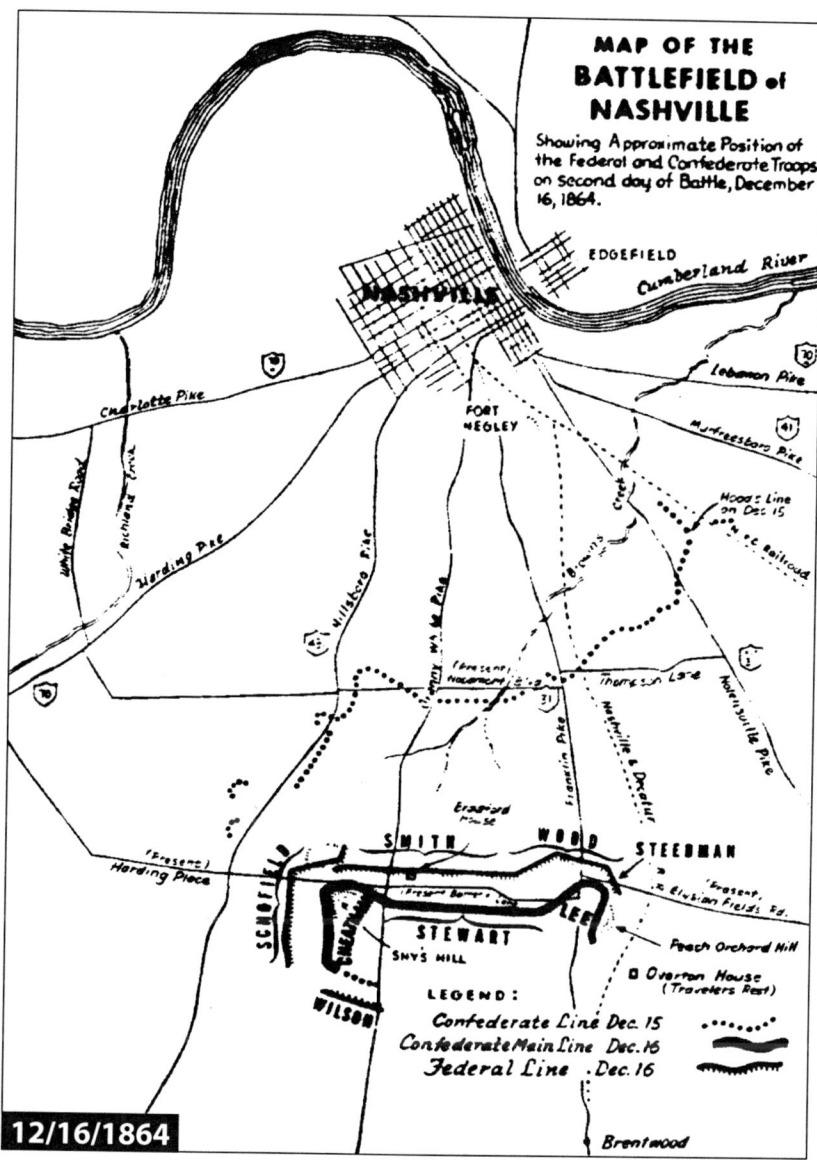

him to strike out from Nashville and quickly attack Hood's weakened army. Thomas was reluctant to do this. His own natural caution and the very inclement weather were against him. Then, a few days after the Battle of Franklin, the Southern troops moved to Nashville. They fortified a defensive perimeter from the Cumberland River near Murfreesboro Pike to the Cumberland River near Charlotte Pike. Roughly, the siege line was strongest along what is now Woodmont Boulevard. The Northern generals argued at the St. Cloud Hotel (Fifth and Church) and refrained from attacking. The reason was primarily the weather. Every day, beginning with heavy dense fogs and rains that for almost ten days straight had muddied the already-denuded hills from which the firewood had been cut to heat the freezing city, mud slicks made it impossible to conduct army exercises with infantry or calvary. The Washington of Lincoln, U.S. Grant, and the War Department of Edward Stanton were wild with impatience and anxiety. When insistence did not move Thomas, a replacement was actually sent. Finally in his own time, with a break in the weather, on December 15, General Thomas attached the besiegers.

From the first day of the Battle of Nashville, the South was foredoomed to failure. The South just did not have enough men to besiege the well-rested and large army already in Nashville. While the numbers are not clear, the best estimates hold forth that there were eighty thousand Federal troops, against about twenty-six thousand for General Hood. The Federal troops, in their defensive position, waited and then attacked the South when they were ready. It is apparent from looking at the map that both the Southern flanks were vulnerable. (See map.) Indeed, early in the morning of December 15 after a feint to the left, a great wheeling action started on the right, centered with Wood and with Wilson overrunning Chalmers and Ector's Brigade, both of whom retreated across present-day Belle Meade to the redoubts that were built on Hillsboro Pike.

Hood's forward position reached its farthest north point near the corner of Hillsboro and Blair. To the Federals, the positions on Montgomery Hill, back of the present-day Catholic Diocese office, looked to be formidable. In fact, it was only a shell. What strength there was in the Southern line lay along Woodmont Boulevard at the crest of Benham Hill. Fighting was delayed on the 15th until almost 10:00 A.M. by a heavy Nashville fog and characteristic military bungling. Smith's troops crossed in front of Wilson's and prevented him from starting his wheel at the farthest perimeter. However, once the Federals were underway, the furious battle commenced. What remained of the Southern troops were under heavy pressure all day.

One by one, the gun positions, or redoubts, fell, and as night descended the Southern troops, in dismay of battle, retreated about two miles southward to what is now Harding Place and Battery Lane. The South was anchored on the morning of the second day at Shy's Hill and at Peach Orchard Hill overlooking Travellers Rest. The ill-fated Ector's Brigade was chosen to defend Shy's Hill, and preparations made during the night were inadequate. On the morning of the 16th, the Federals had surrounded the left side of the Confederate line and, although bloody fighting ensued all day, the outcome was never in doubt. A morning first assault on Peach Orchard Hill, interestingly enough, was led by a Negro brigade. This was their first use in combat during the war. They were not successful in taking the hill, but by all accounts fought with great intensity. At noon on the second day, a cold rain began to fall and, as the position of the Southern troops became untenable, a retreat was inevitable. Somehow the Southerners held out until near dark and as night fell, they retreated along Granny White Pike by Sam Richmond's house. A freezing rain was falling, and the men had neither shoes nor blankets. The best estimate of the dead were ten thousand Southerners in Nashville and about thirty-five hundred Federals. The entire Tennessee campaign of General Hood probably came to twice that number of casualties, making the total for both sides nearly thirty thousand troops. The casualties for the North during the Civil War include 350,000 killed and for the South about 250,000 for a total of 600,000 dead.

This compares to about 47,000 for a country, grown five times as large, in Vietnam. With the completion of the Battle of Nashville, there were ten days of nightmare while the Southerners retreated, harassed continually by the Federals. They finally crossed the Tennessee River on Christmas Day. We can only imagine the intense suffering. It seems clear that during the Battle of Nashville, no sleep and little food was had for as long as seventy-two hours at a stretch. There were no blankets, no shoes, just bloody tracks through the snow and mud. Hood retreated to Tupelo, Mississippi, where he was replaced by P.T.E. Beauregard. The Army of Tennessee rested for the winter until the end in April 1865.

WHAT WAS THE point of the bloody and disastrous campaign of Hood in Tennessee? The desperate and brilliant strategy came closer to succeeding than the above elaboration might suggest. After Atlanta, the only hope for the South was to somehow get up into Northern territory. This could only be done by crossing Tennessee, then moving into Kentucky and Ohio. Had Hood succeeded in reaching into the interior of Ohio and cutting eastward across

Pennsylvania, he might have been able to establish enough of an army to be a threat to U.S. Grant's army in the east. This is exactly the reverse of what Sherman was trying to do in cutting across to the sea and north through South Carolina to eventually attack Lee's rear in the east. One can only conjecture, of course, that if Hood had been able to get by Nashville he would have had fairly clear sailing into the interior of the North. The Northern states were extremely war-weary, and the number of casualties suggest the national horror. There were substantial draft riots in Manhattan in 1863. It was "Hell, no, we won't go" a hundred years before Vietnam. My own guess is that if Hood had succeeded in getting by Nashville, peace would have been negotiated and the secession would have succeeded. Although the South was clearly beaten by the loss of Atlanta, the desperate gamble just might have worked. In Stanley Horn's book on the Battle of Nashville, he concludes that it was The Decisive Battle of the War. Not simply because it was the last, but because it completely destroyed one of the two Southern armies in the field. And had the battle gone the other way, it very well might have been the last battle of the war, as well, with peace being negotiated. One can only conjecture; however, in the end the Battle of Nashville was a bloody battle for all concerned and a disaster for the troops of John Bell Hood.

THEN WHAT, INDEED did the Civil War prove? Six hundred thousand casualties, for what? Here was a nation that had started as a colony, that had been formed by a common and popular revolution at its creation. It had a single homogeneous people, a single language, a single religion, and a single heritage. And yet, six hundred thousand casualties? Why did the leaders fight? And why did the soldiers fight? This was the first modern war. It involved massive amounts of civilian, as well as military, support. One hundred years later we are still trying to discern the lessons of the tragedy.

For myself, I think that there are some things worth fighting and dying for. I am with Patrick Henry in liberty or death. But for me the *raison d'etre* of the Civil War made little sense. The South was wrong on a great moral issue, but six hundred thousand dead is hard to compute.

But even dismissing the whys, the war does not bear forgetting. It was not so long ago and not at all far away. So it is worth the study and the speculation. If Hood had succeeded at Nashville, what would be the state of the world today, a hundred thirty-eight years later? I guess not much different. Who knows?

Just fifteen weeks after the Battle of Nashville and the bloody events just described came the most important month in the history of the United States. At least, so argues Jay Winik. I read his book *April 1865* and found it gripping. I also found it remaindered and cheap at Amazon.com. I bought up a bunch of them and will pass them out as Shamus lagniappe. The fate of the Confederacy (*ovah sholem*) was written with the re-election of Lincoln in November 1864; it was sealed at Nashville in December 1864. Winik's book provides the coda. You'll like it.

Finally, when Joseph Leu deeded his cow pasture to the Abbottsford Homeowners Association, he stipulated a restrictive covenant that one of the lots be preserved. This is Redoubt No. 4. During my tenure as president of the

The Battle of Nashville, 1864

Tennessee Historical Society, at the behest of Mr. Leu's heirs, we placed a marker on this site. On the handout page seven is the inscription on the monument. On page seven is a handsome picture of the Society's president and a picture of Redoubt No. 4. This is the last physical vestige remaining after one hundred thirty-eight years.

A Confetti of Papers

That winter the Southern troop sang a song to the tune of the Yellow Rose of Texas. It went something like this:

So now I am going to leave you, my heart is full of woe
I'm going back to Georgia, to see my Uncle Joe
You may talk about your Beauregard and sing of General Lee,
But the gallant Hood of Texas, played hell in Tennessee.

There are more of these stories. Now they are unpreserved and lost forever. Every family has its *lares* and *penates*, their folklore, nicknames and myths and jokes. Dear reader, write them down! There is more to genealogy than dates.

Old Times Old Tales

Read to the Old Oak Club October 22, 1998

1.

AT THE AGE of nineteen, after a freezing freshman year in New Haven, I went west. This trip required the purchase of a reliable automobile for very little money. Very little money was what was available to me and four companions (Bob, Kim, Donald, and Leon). The first want-ad we answered lead to naught but provided for the trip a watchword, a slogan, and oft-repeated spirit-lifter.

This particular vehicle was in the backyard of a grubby South Nashville dwelling that was at once greasy and scrofulous, while the owner-seller was the same. The car was filthy and dilapidated, unacceptable and unsaleable. The owner could only press his case by genealogy. "This car," he said, "belonged to a Moberly. You probably know them Moberlys of Tennessee Ridge." We allowed as how we didn't, and we didn't buy.

But all across the enormous beautiful country, the surrealism of the man and the car were recalled to our hilarious memory. It was, "You probably know them Moberlys" at the Top of the Mark and "You probably know them Moberlys" at the bottom of Grand Canyon. A Moberly of Tennessee Ridge could provide a snicker or guffaw, whether exhausted picking up apricots in Washington or nervous picking up girls in Yellowstone.

All of which says nothing except that being young, happy, and unpressed is a blessed state, and these little instances of fun are stretched far into the general condition of well-being.

Then twenty-five years passed. I was less young and more pressed. I was trying to run a manufacturing business in a tough apparel industry when on one Thursday, the furious afternoon calm was again broken, now by a man of small stature who burst past the public entrance of May Hosiery Mills. After a brief interval he was directed to my office, which he entered without recourse to introduction. He was dressed in the fashion of a country man come to town. Pressed open shirt, no tie. A once-red neck, now brown, was not hidden. There was no effort to conceal the extent of his agitation.

"My mother-in-law worked here a long time—Sarah Benson. Do you know her?"

"No."

"She is out in Central State. She don't know nothing no more. You know she's got thirty-three thousand dollars. Somebody here got her a will wrote up. I seen it in her box at the bank. Her great-granddaughter in Waverly is a-getting it all. Except what some damn social worker who I can't find has got already. She is some kind of phantom social worker. I can't get her name, even. Phantom, that is all she is.

"Yeah, but somebody here is really the one. Somebody here. I got me a lawyer. Hellfire, I even papered the old lady's, er, Mama's bedroom. Lula and I been married fourteen year now. Mama's out at Central State. She don't know nothing."

At this point, the practiced mill man has two choices. One, offsetting hysterics or two, professional coolness. My composure that afternoon not being up to the former, the second and easier method was applied.

"Sir, I would like very much to help you run this down." I reached for a fresh pad of general utility sheets.

"Could I have your name?"

"P-A-Y-T-E. Payte, Leonard Payte."

"Where can you be reached?"

"Route #2, Tennessee Ridge."

I wrote—then after a pause of exquisite correctness:

"You probably know them Moberlys up at Tennessee Ridge."

"Know 'em! Old Moberly don't stay five hundred yard down the way. Boy, you hunt? You come up soon, we'll fish. Catch some beauts. You can't pass a car in Humphrey County without somebody a-waving howdy-do."

The interview was concluded quickly with no conclusion. The entire mysterious matter was left to my sympathetic discretion. Leonard Payte was at peace when he left me in a world now no longer hostile. I turned to take the call from Sears, Watchung, New Jersey, punching up the delivery of eight dozen tights now two weeks past due.

A Confetti of Papers

———o———

Next year I will be seventy. Me? Seventy? Impossible! Although these seventy years are short in retrospect, they are objectively a long time. We have all accumulated our household gods. We have all participated in our family's jokes, myths, poems, and traditions. Piles of memories that are to be either saved or are forgotten. We are about to be defined by two dates on a tombstone, or if lucky, by ten lines of biography in a newspaper obituary. So, before I become a bony skull without flesh or feature, I ask you, dear Old Oak friends, one evening of personal indulgence whilst I codify some nostalgia and impose on your time in the sharing. The stories are forty to fifty-plus years old. The interspersed wisdom, though of marginal utility is, of course, timeless.

2.

On the bleakest of metallic grey days of January in the late 1940s, I was seated at the back end of a coach car heading from Grand Central Station to New Haven. At the end of the prospective hour-and-twenty-five-minute train ride lay nothing but semester examinations, then cruelly held after the Christmas holidays. Everything inside the railroad car was damp and moist and overheated. I suspect that every person occupying every seat in that crowded car shared the same dull headache. At some point at the front end of the car, the butcher boy entered with a box supported from his neck. He came to serve comestibles to the imprisoned and condemned. As he entered the car he yelled out, "Ham, lamb, cheese and ram, wild buffalo and guinea pig, sandwiches, sandwiches," and as he made his way down the long car, the refrain was repeated, "ham, lamb, cheese and ram, wild buffalo and guinea pig, sandwiches, sandwiches." When he arrived at my chair in the back of the car, I asked, please, could I have a ham sandwich, to which he replied, "Sorry, buddy, I only got peanut butter."

A rather small number of people, some geniuses, some saints, touched my life meaningfully. A quick inventory would include my father, my boss, my camp director, and some teachers. And there are old friends going back to boyhood and young manhood who still provide richness in their association. Of course, one would be amiss not to include five generations of family, relatives, and in-laws, all surviving with powerful love. But this list should not leave out these others, all helpful to me, and some to Ward DeWitt.

> The Duchess of Danvers
> Hall, the Mathematician
> The Sailor of Bude
> The Team of Tom and Louise
> Bruno, the Argentine Gaucho
> A Harlot of Clewe
> An Oxonian Don, Chauncey Dole
> The Maid of Assizes
> The Scot McGlurcken
> The Plumber of Dundee

3.

In 1946 or 1947, a year or two after we had been initiated into the American tribe by virtue of our driver's licenses, a group of us set out on our continual exploration of Tennessee. We went to the Old Mulky Meeting House, to the riverside opposite New Madrid, Missouri, that is in Kentucky but only reachable from Tennessee. We went to the top of Mount LeConte and to the bottom of Higgenbottom Cave. This Saturday, Donald, Kim, Frank, and I headed toward Falls Creek Falls. In those days it was a primitive undeveloped area. Today it is really a wonderful resort with excellent facilities for golf and beautiful cabins for rent. Nothing of the type existed then. It was only one rough road that led into the falls, which plunge 256 feet into a deep ravine. At some time in the past a half-inch cable had been put from the top of the cliff so that one could back down holding onto the cable and reach the bottom of the falls. I do remember that the cable was rusty and had many breaks in the strands, which if you were not careful could cut your hands badly as you gripped the cable. We descended the steep path on a hot day, and when we reached the bottom, the pool under the falls looked so inviting that we decided to have a swim. In such isolation, there could be no need for swim wear. How could we have foreseen that a Baptist church in Spencer County would choose that same day and time to have a picnic at the crest of the falls? The next thing we heard was the voice of the law, who had descended down to the deep pit, telling us to get our clothes on and to follow him back up top.

The lawman was sheriff of the smallest county in Tennessee. He told us to get in our car and follow him. He took us to his very modest frame home. It had a front porch, and we were told to sit down in the wicker chairs and wait. His wife came out and asked us if we would like a drink. We said, "Yes," and she brought us absolutely delicious lemonade. The sheriff then returned with an ancient volume of the criminal code of the State of Tennessee, 1922. He handed the book to Donald, who looked most intelligent of the bunch, and told him to "Look up in 'are and see what it is you boys done." With Frank leading the conversation with the sheriff, Donald searched. He then said he could find no such offense in the book. The sheriff, apparently stumped by this response, said: "About how much money you boys got anyway?" We pooled our pocket money and found we had among us $14.85. The sheriff then said, "You know, they had something like this happen over in the next county and the judge fined them people fourteen dollars even. You give me that fourteen dollars, and that eighty-five cents might get you enough gas to get back to Nashville. Now yawl git."

———o———

It is conventionally reckoned that the law is good training for anything and everything. I don't think so. Law school is wonderful training for a career in the law, but among all of the graduate schools it is perhaps the most specializing. Business school is much better preparation for the generalist.

However, I have found that businessmen give enormous to deference to attorneys. It is as if through their arcane mumbo jumbo that the law has curative powers. The law doesn't. It is slow and expensive, and if you are looking for justice at the courthouse, it may be found etched in the marble above the door. Once you pass through, there is a lot of unpredictability, luck, and just plain idiocy.

The cross-reference here to the O.J. Simpson case.

4.

In the 1960s, Natalie May would leave her children on a Saturday afternoon and go with the greatest of all Nashville bargain-hunters, Lucille Loveman, to East Nashville to an antique furniture warehouse. On one such occasion, Nat, who had a sharp eye for form, spotted a dusty desk and bought it for two hundred dollars. The desk was not only covered with dust but was painted in a tarry black with ugly swirls. On top of the black were the remains of gold fat angels and cherubs and festoons of garland that covered the outside of the desk. Nat shrewdly reckoned that a desk this beautiful must have a fine finish and found a master furniture finisher to remove the ebon layer and see what was underneath for another two hundred fifty dollars. The furniture in due course was stripped and there revealed a magnificent inlaid desk, which the refinisher reckoned dated from England in the 1790s. The proud purchase was brought home, thanks to a keen eye and a bit of good luck. We proudly told this story to all who admired the piece of furniture in our living room.

The curtain is here lowered to denote a passage of time.

A few years later on our annual fall pilgrimage to the hills of Kentucky to revisit Shakertown and Keeneland, we stopped at the antique shop at the Beaumont Inn in Harrodsburg. There, incredibly, in the shop was the self-same desk, but with a price tag of fourteen thousand dollars. And the desk was not the beautiful refinished inlaid object in our living room, but was again the black tarry paint with the angels and cherubs blowing trumpets and festooned thereon. I

The eighteenth-century desk, after refinishing

asked the knowledgeable proprietor what the story was as to the desk. He said, "Sir, this is one of the last five desks on earth that were hand-painted in England by the great eighteenth-century Swiss artist Angelica Kauffmann." To which I replied, "No, sir. It is one of the last four."

———o———

With antiques or any other collectibles, you are always buying at retail and selling at wholesale; ergo, what you have bought has to double in value before you have broken even. However, if collecting gives you pleasure, at least the pleasure cannot be taxed.

There are just two things that keep most Americans broke: cars and interest. Americans love cars and don't understand interest. Unfortunately, they are too often connected. My advice is never buy a car unless you can do it for cash. You can buy a car in this country for as little as two weeks' pay at minimum wage.

For many of us it isn't cars but Wall Street that fascinates.

Regret is when you buy a stock and it goes it up—you should have bought more. However, the consolation is that there is something just as good today if you can find it. From Mark Twain: If you buy stock and it goes up, sell it. If it goes down, don't buy it. My favorite of all advice of little value is from Bill Turner's Old Oak paper: "The future will resemble the past more or less."

5.

On our 1948 trip around the western United States we would solve disputes by drawing straws. Straw-drawing, like life, is not always fair. When deciding who would drive the Chevy four hundred fifty miles around from the north side of the Grand Canyon to the south, while the other four hiked across, Donald Maynard picked the short straw. This was unfortunate because Donald was the naturalist in the group and wanted most to take the remarkable hike across the canyon. Naturally he lost and had the long drive. We walked across the canyon, and it was magnificent. It is the opposite of mountain climbing. The hard part of a canyon walk is the end. You have gravity with you in the beginning, and it gets hotter as you go down. You, in effect, disappear into thick air. We slept at the bottom of the canyon on warm rocks and then climbed out the next day. And there was Donald, cheerful, to greet us.

Donald also figured in a second raffle. In a farm field near Kelso, Washington, we set up our cots for the night and started cooking our beans on a Coleman stove. When the late summer sun began to set, down the road walked two farmer's daughters. Yes, those farmer's daughters. We asked them to share our dinner, and they seemed ready to accept. In fact, in most respects, they seemed ready. We had been out about five weeks with five men crammed into a small car.

And crammed into the five men in the car were hormones, which made palpable the thirst for all things female. Girl No. 1, thinking the better of staying much after dinner with these five men, left. But Girl No. 2, one Laverne McCoy, stayed and asked only that one of us give her a ride home. Again we drew straws for the honor, and again Donald Maynard won. Donald was less interested in human fauna than he had been canyon flora. I seized the opportunity to do the honorable thing and offer to exchange the right to Ms. McCoy for my orange juice at breakfast the following morning. Donald accepted this exchange as fair. However, while these honorable gentlemanly negotiations were ensuing, the dastardly Robert jumped into the Chevy, dragging Laverne, and took off. You can imagine my state of wrong, betrayal, frustration, anger, and despair. Little have fifty years muted their flavor. Bob did not get back to the campsite until very early the next morning. He explained that he spent the evening trying to convince her that it would be unwise for her to drop out of high school and that her life would be more fulfilled by graduation. Bob said that she seemed somewhat responsive to his sermonizing, and that was all. Oh, the waste. Oh, the desolation.

———o———

Remembered Conversation

Jack: (ever bitter) You know I haven't seen Sue in ten

years. She just ran into me in the parking lot and said, without greeting, "Get the bags out of my car, Jack, and bring them in! I don't want to be late for the reception!" She must be the worst person in the world.

Kim (ever-tolerant): I don't know about that, Jack. She has achieved mightily, written books, gained access to the Oval Office, and turned Ronald Reagan around on the Soviet Union. That's not a small thing, bringing détente to super powers. She defused a possible nuclear holocaust, thus saving millions of lives. You might say that Sue has saved Western civilization.

Jack: It's just not enough.

6.

On our westward travels we reached the Bonneville Dam and toured it extensively. There on mammoth turbines the size of a small house were plaques describing the characteristics and capacities of each. These were heavy metal plates, which were welded to the side of the giant electrical generators. The plate detailed the technical characteristics of each turbine such as the millions of cubic feet per minute that passed through them and the thousands of kilowatts produced and generated as the dam provided power for the Northwest. At the bottom of these specifications cast in brass was the statement, "Please read instructions carefully before installing." Was this the work of bureaucracy or of a comic genius? Who knows, but it was funny.

Advice to Kids

Marry brains and live modestly. Don't take too much

credit for your children's success or too much blame for their failures. It almost all happens at conception.

From Errol Flynn: You think marriage is about love love love, but no, it's about house house house.

From Herman Kahn: The IQs of spouses correlate more closely than the IQs of siblings.

From Dan May: I'm comforted by old age because it gradually assuages those two lifetime bothers, sex and ambition.

Lessons of the 20th Century

1. It takes two to tango but only one to make a war. Remember Pearl Harbor. Remember 9/11.

2. The ability of governments to do good has developed fitfully and uncertainly. The proposition is still in doubt. However, the ability of governments to do evil has progressed at a rapid rate in the century. Remember the cleansings, massacres, killing fields, and holocausts. You may love your pacifist and your socialist, but beware, they are deadly dangerous.

7.

One summer in the 1960s I packed my Volkswagen Beetle and headed west for one week's seminar at the Menninger Clinic in Topeka, Kansas. Nat and the kids had gone for the usual month visit to her parents in Brooksville, Long Island. I left work in mid-afternoon on a Friday and drove northwest, crossing the Ohio at Shawneetown. Then across southern Illinois to Marion and DuQuoin. This little town was the home of the Hambletonian trotting race and possessed one drive-in A&W Root Beer stand. I had a hot dog and root beer and continued on Illinois Highway 13.

A Confetti of Papers

Somewhere between Pinckneyville and Coulterville on a very flat road in the soft late twilight of summer there appeared in my headlights a cyclist weaving down the middle of the road. I swerved into the path of the oncoming cars to avoid hitting the cyclist. But I did hit him. His left pedal sliced through my right front hubcap and he flipped off the road onto the flat grassy shoulder. I stopped as quickly as my moderate speed allowed and rushed back, expecting to find him dead. But there he stood and said, "I dropped my groceries." The frightening part was swerving into the left side of the road into the path of oncoming vehicles. Again, fortunately, the shoulder was flat, and the oncoming vehicles swerved off the road to avoid me. There was apparently no one seriously hurt. The cyclist had lacerated his left arm somewhat when he hit my aerial, but everyone was apparently okay. Again, fortunately, one of the oncoming cars was an off-duty highway patrolman who radioed for police help. He was able to get an ambulance and to be a witness, describing what had happened. It turned out that the injured cyclist who pedaled one-armed on the highway at night was a parolee and slightly retarded.

Cleaning up the excitement probably took a couple of hours, and I left the scene of the accident about eleven o'clock and drove through St. Louis and found a motel where I checked in for the night. Before going to sleep in my keyed-up state, I walked across the highway to a driving range and hit golf balls to relax. I stroked the balls long and straight as if I had been a professional.

The next morning I continued on across Missouri to Topeka. I checked in with my fellow executives and found everything pre-planned and comfortable. The comfort and the detailed agenda, they explained later, was to create a sense of dependency. The dependent are less likely to resist and more likely to absorb what was to be taught. The other participants were all older than I and were hardened and experienced businessmen. They all did as they were told, so the strategy was apparently successful.

The teaching was along Freudian lines. Everything was put in terms of the family; thus, the boss was the father figure and the conflicts between the manufacturing and the sales departments were put in terms of sibling rivalries. The whole thing was of a piece and effective. I remember certain admonitions to this day. After a promotion, increase supervision; dealing with an alcoholic, give one warning only, and then you must fire no matter how valuable.

While I was in Topeka I did two things that I have never done before or since. The first night of my arrival, taking a shower, I slipped in the bathtub and hit my knee hard on the edge of the bathtub. Later in the week, when we had some free time, I was exploring the psychiatric museum and went into a restroom. It was only when I came out that I realized that I had been in the women's restroom.

Since I was alone in the museum and there were generally only men around, no embarrassment happened nor was even likely. When I had an opportunity to discuss my week with an assigned doctor, I described much of the above. He looked at me over his glasses and chuckled knowingly. The fall in the bathtub was of course to punish myself for the traffic accident. Even though it had not been my fault, there was pain inflicted and expiation was necessary. The fact that I was hurt and my knee dully ached for a few days provided a needed psychic comfort.

Yeah, but what about the women's restroom? Well, of course, he opined, this was the same symptoms that send criminals back to the scene of the crime. You just wanted to put yourself in another dangerous situation. You chose one that was benign but that rekindled the excitement.

Well, maybe. I do know that we are living in the dark ages of mental health and mental knowledge. That the mind is subtle and complex beyond our present understanding is wonderfully apparent.

———o———

A THOUGHT ON the end of the game. Death really isn't so bad when by aging we have lost those things that have made life meaningful and a pleasure. If we have lost the ability to sense, taste, see, and touch, the eyesight to read, and the joys of elevated thought, and friends, and the stamina to maintain, why stay? With these gone, what else is there? Death will come to the old as welcome as sleep to the tired.

In closing, you can be thankful I did not tell you about my perfect grandchildren. But there was the time off the North Korean shore at night when we thought we had run aground on a small island and were terrified with realization when a freight train went by a few yards inland. And then there was the time at Yale we stopped forever the century-old ceremony of Tap Day. But that, too, will be for another time. This is all quite enough for now.

Charles Burson, a Shamus brother, along with his wife Bunny had just announced that they were leaving Nashville for Washington for Charles to become Vice President Al Gore's Chief of Staff.

Why Jacob May Was a Republican

Read to the Shamus Club February 11, 1997, at the home of Bernard Werthan

JACOB MAY WAS born in 1860 in Höchst in a small village of eight hundred people in Odenwald, about forty miles southeast of Frankfurt. At the age of twenty-one he departed the May home, where the family had lived for over two centuries, and became the first of his family to sail for the United States.

He landed at Castle Garden, Manhattan, in 1881. He went to New England, first as a peddler, then as a store-owner, then as a supplier to the hosiery industry. He won a contract with the State of Tennessee to use prison labor to

Jacob May

set up a hosiery plant in Nashville. He arrived in Nashville in 1895, and by 1905 his company was the largest employer in Davidson County, and he was perhaps its richest citizen—this only twenty-five years after landing in New York without money, language, friends, or relatives. His immigration and success are not novel. This, however, should not moderate one's admiration for the courage and daring of Jake and for all those people who came and built America. Perhaps he was helped in his success because there was no income tax and little bureaucracy. Then the word "wealthy" was not said with a sneer, nor had the successful yet become society's enemy, nor was envy yet used to build an electoral majority.

Jacob May learned his Republicanism in New England. The economic issue of the day was the need for high tariffs to protect the new-born manufacturing companies spawned by the Industrial Revolution. This was the Yankee Republican view, and Jake agreed. When he moved to the South, he found enormous hatred of Yankees and the newly freed slaves. The Democrats were the "white man's party." Jacob May's sense of justice had to have been piqued by coming to a part of the country that was on the wrong side of the great moral issue of the century. So, in Nashville, in order to protect his economic interests and to salve his sense of outrage at social injustice, he became and remained a Republican. It was not a popular thing to be in that time. It was more like an underground movement. He wore his campaign buttons on the inside of his lapel. Parenthetically, I remember the first

May Hosiery Mills

time I voted in a Republican primary in about 1960, the registrar at West High said as a joke, I suppose, "Here's another one; get his picture." Jacob always hired, to the extent possible, black Nashvillians. This was novel, even daring, at the time. He also sought refuge from foreign competition and embraced protectionist views. Thus was this immigrant Jewish Yankee a Lincoln Republican.

MY DEAR SHAMUS friends, the paper tonight is indulgent, embarked upon to please no one but myself. So humor me in these memories and apologia. The purpose tonight is not to convince or convert anyone, for that is quite impossible. But I do need to vent. Among my closest friends and even in the confines of our collegial group, I find that I am indulged as an eccentric, thought to be at best quaint by those of you who are more brilliant and more disposed to the Democratic Party. I don't mind this, of course. It is rather flattering in a way. But you fellows must know that you are wrong in a fundamental sense. Surely you all have been joking.

Why Mortimer May Was a Republican

My uncle, Mortimer May, was born in 1892, was raised in Nashville, graduated from Hume-Fogg High School, and went on to Columbia College in New York. Mortimer was a brilliant man. He was a linguist, an orator, and a horse player. He devoted his life to Jewish causes worldwide. For a small-town Southern Reform-Jewish Republican to attain the presidency of the Zionist Organization of America was an anomaly. But Mortimer was a man of zeal and dedication. By personal intervention he saved several hundred Jews from the German Holocaust. He was a frequent visitor to Palestine, and worked tirelessly with the early leaders of that state to bring its dream into a reality. As early as the 1930s, he and Golda Meir would "schnorr" around Nashville trying to fill blue boxes with coins for the Jewish homeland. And yet Mortimer May was a Republican.

Mortimer May, 1961

Mortimer felt that the intrusion of Government into the lives of the citizenry was a poor course of action. The great programs of the New Deal offered hope to America when it needed hope, and yet those promises would in time prove hollow and fruitless. I can recall him arguing against TVA at a time when that was unthinkable in Nashville. The program was instituted to act as a standard to which the private utilities should aspire. He was prescient in saying that in time it would be the private utilities that would create a standard to which TVA would have to aspire. He saw that TVA could sell electricity cheaply, but since no one knew what it cost, it is impossible to say that it was low-cost power—and, of course, TVA pays no tax. He foresaw that Georgia Power and Duke Power would permit their home states to grow faster than Tennessee because of the nimbleness inherent in the private sector. As early as the thirties he was skeptical of Social Security. I recall him saying that it was no more than taking money from the productive young, running it through the leaky conduit of government, and giving it to the nonproductive old. This would be fine until the inverted pyramid would topple, as all such schemes must.

Mortimer was a Jew by profession. He saw the political concentration of Jews within the Democratic Party as potentially damaging to the cause of our people. His point here was not ideological, but tactical. He foresaw that when any group gets too much aligned with any one party, then that party has very little incentive to cater to that group. Likewise, if none of the group is involved in the party, it likewise can ignore the group. In this case, the Jews, overwhelmingly members of the Democratic Party, lost their leverage with both parties. Mortimer was extremely dismayed at the duplicity that Franklin Roosevelt showed toward the Jews. He talked in sweet tones, but when the chips were down, he was not their savior nor rescuer. His arm was around the shoulders of Ibn Saud while he whispered liberal pieties and claimed the Jewish vote regardless of his actions. FDR had knowledge of the Holocaust but was not moved to communicate outrage nor to act. Put not thy trust in princes, saith the psalmist. Yet the Jews idolized Roosevelt.

The Jews were attracted to the liberalizing forces of socialism in nineteenth-century Europe. Indeed, it was the socialists who raised the only voice in the defense of Jewry. Perhaps this bent the twig that has kept the Jews on the liberal side of the spectrum. It is ironic, however, Mortimer once observed, that the unspeakable events of the twentieth century with regard to the Jews came out of National Socialism in Germany and Soviet Socialism in Russia. With modern techniques of communication and suppression, the capacity of governments to do evil was magnified in the twentieth century, while the ability of governments to do good has been an ambiguous process, to say the least. Mortimer may have voted Democrat in 1936, but never thereafter.

Why Daniel May was a Republican

Dan was born in Nashville in 1898. He attended Nashville public schools, Hume-Fogg, and Townsend Harris Hall in New York, and then returned to Nashville for a degree at Vanderbilt, after which he started medical school. After a year his father insisted that he leave medicine and return to the family business, which needed his talent. Over the eighty-seven years that May Hosiery Mills existed, it produced about a million socks per week. The hosiery industry is a perfectly competitive market. Price competition in this type of interesting market has some bad side effects, but the good results were high quality, low cost, and plenty. Dan was also active in government. He spent many years on the school board, the county court, and in the City Council. He was a bright man with a sharp eye for reality and an aversion to cant. He was deeply experienced both in the public and private sectors. My nephew Willie Stern's book includes the following short quotes:

Daniel May, 1961

A Confetti of Papers

"Free market capitalism is the only way to improve mankind's lot."

"Any tinhorn dictator from any centralized government, left or right, can make the rich poor. This will always be popular with the already poor. However, it is only through free-market capitalism that the poor have been made rich."

"The only thing that Jews need fear in western democracies is economic collapse. This can result from stagnation brought about by government, which stifles growth and economic activity. Therefore put not thy faith in princes but in freedom, which will bring prosperity, growth, and hope. In such an environment the Jews need not fear."

Dan did not like liberals as a group.

"Too many American liberals are under the impression that they have a monopoly on morality. It dulls subtlety."

"A liberal is someone farther away from the situation than you are. I have always been troubled by the white liberals of Nashville who are strong advocates of busing when it is a Mississippi issue but are quick to enroll their kids in private schools when integration came to Tennessee."

"I don't know who has done more harm to

America—the out-and-out scoundrels or the well-intentioned damn fools."

Dan always considered himself a little "l" liberal in the eighteenth-century sense. Such a person is willing to approach present problems with a free and open mind and willing to accept change. It is the little "l" of liberal arts. The capital "L" liberals in his lifetime had become doctrinaire, predictable, and as such reactionary. It was as if liberals knew the answer could be found only in the conventional wisdom of the left. The liberals embraced the politically correct and refused to accept different points of view. Dan always hated the bigotry of the doctrinaire left. He always championed education because without it we could not use the liberties that we have been granted. It is only by freedom that any nation can achieve its true potential. The clumsy intervention of government diminishes freedom and so is an obstacle to human enlargement. Lordy, was he a Republican!

Why Jack May is a Republican

I was born at Vanderbilt Hospital in 1929 and attended Peabody Demonstration School for thirteen years. After college, I joined the Central Intelligence Agency. I reckoned that there are few things worth fighting for, but at the top of my list is the United States of America. After my experience in Korea, I returned to work at the May Hosiery Mills, and to go to night law school at New York University on the GI Bill. Yes, the GI Bill. I gladly accepted this money that had belonged to and was taken from someone else. I worked for the CIA for about four years and for May Hosiery Mills for about thirty years. Here I would like to quote from a paper about Jack Downey, which I read to this Club in 1976.

> *My decision to leave the intelligence business after only four years was a matter of principle. First of all, I did not want to spend my life making war, hot or cold. Secondly, I detested the bureaucracy. Those organizations that are not subject to the discipline of the marketplace are always political and often in the worse sense. Since there is no objective way to evaluate personal performance, life becomes one of convincing the echelon above of the worth and merit of the individuals and projects of the echelon below. It is not how good you are, for indeed there is really no way to measure that. It is how good your superiors think you are. It is this impossibility of performance evaluation that makes so fundamental the manure, both chicken and bull, that is commonly associated with the bureaucratic structure. Never have I known as many able men assembled in one place, and never have I known so many motivated together in one organization. At the same time, never did I see so much waste of talent as within the bureaucracy, and the profligacy with money was incredible. If this is true of the CIA's dedicated, even inspired, workers, what must it be like at the Bureau of Mines? A typical CIA professional was brilliant, scholarly, and serious. If you were to ask me who among our members is most stereotypical of my colleagues at the CIA, I would point to the brilliant, scholarly, and serious Sam Richmond. Instead of the attention and energy of these men being focused on the external tasks, our heads were always turned backwards as if swept along by the paper*

Why Jacob May Was a Republican

blizzard of reports, always self-serving, blowing toward the great wastebasket on the Potomac.

So I did at least two things in my life on principle. For patriotism, I joined the CIA. And I got out of it because I could not bear it and went to making socks. The scope of manufacturing socks is exceedingly narrow compared to the world-view problems of the CIA. But nevertheless the frustrations are less, decisions are possible, and the result is a humble but useful product. Socks function well and sell at a low price. And at the end of the year you can look at some numbers and see how well you did. For those of you outside of the marketplace, you can never be sure.

And so I am a Republican. I believe the less money allocated through the bureaucracy and the more funds allocated to the private sector will end in a greater good for the greater number. Taxation, whether to Pharaoh or to the welfare state, is an act of constriction that will ultimately lead down the road to serfdom. Moses understood. And finally, I am a Republican because I feel they are the best hope for that most precious of gifts—peace. Peace is more likely reached in two ways. One, have a strong military

Jack May

in the hands of a free democracy, and two, have free commerce internationally. These have been two traditional Republican tenets. Weakness encourages the aggression of evil men. This century Republicans have generally been more hawkish in the development of our military. Doves were in control in the lead-up to World War I, World War II, Korea, Vietnam, [and 9/11] with disastrous results. The maintenance of our military has maintained the peace in the second half of the twentieth century. To have a peaceful world in the next fifty years, it is essential that our democracy be preeminent in military strength. Peace will come through God's beneficence and through our vigilance.

On a more positive note, peace, once attained, can be sustained. Free markets work as well worldwide as they do intra-country. If we enlarge the marketplace we will increase the prosperity. If we increase the prosperity it is likely that peace will grow. Once when I visited Wal-Mart with a satchel of socks, I drove from Bentonville, Arkansas, over to the Federal monument at Pea Ridge. It was here the Rebels attacked the Yankees. I speculated that another Rebel charge is not apt to happen. Wal-Mart too much depends upon merchandise provided by the factories of the North and of the Midwest and their customers who live there. Thus is anger defused by commerce.

Political parties exist for one reason only, and that is to elect candidates. In some general way they do have an ideological bent. The United States was built upon two great ideals, freedom and equality. In our time conservatives have put freedom ahead of equality, while liberals have put equality first. Generally, those societies that put freedom first have done better by equality than those that put equality first have done by freedom. The shadings are subtle. So one must seek and vote fundamentals, not platform rhetoric. It is most disturbing to me to see ascendance of know-nothing populism as exemplified by both Pat Buchanan and Ross Perot. The rise of protectionism, nativism, and suspicious ill-will is most disturbing. Perhaps we will see Mortimer's prophecy fulfilled when one party sees it can get more votes by being anti-Jew and anti-black than it can get from those groups by being pro-Jew and pro-black. If such a trend should become ascendant, I would switch parties in a minute. After all, I am not a virgin. I did vote for Lyndon Johnson because of Goldwater's stand on the public accommodation section of the Civil Rights Act of 1964.

Parties do change through time. In my paper to the Shamuses on the Hasmoneans, I tried to figure out what the Pharisees and the Sadducees stood for in the hundred fifty years leading up to the birth of Christ. The reason I had a hard time figuring it out is that over that time period the groups changed. The conservatives became liberal, and the liberals became conservative. And it is going on now in our time. The Democrat President tells us the era of big government is over, and the Populists in the Republican Party say that free enterprise and free trade are bad. It will be most interesting to see how this plays out in the next few elections. In the meantime, don't forget the watchword, "Government can't do anything." As I am writing this paper today's news tells us that the FBI crime lab is guilty of corruption and faulty practice and that the IRS is incapable of putting in modern computer systems that one would suspect would have been in place for a generation. The Government can't do anything!

A Confetti of Papers

I close this paper with a fare-you-well and God-speed to Shamus Charles Burson. You are going to a city that is financially bankrupt and beset by the corruption that power engenders. As you enter the vortex, remember: You always have a lifeline back to Nashville and Shamus. Don't become cynical about the process. That is just too easy a course. I speculate that the best of men, e.g., George Bush and Jimmy Carter, made indifferent Presidents, and the most cynically pragmatic of men, e.g., Tricky Dick Nixon and Slick Willy Clinton, have made quite good Presidents. It is all very off-putting. Don't be put off. In such an environment one can lose his way. So keep your eye on the ever-fixed star. Know that you have our thanks and admiration for taking this tough assignment. It is said that God takes care of drunks and the United States of America. Surely He is assisted by the commitment and application of fine men such as you. Goodbye, Charles, and good night all.

A quick, less-boring recapitulation of the papers, some now in the canon (excuse some redundancy here), others relegated to the apocrypha. They will remain forever in that desert. Subjects there wandering include: sex differences, tribes, welfare failure, the one-time pad, Khazars, prints, media bias, Lebanese politics, and homelessness.

Shamus Synopsis

*Read to the Shamus Club April 27, 2005,
at the home of Daniel Casse*

OF COURSE BEING in Shamus is a treat. There is always the food and the friendship, but the papers are the glue. Over the course of a couple of years we will hear twenty-four more papers on various topics of general interest. They are of varying qualities, but I have never had a Shamus evening where there was not something I learned. Looking back over the papers that I have written, at least those I can find, during the past thirty years, I find the same thing to be true. So, I will review tonight some of the paragraphs from these various twenty-four papers. See if you can find something of interest. It's two years of Shamus in one night.

A Confetti of Papers

My greatest failure was a paper I wrote in 1987 entitled "The Draft Riots of the '60s, Tet, and the Battle of Nashville." My point was that it is not important who wins military victories but only how those military victories are perceived. We had draft riots in the 1960s, but much worse ones occurred in the 1860s. The four days of rioting in Manhattan during and just after the Battle of Gettysburg were violent and widespread—even Brooks Brothers was burnt. Two thousand were killed. The North was rife with discord, as was John Bell Hood's plan to get past Nashville and his northward sweep at Atlanta and drive into Kentucky and Ohio. He doubted the farm boys of Ohio would continue to fight. Like the Battle of Nashville, Tet was an enormous victory for the United States, but the perception of those victories was enormously different. The will of the enemy to continue the fight was seen, I think, incorrectly in Vietnam. The will of the enemy to fight after Nashville was perceived, I think, correctly. The correct perception of Nashville led to the end of the Civil War without serious additional military engagement. The perception of Tet as a failure also meant the end of serious military involvement.

My feeling is that the failure to perceive Tet correctly resulted in the holocaust of two million Cambodians. The correct perception of Nashville led to the preservation of the Union and the effective end of slavery. The point may have been well taken, but the argument with regard to perception was never really met in this presentation to the Club.

I did better with a paper in 1990 entitled "The House of Hasmon." The genesis of this paper was a sermon in mid-November by the excellent Rabbi Beth Davidson. She reminded the congregation that the holiday of Thanksgiving, while a tribute to God for His bounty, was the tribute of a very narrow religious sect that had settled in the United States. The Puritans were intolerant of any outside religious view. Beth felt that the Puritan bigotry toward others was a trait that diluted the essential aspect of the Thanksgiving holiday. I took umbrage at this. Early on in our history, Roger Williams broke off and founded Rhode Island based on religious freedom. The result of the Pilgrims' settlement was nothing less than the United States of America. The Jews have fared best in the liberal capitalist democracies of Northern Europe and the U.S. where Protestantism took hold. At the same time I wrote Rabbi Davidson, "Perhaps we should take a closer look at our celebration of Hanukkah." I realize that the rise of this non-Biblical holiday is a defensive measure to the general and commercial successes of Christmas. Christmas is essential and germane to Christianity, where Hanukkah is neither to Judaism. For the most part Judas Maccabee was not fighting the Romans but was fighting and killing what might have passed in those days for reform Jews. The next hundred years under his successors was a disgraceful period in Jewish history and one of the most disgraceful periods in the history of the world. The Hasmonians were brutal and barbaric. Their rule should not be the basis of a joyous celebration at the solstice that it has become. Better join the Christians and then adopt the pagan Saturnalia.

Early in 1976, I wrote a paper on Meriwether Lewis. As far as I could tell, Lewis spent only one day of his life in Middle Tennessee. It was a beautiful October fall day. Unflatteringly, he chose to conclude this day by shooting himself in the chest. Lewis at the time of his suicide was our greatest hero. I don't know that we have had one as great before or since—maybe Lindbergh, maybe Neil Armstrong, Admiral Byrd, or Daniel Boone. But for my money, Meriwether Lewis was the greatest. Three hundred-plus years after Columbus, he ended the search for a way to the Orient. At the time he went west no one knew of the existence of the Rocky Mountains. Imagine. There recently have been a number of excellent biographies of Lewis—*Undaunted Courage* by Stephen Ambrose comes to mind. None of his biographers has suggested the basis of his mental depression. I rather suspect he was what we would call a twenty-first-century gay. I hate to use this abominable corruption of a fine English word, which is presently used to describe the sad lifestyle of the homosexual. But something was clearly wrong with Lewis, and my suspicion is that it was just this. Lewis's father was killed when he was at an early age, and he was raised by a strong domineering mother and unsympathetic stepfather. He was chosen by Jefferson to lead the corps of discovery but said he would not go unless Captain Clark was along. When the two men returned after their remarkable three-year adventure, Clark married right away. Lewis tried many relationships with women. After all, he was a dashing hero. None of these was able to reach fruition. Alone as Governor of Missouri, he became more and more depressed and irrational. His suicide in Tennessee was a climax of his unhappy life after his return. There is today at Lewis State Park near Hohenwald an obelisk that is truncated. The symbolism here is of a young life broken off at its prime. Perhaps. I suggested that the incomplete shaft might have other symbolism.

Over the course of these thirty years since my first

paper in 1975, I have done biographical profiles of four diverse and astounding Jews. They are Karl Marx, Marilyn Monroe, Meyer Amschel Rothschild, and Moe Berg. What a group! Karl Marx was a selfish, mean-spirited, cruel economic philosopher who changed the course of history for a hundred fifty years after his greatest writings. He was powerfully persuasive and did touch a strain in humankind. He was wrong about everything. He did not foresee Stalin, the rise of the middle class, the economic opulence of the West, which extended to all levels of society. He could not have foreseen the gulags or Mao's great leap forward. His idiotically wrong economics deserves credit for these excesses. He deplored the exploitation of the working classes. He found them to be underpaid, but so far as I know he found none that were paid nothing at all. However, such a person did exist. It was a servant girl in his own household who was virtually enslaved and abused. Thoroughly, an awful man.

Marilyn Monroe, with the possible exception of Mohammed Ali, may have been the most widely known celebrity of the twentieth century. She, like Meriwether Lewis discussed above, was a young suicide at about the same age. She had been married to an excellent centerfielder and a mediocre playwright. She had been a prostitute as a teenager. She had been sexually exploited by many, not the least of which at the end were Jack and Bobby Kennedy. She was a good actress and a fine comedian but always desperately unhappy. What could cause a suicide to such a celebrated figure? My only explanation was she was not loved as a child.

The rise of the Rothschilds from the unspeakable conditions of the eighteenth-century ghetto is a story that defies imagination. What the Rothschilds became and where they came from in two generations is a tale told by a fabulist or a mythologist. I went back and looked at the book *Founder*. I found myself still unable to read the early days without a sickening in my stomach. The heights to which the family rose are the stuff of fable. This was a good story and a good Shamus paper. The family sustained itself for many generations until some recent decadence. On the occasion of a modern young Rothschild suicide I got the poem "Richard Cory" from Sam Richmond.

The Moe Berg story is also remarkable. He was the third child of a druggist in New Jersey. He went on to Princeton where he excelled in academics and athletics. He played major league baseball for over twenty years. He became fluent in seven or eight languages. Besides being a pretty good catcher, he was a good enough physicist to deal one-on-one with Heisenberg. Berg's espionage figured in both the Pacific and European theaters. He photographed Tokyo from the top of his hotel while barnstorming with Babe Ruth, *et al.* These pictures were used by Jimmy Doolittle on his bombing raid. He was sent to Switzerland to assassinate Werner Heisenberg if he thought that the Germans had made or were close to making an atom bomb. This is a fabulous life. You can't make this stuff up.

More recently in the year 2000, we looked with James Reston Jr. at a parallel biography of Pete Rose and Bart Giamatti. Giamatti was a brilliant academic, a much-loved President of Yale, and a failed Commissioner of Baseball. Pete Rose was a low-life scuzzball who had a genius for competition and hitting, and a history of gambling with men and abusing women. The two men are fascinating in contrast. There is little doubt in my mind that Pete Rose caused the death of Giamatti. It was because he had to ban this hero from the game. Of course, Giamatti weighed three hundred pounds, smoked three packs a day, and always had a pressure-filled job, but I still think it was Pete Rose who performed the *coup de grâce*. As a sidebar it is Giamatti's son, Paul, who is the star of an excellent movie this year, *Sideways*.

In 1979, I wrote a paper on the Battle of Marathon. It was a good paper for me to write. I went back to my Herodotus. This tale started around 590 B.C. in the rule of Nebuchadnezzar. He had subjugated all the world worth subjugating. This included the Jews. He destroyed the Temple and led them off to Babylon. About forty years later, his successor Cyrus restored them and let my people go. Cyrus was the Mede who conquered Persia. One man's Mede is another man's Persian. This was the first victory of the Northern Aryans over the Semitic people of the south. His successor Darius, hearing of some skirmishes along the Ionian Coast with some Greeks, set about to enslave them as well. He did not. He was defeated at the Battle of Marathon. After which Pheidippides ran about twenty miles from the battlefield at Marathon back to Athens, told them that we had won, and dropped dead. The balance of this paper dealt with my own running on my fiftieth birthday of a twenty-six-mile race in Terre Haute, Indiana. I ran the race in a Shamus and Old Oak Club T-shirt. I did finish and was not last. It did not kill me, but it did kill two evenings.

I wrote a couple of personal papers. The May Family has been in Nashville since about 1895. I have known many of them through five generations. Though the personalities are all quite different and the times have changed enormously, to my knowledge every one of them has been a Republican. The paper attempted to explain this strange phenomenon. I spoke in the voice of Jacob May, a Lincoln Republican, Mortimer May, a Zionist Republican, Dan May, a businessman Republican, and me, the all-knowing Republican. The philosophies were varied, but all were interesting and profoundly held. A couple of my children married outside of the party. To my certain knowledge none of these mixed marriages has produced anything but more Republicans. This paper was received with extraordinary grace by my fellow Shamus members.

I also wrote a personal remembrance of anecdotal stories and old-time tales that have been indigenous to my family. The Club indulged me by listening to these tales of old times. It was a paper of great fun to write and to read. These papers are a good time to record family remembrances, and I encourage the members to do so. For instance, ham, lamb....

I have written a number of papers on topics of general interest of the moment: one on sex differences; one on welfare reform; another on media bias; and another on the politics in Lebanon. With regard to the latter—when I wrote that paper in 1984 I knew nothing about the Shiites or Sunnis. I knew very little of the Maronite Christians and did not know any thing then or now about the Druze. It was interesting to do research on these four religions. At that time Lebanon was in chaos, and my son had very nearly died there. Since then, the lid has been held on this boiling pot by the Syrians via *force majeur*. Now it appears that they are leaving and these strange factions will again try to organize a government. I wish them well, but I am not sanguine about the prospects.

Shamus Synopsis

The paper on media bias in 1988 was much derided by the Club. I was accused of shallow paranoia. The media may have their own ideas, but the main thing is viewership and readership, and all else takes a back seat to that. It should have appeared obvious to me. However, in the wake of running off a president who had won forty-nine states and the withdrawal of support of our troops in Vietnam after the victory at Tet, I should have known that something was at work. There is always a bias towards bad news. If a thousand planes take off a day that is not news; if one crashes, it is. The local news maxim of *if it bleeds it leads* is almost comic when watching the repetitiveness of local news. As far as the left bias, I am now somewhat consoled even though Dan Rather had a eighteen-year run after my Shamus paper.

In 1985, I reviewed Charles Murray's book entitled, *Losing Ground*. Murray's thesis was that during the sixties and seventies social pathologies rose at an increasing rate. Crime, homelessness, poverty, single parenthood, and SAT performance, to name a few. He felt that this was because the incentives set by social welfare systems were wrong and encouraged failures. We were a society that was led by concern for the losers. Of course, Murray was right. With Bill Clinton's promise to change welfare as we know it and with the complicity of Newt Gingrich, the welfare system was changed and the benefits were not only enormous, they were almost instantaneous.

I more recently wrote a paper on homelessness, about which I had seen a little of first-hand in working with Father Strobel. My conclusion was that this was not an economic problem but a mental health problem. With the best of intentions, feeling that psychotropic drugs could control the situation, we closed asylums and institutions and turned the mentally ill loose. That, combined with a drug culture and the abundance of alcohol, led to a problem of homelessness that did not exist when we were young. Repeal of the vagrancy laws didn't help. I don't know how the problem will be solved, but it will not be with money.

In a paper twelve years ago, I tried to define the meaning of the word "tribe" as in MOT. There are a number of tribes in the world. Besides the Jews, I suggest there are the British, Chinese, Japanese, and Asian Indians. I looked at some smaller groups—the Armenians, the Mormons, the Palestinians. Some of these have become more a tribe and the Jewish/Americans probably less. Is the Diaspora over? What say landsman?

Another book on tribalism came from Arthur Koestler's book on the Khazars. After all, in the twelfth century the expulsion of the Jews from England involved a few hundred people. The expulsion later from Spain in the fifteenth century involved a few thousand. Yet there were six million Jews killed in the Holocaust. Where did they come from? If the Jews of today are not Semites but Aryans, does that mean we are less chosen? Aryans did not come from the Valley of the Jordan but from the Valley of the Don. Does that render our covenant with the Almighty any less binding? We are now in the Passover season celebrating our exit from Egypt. But whose exit? Could we as well claim the Trail of Tears? All of this involves the conversion of the Khazars in the years around 965 BCE. This is a fascinating and astounding concept. I loved exploring it. There is one quotation from a Muslim empyreal document of the tenth century that says,

"In Khazaria, sheep, honey, and Jews exist in large quantities." What is to be made of this?

I reported on a very interesting book by professor Steven Goldberg with the provocative title *Why Men Rule: A Theory of Male Dominance*. He looked at gender differences physiologically, neurologically, and culturally, and came to interesting and anti-politically correct conclusions. Why, my friends, is it that through all history and all geography, are men almost always (well over ninety percent) in charge? Why do women almost always wear their hair longer? Why? Many whys. Goldberg quotes from Cicero: "Custom will never conquer nature, for it is always she who remains unconquered." Perversity will be challenged.

My final two papers that I will review for you were self-indulgences. I have always loved and collected prints. They are affordable. One can get a Rembrandt or Durer for less than five thousand dollars, so it is a good hobby. When I get a little money together, I buy prints. The prints and the pauper. Also, their personality suits mine. They are sardonic, sarcastic, bitter, mordant, and humorous. All prints are copies of something, so these are Xeroxes of some famous prints that I liked and discussed. Xeroxes are not valuable, but perhaps you will enjoy looking at them. At least they are understandable and do not need learned explanation for us to get it. Maybe one day I will catalog them in a book.

And finally the brief, sad, and lower case of e.e. cummings, who lived his life in Boston and Greenwich Village, New York. Now I am not going into the details of his life, which are interesting, but on his worst day he could write circles around Wallace Stevens and William Carlos Williams. I only bring up this paper because of the really superb job

A Confetti of Papers

David Steine did on Williams. I put this paper last because I enjoy reading his poems so much. I will comment a little further as time permits as we go through this small compilation. Thanks for listening.

rain or hail
sam done
the best he kin
till they digged his hole

:sam was a man

stout as a bridge
rugged as a bear
slickern a weazel
how be you

(sun or snow)

gone into what
like all them kings
you read about
and on him sings

a whippoorwill;

heart was big
as the world aint square
with room for the devil
and his angels too

Shamus Synopsis

yes,sir

*what may be better
or what may be worse
and what may be clover
clover clover*

(nobody'll know)

*sam was a man
grinned his grin
done his chores
laid him down.*

Sleep well

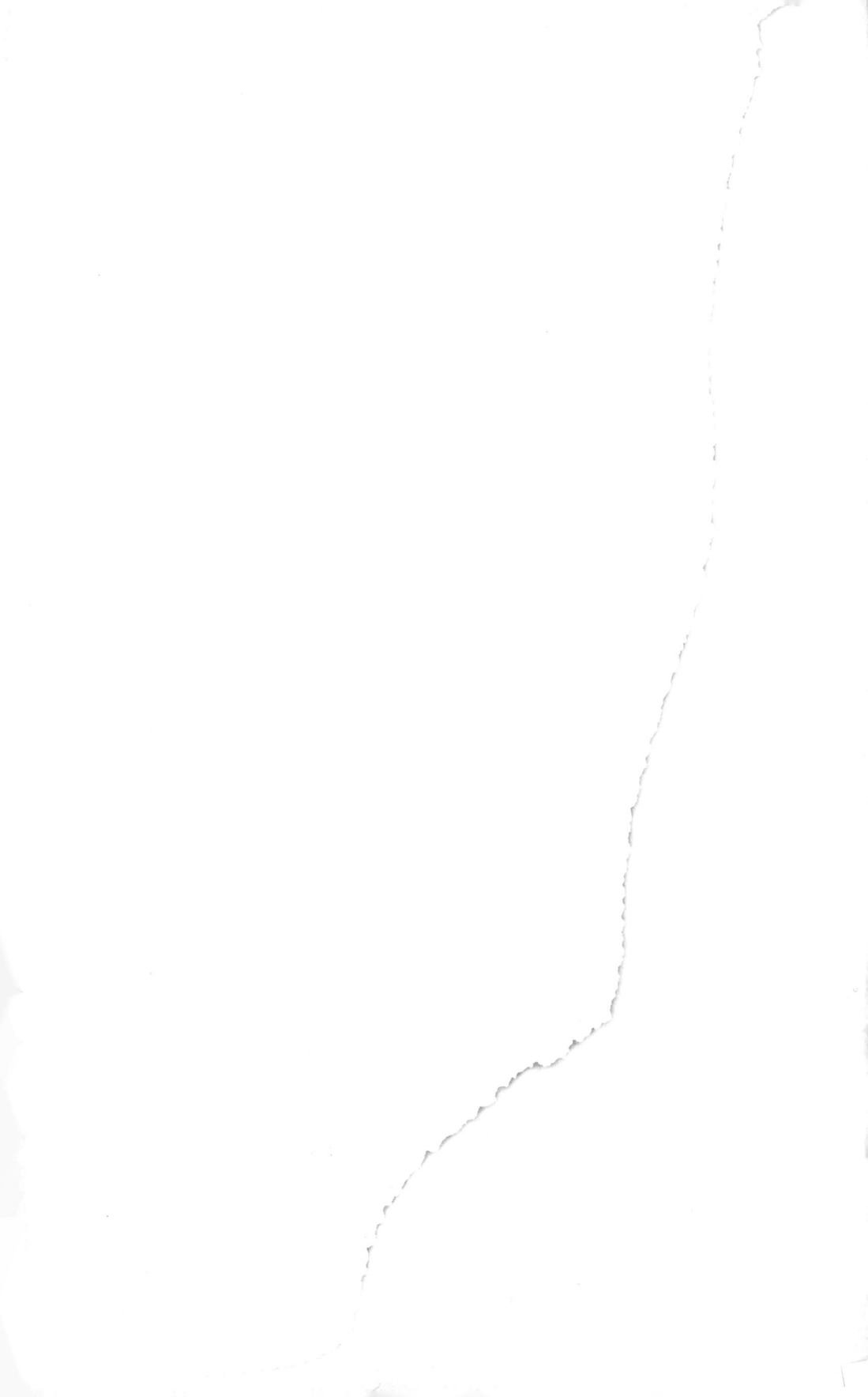